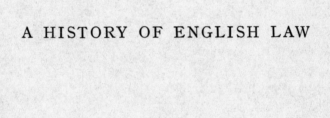

A HISTORY OF ENGLISH LAW

A HISTORY OF ENGLISH LAW

IN SIXTEEN VOLUMES

For List of Volumes and Scheme of the History, see pp. vii-viii

A HISTORY
OF ENGLISH LAW

BY

SIR WILLIAM HOLDSWORTH

O.M., K.C., D.C.L., Hon. LL.D.

LATE VINERIAN PROFESSOR OF ENGLISH LAW IN THE UNIVERSITY OF OXFORD; FELLOW
OF ALL SOULS COLLEGE, OXFORD; HON. FELLOW OF ST. JOHN'S COLLEGE,
OXFORD; FOREIGN ASSOCIATE OF THE ROYAL BELGIAN ACADEMY;
FELLOW OF THE BRITISH ACADEMY; BENCHER OF LINCOLN'S INN

VOLUME XVI

EDITED BY

A. L. GOODHART

K.B.E., Q.C., D.C.L., LL.D.

AND

H. G. HANBURY

Q.C., D.C.L.

*To say truth, although it is not necessary for counsel to know what the
history of a point is, but to know how it now stands resolved, yet it is a
wonderful accomplishment, and, without it, a lawyer cannot be accounted
learned in the law.* ROGER NORTH

LONDON
METHUEN & CO. LTD.
SWEET AND MAXWELL

PREFACE TO VOLUMES
XIV, XV AND XVI

A DECADE has passed since volume XIII of Holdsworth's great history appeared. The material for that volume was in typescript, but the remainder was in manuscript, and Holdsworth's handwriting, like that of many men who wrote much, and always by hand, was very difficult to decipher. A further difficulty was its sheer bulk. He clearly underrated its inevitable proportions. Even with the omission of Part II (The Rules of Law), which was incomplete, a single volume would have comprised well over 1,000 pages. We have, therefore, been constrained to divide the material into three volumes, which cover the period 1832-1875.

The introductory chapter demonstrates Holdsworth in the light, not only of a profound legal historian, *facile princeps* among his contemporaries, but also of a shrewd political historian. The interactions of Peel and Melbourne, and later of Disraeli and Gladstone, are sketched by a master hand.

The rest of volume XIV deals with Public Law. It begins with a subject on which Holdsworth was always fond of lecturing, the relation of English law to international law. He goes on to deal exhaustively with Acts of State, the legal position, in relation to English Courts, of ambassadors and foreign sovereigns, and the treaty-making power of the Crown, foreign enlistment, foreign jurisdiction and extradition.

He then passes on to the growth of the practice of the bestowal by Parliament, on the executive, of law-making powers, and to a review of the whole machinery of central government, the departments of state, legislature and judiciary. This vast survey is followed up by an analysis of local government.

The volume ends with a review of the Empire. Much of it is, of course, now out of date, but to the legal historian it is indispensable, and all has been preserved, excepting only the relations between the British government and the Indian States. Valuable as his account was, it ceased to have much bearing on the modern situation when the last of the States " acceded " to India or Pakistan.

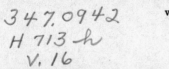

v

Volume XV deals with the enacted law, the legal profession, legal literature and the common law judges. Volume XVI, deals with the Chancellors, Masters of the Rolls, Lords Justices in Chancery, and Vice-Chancellors, and finally with the civilians.

We are deeply grateful to Mr. W. W. Budden, B.C.L., M.A., St. Edmund Hall, who has discharged the onerous task of compiling the indices, and tables of cases and statutes.

A. L. GOODHART
H. G. HANBURY

Oxford, 1966.

PLAN OF THE HISTORY

CONTENTS

BOOK V (*Continued*)

PART I

SOURCES AND GENERAL DEVELOPMENT (*Continued*)

CHAPTER V

THE AGE OF REFORM—THE FIRST PHASE (1833–1875) (*Continued*)

VIII. THE CHANCELLORS, THE MASTERS OF THE ROLLS, AND OTHER JUDGES OF THE COURT OF CHANCERY

TABLE OF CASES

References are to page numbers

TABLE OF STATUTES

References are to page numbers

THE CHANCELLORS, THE MASTERS OF THE ROLLS, AND OTHER JUDGES OF THE COURT OF CHANCERY

CHANCELLORS

LYNDHURST

(1827-1830, 1834-1835, 1841-1846)

Brougham's predecessor and successor as Chancellor was John Singleton Copley, Lord Lyndhurst.[1] He was one of the most eminent of the Chancellors of this period, both as a lawyer and as a statesman. Copley was born at Boston, on May 4, 1772. His father was a distinguished painter, and, when the war of independence broke out, he was making a tour of Italy. He was joined in England by his wife, whose family were loyalists, and his son and daughters. They made their home at 25 George Street, Hanover Square, and Copley continued to make it his home throughout his long life. From Trinity College, Cambridge, he graduated as second wrangler in 1794; and besides mathematics he studied both chemistry and the classics. He became a fellow of Trinity in 1795. Having been appointed a "travelling bachelor" by the university he visited America in 1796-97.[2] He had become a member of Lincoln's Inn in 1794, and in 1797 he began his legal studies in Tidd's chambers.[3] Having practised as a special pleader from 1798 to 1804 with but indifferent success, he was called to the bar in 1804. He diligently attended court, and soon began to acquire some practice. In 1812 he brought himself into the notice of the public by his success in discovering a formal defect in the indictment of one of the Luddite rioters, and in getting the court to quash it on that ground.[4] In the following year he became a serjeant-at-law. As a serjeant he had a steady practice, and in its

---

[1] Theodore Martin, Life of Lord Lyndhurst; Atlay, The Victorian Chancellors i 1-167; Foss, Judges ix 178-183; Quart. Rev. cxxvi 1-35—an article by Abraham Hayward; Ed. Rev. cxxi 556-572; Campbell, Lives of the Chancellors viii 1-212; Campbell's book is a posthumous volume which is notorious for its inaccuracies and malice about both Brougham and Lyndhurst, more especially about Lyndhurst; but it is sometimes useful, more especially when he is constrained to praise, since it gives the impression of a contemporary and an eye witness.

[2] The Latin letters describing his travels, which, as travelling fellow, he was obliged to send to the Vice-Chancellor, are set out in a translation by W. H. Bennett, Biographical Sketches from the Note Book of a Reporter 182-196.

[3] Tidd was the author of the great book on practice which was studied by Uriah Heep; many famous lawyers read in his chambers, including Denman, Campbell, and Cottenham; for an account of Tidd and his chambers, see Life of Lord Campbell i 148, 158-160. For Tidd's Practice, see vol. xiii 452.

[4] Martin, op. cit. 116-117.

conduct he showed the qualities which later made him a great judge. Hayward said of him that,

he was never a brilliant or showy advocate; his strength lay in his clear strong subtle intellect; his highest forensic qualities were of the judicial order; and his want of early popularity amongst the dispensers of briefs was in a great measure accounted for by the friend (Sir Samuel Shepherd I believe), who remarked that he had no rubbish in his head.[1]

The case which made his name as a great lawyer and advocate, and influenced the whole future course of his life, was his successful defence of Watson, who was indicted in 1817 for high treason as a result of the Spa Fields riots.[2] Campbell, who heard his speech, said that it was one of the most effective that he had ever heard.[3] It is said that Queen Elizabeth I, after hearing an argument by Egerton against the Crown, said that he should never plead against her again.[4] The government took the same view of Copley's abilities.[5] Later in 1817 he was retained by the Crown in the case of Brandreth and other rioters;[6] in 1818 the government found him a seat in Parliament; and in 1819 he became solicitor-general. We shall see that his act in joining the government was made the foundation of baseless charges of apostasy and political cynicism which persisted during the greater part of his life and after his death.[7]

As solicitor-general he showed his ability as an advocate in his prosecution of Thistlewood and his gang.[8] But it was in the Queen's trial that he scored his greatest success.

His handling of one of the Queen's witnesses, a certain Lieutenant Flynn, dealt a blow to her case from which it never fully recovered; and the speech in which he summed up the evidence for the Bill went a long way to destroy the effect produced by the furious cross-examinations of Brougham and his colleagues.[9]

In 1824 he became attorney-general. As attorney-general he brought in an abortive bill to give effect to some of the recommendations of the Chancery Commission, and his speech in introducing it, though he had little knowledge of equity practice, won much applause.[10] He opposed the Prisoners' Counsel Bill, which he afterwards supported.[11] But, unlike Vicary Gibbs, he filed no informations for libel.[12] In 1826 he became Master of the

---

[1] Quart. Rev. cxxvi 11.   [2] 32 S.T. 1.
[3] Lives of the Chancellors viii 17.   [4] Foss, Judges vi 138.
[5] The fact that in the case of *Thorpe v. The Governor of Upper Canada*, when Castlereagh was present in court, he successfully prevented the disclosure in evidence of an official document, may have helped the government to make up its mind, see J. P. Collier, Criticisms on the Bar 189-190.
[6] 32 S.T. 755.   [7] Below 14, 15.   [8] (1820) 33 S.T. 681.
[9] Atlay, op. cit. i 35.   [10] Atlay, op. cit. i 43; below 6.
[11] Below 9.   [12] Atlay, op. cit. i 73-74; Martin, op. cit. 205-206.

Rolls; and in that capacity he reintroduced in an amended form his Bill for the reform of the Court of Chancery, which, like its predecessor, never became law.[1] In 1827 he was involved in a famous altercation with Canning in a debate on Catholic emancipation. But this quarrel was short-lived, and later in the year Canning offered him the Great Seal. Copley accepted, and became Lord Chancellor with the title of Lord Lyndhurst. The appointment was generally approved—we shall see that his qualities as a lawyer, as a judge, and as a member of Parliament were so preeminent that no one could question his fitness to hold the highest office in the law. "A discriminating observer would have said of him what Talleyrand said of Thiers, 'il n'est pas parvenu; il est arrivé'."[2]

Lyndhurst's first Chancellorship lasted till the fall of the Tory government in 1830. He soon acquired an influential position both in the cabinet and the House of Lords. One of his first acts as Chancellor was to remedy Eldon's reluctance to give silk to leading juniors by giving it to Campbell, Brougham, and Bickersteth,[3] the fact that these men were promoted shows that, in exercising his legal patronage, he was not guided by political considerations; and the same absence of political bias is apparent in his appointment of Macaulay to a commissionership in bankruptcy, and Sydney Smith to a canonry at Bristol. His support of the Dissenters' Marriage Bill [4] and the repeal of the Test and Corporation Acts [5] showed that he had little sympathy with the diehard Toryism of the Eldon type. He supported two other bills,[6] which failed to become law, to reform the court of Chancery, and, in his speech on the second Bill, he outlined further extensive measures of law reform in addition to the reforms which, as he pointed out, had already been made.[7] He made as skilful a defence as it was possible to make of the *volte face* of the government on the question of Catholic emancipation. As judge of the court of Chancery he did the best he could with the as yet unreformed system of equity practice, and his efforts won the approbation of the legal profession.[8]

There were rumours that on the change of government in 1830 Lyndhurst "would keep the Seals";[9] and perhaps Grey would have

[1] Below 16, 17.   [2] Quart. Rev. cxxvi 23.
[3] Afterwards Lord Langdale, M.R.   [4] Atlay, op. cit. i 60.
[5] Ibid 60-61.   [6] Ibid 68-71.   [7] Ibid 70.
[8] In 1835 the Law Magazine xvi 15, cited Atlay, op. cit. i 72, said that "his name as a great Equity judge may not undeservedly be associated with those of the brightest of our Chancellors"—though it added that in his early days "he brought more of ornament than of very powerful relief to the then oppressed Court".
[9] Greville, Memoirs ii 65.

liked him to keep them. But the Whig party did not approve,[1]
and it became necessary to secure Brougham by making him
Chancellor. It was felt, however, that something should be done
to secure Lyndhurst's services as a judge. Grey offered him the
post of Chief Baron of the Exchequer which, after consulting his
political friends, he accepted. To his capacity as a judge of his
court and to his popularity with the bar Campbell testifies.[2] In
fact he restored the reputation and efficiency of the court.[3] The
Commission on the courts of common law had reported that so
few cases were heard in the court of Exchequer that the position
of Baron was almost a sinecure.

Lyndhurst effected a rapid change, and with the assistance of such able
puisnes as Bayley and Alderson brought back the flow of business until,
in Brougham's language, he had founded anew the Exchequer "with an
éclat and lustre which the Committee on the Courts could hardly have
expected when they made their report." [4]

It is said that when Lyndhurst was made Chief Baron it was
understood that he was not to oppose the government.[5] But the
introduction of the Reform Bill changed the face of politics, and
all understandings, if any such there were, disappeared. In the
House of Lords Lyndhurst was one of the leaders of the opposition
against the successive Reform Bills. It was his amendment to the
third bill, which proposed to postpone the disfranchising clauses,
that caused the resignation of the government, and the unsuccessful attempt, in which Lyndhurst played a considerable part, to
form a Tory government.

In the first reformed Parliament Lyndhurst was the leader of
the opposition in the House of Lords. His opposition was sometimes mistaken, certainly in the case of Brougham's Local Courts
Bill ;[6] and at a later period he saw his mistake.[7] In 1835 he became
Chancellor for the second time in Peel's short lived ministry. It
was in the July of this year that Lyndhurst made the acquaintance of Disraeli, whose genius he from the first recognized. As
Atlay, says[8] there were affinities between them:

they were at one in their dislike for the "Venetian Oligarchy" of the
Whig families, both had a strong strain of the modern spirit of imperial-
ism, neither of them, to put it mildly, had very pedantic scruples in
political warfare; and, one of them a Hebrew by descent, the other a
North American colonial by birth, they both looked at English party
traditions and conventions with a detachment that finds no parallel
amongst their contemporaries. Lyndhurst felt by intuition the extraordinary qualities which lay hidden beneath the bizarre and dandified

---

[1] Quart. Rev. cxxvi 48; see Greville, Memoirs ii 91.
[2] Chancellors viii 71.   [3] Martin, op. cit. 277.   [4] Atlay, op. cit. i 82-83.
[5] Greville, Memoirs ii 92.   [6] Below 17.   [7] Below 17, 18.   [8] Atlay, op. cit. i 112.

exterior of his young friend; had Peel been possessed of equal discernment the history of the Conservative party would have been very different.

When Peel resigned Lyndhurst occasionally heard appeals in the House of Lords and in the Judicial Committee of the Privy Council. His chief occupation was political. He led the opposition to the Municipal Corporations Bill, which he regarded unjustly as a Whig job, and succeeded in making at least one amendment which has been recognized as an improvement.[1] His conduct of the opposition to this bill increased his reputation, and it "exposed the vulnerable spot in the Government harness. They had no longer sufficient popular feeling behind them to browbeat the Press."[2] The government were still further weakened in the House of Lords by its quarrel with Brougham, who joined forces with Lyndhurst and the opposition. Lyndhurst did good service as a critic of crude legislative projects,[3] but, that he was by no means an undiscriminating opponent of reform can be seen from the fact that he had supported the Prisoners' Counsel Bill.[4] He opposed the Irish Municipal Corporations Bill on the ground that it was meant to be a stepping stone to a repeal of the Union;[5] and he did good service to his party by his surveys in 1836 and 1839 of the conduct of the government, and his criticism of its failure to pass its principal measures.[6] In 1841 Peel carried his vote of no confidence in the government, Parliament was dissolved, the conservatives got a majority, and Lyndhurst entered upon his third and last Chancellorship.

We shall see that during Lyndhurst's third Chancellorship several useful measures of law reform were passed.[7] "Any genuine measure for the amendment of the law received his support."[8] His conduct as judge of the court of Chancery during this period has been criticized. It has been said that "his heart was not in the business".[9] We shall see that this is not wholly true.

---

[1] "The retention of the aldermen has been found most beneficial in practice, and has been followed in the creation of the county councils", Atlay, op. cit. i 124.
[2] Ibid.
[3] Hayward says, Quart. Rev. cxxvi 29, "he originated little, but he corrected, perfected, or improved much; and it is no slight praise to say that, without his controlling care, the statute book and the jurisprudence of England would be much more imperfect than they are".
[4] Atlay, op. cit. i 127.   [5] Ibid 128.   [6] Ibid 132, 136.
[7] Below 19.   [8] Atlay, op. cit. i 140.
[9] Selborne, Memoirs ii 372, cited Atlay, op. cit. i 142, says, "my knowledge of him in that character was only during his last Chancellorship from 1841 to 1846, where he took things very indolently and easily, affirming almost indiscriminately the judgements brought before him on appeal. It was depressing to argue before a Chancellor whose heart did not seem to be in the business, however famous he might be as an orator or statesman."

But it is true that in his court he was a judge for the parties rather than a judge for the lawyers.[1] He was,

an acute discerner of fact, an accurate weigher of testimony, a nice discriminator of argument. He was content to deal out justice in the particular matters in Court without laying down principles applicable to other disputes. . . . As Brougham concisely puts it, he possessed the faculty of splitting the nut, throwing away the husk and getting at the kernel.[2]

But there is no doubt that he was a great lawyer. "When Lord Westbury, towards the close of his long life, was once asked at Jowett's table whose was the finest judicial intellect he had ever known, he replied Lord Lyndhurst's; and Lord Grimthorpe was of the same opinion.[3] In the House of Lords he took part in some notable decisions—*Viscount Canterbury v. The Attorney-General*[4]— a rather unfortunate decision,[5] *R. v. Millis* [6]—in which he upheld the majority and probably incorrect view,[7] and the *O'Connell Case*[8] —chiefly notable as the last attempt of lay peers to take part in a judicial decision of the House.[9] He was scrupulously just in his dispensation of patronage, and his judicial appointments were all excellent.[10] With the fall of Peel's ministry in 1846 his last Chancellorship came to an end.

He was glad to retire. He was growing old, and a cataract in one of his eyes threatened him with blindness. But in 1849 he returned to the House of Lords to support a motion to ask the Crown to refuse to assent to a bill passed by the Canadian Parliament, which compensated those who had suffered loss in the Canadian rebellion, on the ground that it applied to the rebels as well as to the loyalists. The cataract was removed; he was able again to resume his activities in Parliament; and his services were so valuable that in 1852 Derby offered him a seat in his cabinet without office. But he refused; a cataract had appeared in the other eye, and it was not till July that it was successfully removed. In 1853 he took part in the decision of the famous *Bridgewater Case* [11]—the leading case on the question of the avoidance of contracts and disposition of property on the ground that they are contrary to public policy.[12] To the end of his

---

[1] This distinction is made by Bagehot, Biographical Studies 67.
[2] Atlay, op. cit. i 143.   [3] Atlay, op. cit. i 85.
[4] (1843) 4 S.T.N.S. 767; 1 Phil. 306.   [5] Holdsworth, H.E.L. ix 43 n. 3.
[6] (1843) 10 Cl. and Fin. 534 at pp. 831-873.   [7] Vol. i 622; above.
[8] (1844) 5 S.T.N.S. 1.   [9] Holdsworth, H.E.L. i 377.
[10] Erle, Cresswell, Alderson, Bolland, Platt, Parke, Taunton, Patteson, Coleridge, Atlay, op. cit. i 146.
[11] *Egerton v. Brownlow* (1853) 4 H.L.C. 1 at pp. 155-164. (The case is commonly treated as a contract case, but it almost entirely concerned the disposition of property. Eds.)   [12] Holdsworth, H.E.L. viii 54-56.

days he did good work, as even Campbell admitted,[1] in committees or on bills for the reform of the law.

Contrary to all experience, his grasp and view seemed to broaden with the increase of years. Free from all party obligations, he was able to view men and measures on their merits alone. In the non-contentious sense of a much abused term he had become a true "Liberal", and the man who had been Solicitor-General to Sidmouth and Castlereagh was found, after a lapse of nearly forty years, joining heartily in the manifold reforms of the mid-Victorian epoch.[2]

In 1857 his opposition in a very witty speech to an ill-drawn bill of Campbell's for the suppression of obscene literature,[3] in which he was supported by Brougham, Cranworth, and Wensleydale, produced a serious quarrel with Campbell, who had uttered some very offensive words in his reply. But the quarrel was made up, and it was chiefly due to Lyndhurst that Campbell was made Chancellor. To the end of his days also he maintained his interest in mechanical scientific inventions and in the classics. His interest in the former is illustrated both by one of his earliest cases, in which he successfully defended his client in an action for the infringement of a patent,[4] and by the interest which he took in patent cases which, under an Act which he had promoted, came before the Judicial Committee of the Privy Council.[5] His interest in the classics is illustrated by a letter which he wrote to Gladstone on the latter's translation of the first book of the Iliad.[6]

He kept his high spirits and his great mental powers to the end. Campbell prints some letters which he received from him in 1859, when he was eighty-seven, which might have been written by a young man full of the *joie de vivre*.[7] Gladstone tells us that Brougham, having heard Lyndhurst, who was over eighty, explain a legal point to him (Gladstone), said, "I tell you what Lyndhurst, I wish I could make an exchange with you. I would give you some of my walking power and you should give me some of your brains".[8] Those mental powers were displayed in the speeches with which on great occasions he astonished and delighted the House of Lords. Of his speech on the Wensleydale peerage case in 1856 Campbell said that it was the most wonderful speech he had ever heard.[9] His great speeches on national defence in 1859 and 1860, in which he advocated a "two power standard", most necessary in the days when the influence of Cobden and

[1] Chancellors, viii 182.
[2] Atlay, op. cit. i 158-159.　　　　　[3] Below 22.
[4] *Boville v. Moore* (1816), Martin, Life of Lyndhurst 123-125.
[5] Ibid 395.　　　　　　　　　　　[6] Ibid 503-504.
[7] Life of Lord Campbell ii 381-382.　　[8] Martin, op. cit. 505.
[9] Chancellors, viii 192-193.

Bryce was at its zenith.[1] In the latter years he argued also for the
constitutional right of the House of Lords to reject the bill
repealing the paper duties.[2] This must have been the speech which
Sir Edward Clarke heard him deliver, for he says that the date
was May 21. Clarke says:

I remember little of the debate, but no one could forget the scene while
he was speaking. He had reached eighty-eight years of age that day; he
could not stand unaided, so a rail had been built for him, and folding
his arms across his chest he hung upon it while he spoke. But the voice
was full and resonant, the argument was closely reasoned, and the perfectly turned sentences were rhythmical and pointed.[3]

His last speech was delivered in 1861 in support of Lord
Kingsdown's Act—"There was no sign of mental failure, but the
physical weakness was sadly evident."[4] He died October 12,
1863, in his ninety-second year.

Lyndhurst's personal characteristics were striking. When he
was a young man waiting for briefs he was described by an
observer as

Sitting in the old Court of Common Pleas, always occupying the same
seat at the extremity of the second circle of the Bar, without paper or
book before him, but looking intently—I had almost said savagely (for
his look to me at this time bore somewhat the appearance of that of an
eagle)—at the Bench before him, watching even the least movement of a
witness or other party in a cause, or treasuring up the development of the
legal argument brought forward by the eminent men who then formed the
inner circle of the Bar of learned serjeants.[5]

When he was beginning to make his way at the bar the same
observer said of him:

In person he was eminently handsome—his voice strong and melodious
—with an eye deeply set, and from which nothing escaped—with a
dignified presence far in advance of his years; his intellect clear, his
memory most tenacious, and his thirst for knowledge unbounded.[6]

Throughout his life his handsome appearance set off by his
perfectly cut garments, and the smart cabriolet which he drove
about London, made him a unique figure amongst the lawyers,
and shocked the staider lawyers of Eldon's school. His own social
gifts and those of his wife increased his popularity with his
professional brethren,[7] and made his house a centre of fashionable
society—literary, scientific and political—though some thought

---

[1] Atlay, op. cit. i 159-161.   [2] Ibid 161.
[3] The Story of my Life 48; Hansard (3rd Ser.) clviii 1463-1473.
[4] Atlay, op. cit. i 161.
[5] W. H. Bennett, Biographical Sketches from the Note Books of a Law Reporter
197.   [6] Ibid 212.
[7] Campbell, op. cit. viii 24; Quart. Rev. cxxvi 16.

he would have been wiser if he had lived in a less extravagant style.[1]

His mental characteristics were no less striking. However complicated the facts of a case he could analyse them, arrange them in his mind, and expound them, in such a way that the legal consequences for which he was arguing seemed natural and inevitable. This power was due to the fact that he had not only a clear logical intellect which could see straight to the heart of a problem, but also a most wonderful memory.[2] When he was at the bar it was said of him, as it was said of Mansfield,[3] that his opening statement was worth any other man's argument;[4] and when he was on the bench the way in which in his summings up to the jury he presented a reasoned analysis of the effect of the evidence was unique.[5] But mental gifts made him somewhat intolerant of shams—like Disraeli he saw through the shallowness of many of the theories of the philosophic radicals; and they made him ready to criticize persons and policies in a way which gave him a reputation for holding radical views, or for a cynical scepticism on political questions.[6] His appearance at some of his utterances on these questions led men to call him Mephistopheles —though in fact "he presented the rather uncommon contrast of a sneering propensity combined with a singularly genial character".[7] With these mental gifts he was, as might be expected, a good judge of men. We have seen that he from the first recognized Disraeli's genius,[8] and that his appointments to the bench were all good.[9] These personal and mental characteristics have been summed up by Bagehot with his usual penetration and felicity. He says:

The characteristic of his intellect was the combination of great force and great lucidity. Every sentence from him was full of light and energy.

[1] Greville, Memoirs ii 110, speaking of his appointment as Chief Baron, says that Lyndhurst talked of himself as standing on neutral ground, disconnected with politics; he adds "It is certainly understood that he is not to fight the battles of the present Government, but of course he is not to be against them. His example is a lesson to statesmen to be frugal, for if he had been rich he would have had a battle ground before him."   [2] Below 22.   [3] Holdsworth, H.E.L. xii 468.

[4] Quart. Rev. cxxvi 21; Martin, op. cit. 203; Atlay, op. cit. 30-31.

[5] "When at the Bar he had frequently observed that the prevailing practice of the presiding judge reading over his notes of the evidence to the jury, when making his charge, instead of clearing and assisting their minds, more commonly, especially in long cases, tended to deaden and confuse them. He therefore resolved, if he were ever raised to the bench, that he should not follow the practice, but should endeavour to present the evidence in a condensed form, and so classified and arranged that the jury might more readily appreciate its bearings upon the points at issue. . . . Only with a judge of the highest order of judicial intellect would such a process be possible, for only such could escape the hazard of losing in the advocate the functions of the judge", Martin, op. cit. 281-282; cf. Atlay, op. cit. i 85.

[6] Ed. Rev. cxxix 567-568.   [7] Ibid 564.   [8] Above 8.   [9] Above 10.

His face and brow were, perhaps, unrivalled in our time for the expression
of pure intellect, and he preserved the physical aptitude for public oratory
to an old age when most men are scarcely fit for mere conversation.[1]

It was because his intellect was a "disciplined" intellect, that
his style of oratory—clear, cogent, logical, unornamented—was
as unique as his personal and mental characteristics. Those who
turn to his speeches will find, says Bagehot,[2]

some of the best, if not the very best, specimens in English, of the best
manner in which a man of great intellect can address and enlighten the
intellects of others. Their art, we might almost say their merit, is of the
highest kind, for it is concealed. The words seem the simplest, clearest,
and most natural that a man could use. It is only the instructed man
who knows that he could not himself have used them, and that few men
could.

And it could suit itself to its environments. His legal arguments
delighted the lawyers. He could interest the House of Commons;
and in the House of Lords his sway was almost absolute.[3] He was
able to expound lucidly or to criticize in committee the details of
a proposed legal reform, to argue clearly, forcibly and learnedly a
complicated constitutional case such as the Wensleydale peerage
case, to expound eloquently a political or a legal principle, to
deal trenchantly with those who attacked him, or to kill with
ridicule proposals which he considered to lead to absurd results.

Both as a statesman and as a lawyer Lyndhurst has left his
mark on English legal history.

For a long time Lyndhurst's reputation as a statesman was
under a cloud. The prevailing opinion was that he was a political
apostate, in spite of his repeated assertions that till he came into
Parliament in 1818 he was connected with no political party; and
Campbell bolstered up these rumours by many inaccurate and
malicious statements. It is quite true that when at the University
and perhaps later he may have exercised his powers of debate in
upholding some of the Jacobin tenets, and in criticizing the
government. His keen critical mind and powers of exposition may
well have been employed, at a time when he belonged to no
political party, in exposing the errors of politicians of all parties.
To a man with his social gifts, sense of humour, and critical
powers "there must have been many temptations to shock a

[1] Biographical Studies 324—a short sketch written just after Lyndhurst's death
in 1863.   [2] Ibid 328-329.
[3] Disraeli, writing on the day of his death October 13, 1863, said, "unsuccessful
in the House of Commons, he rose at once in the House of Lords to a position of
unapproached supremacy. . . . His stately and humorous exposition in a voice of
thrilling music were adapted to a senate of which he caught the tone with facility".
Monypenny and Buckle, Life of Disraeli (revised ed.) i 330.

literal-minded Scot [like Campbell] and go one better than the
enthusiastic Denman".[1] At all periods of his life he had a keen eye
for the mistakes of politicians—it is said that in 1830 he condemned the Duke of Wellington's impolitic declaration against all
reform, though he was Chancellor in his government;[2] and this
characteristic was made the basis of a charge of political cynicism.
But many men in that age of changing conditions saw reason to
alter their political views—Peel, for instance, and Gladstone
amongst statesmen, and Southey, Wordsworth, and Coleridge
amongst men of letters. But Peel and Gladstone never acquired
the reputation which Lyndhurst, in the opinion of many, deserved
of political apostasy or of political cynicism. That neither of these
charges can be substantiated against him is, I think, clear from
the record of his life. Southey once said that he was no more
ashamed of having been a republican than of having been
eighteen;[3] and if the fact that the youthful Gladstone was by
conviction "a stern and unbending Tory" is not remembered
against him, still less should it be remembered against Lyndhurst
that, when an undergraduate or a young barrister, he expressed
sympathy with Jacobins or radicals or Whigs; for it is clear that
"no one who knew him after his entrance into public life could
discern a trace, a sign, a feature of the democrat".[4] As Atlay
says, in political life the general rule is to judge a man by his
public utterances only, and that "it would be hard to find an
instance, save in the case of Copley, where this rule has been
violated".[5] Why was this exception made in his case?

The explanation of the fact that the treatment meted out to
Lyndhurst was different to that meted out to other statesmen,
such as Peel or Gladstone, is, I think, this: the modifications of
their opinions was from Tory to Liberal. They were therefore
treated by Whig historians or sympathizers, who regarded their
opponents as fools, as signs of grace and enlightenment. But, if it
be true that Lyndhurst's early sympathies were radical or Whig,
the modification of his belief was in the opposite direction. His
abilities could not be denied, and therefore his change of view was
ascribed to a political apostasy or cynicism, which induced him
to desert his principles for office. This was the line taken by so
acute a critic as Bagehot. He says:[6]

We do not mean to charge him with acting contrary to his principles—
that charge was made years ago, but was the exaggerated charge of
political opponents, who saw that there was something to blame, but

---

[1] Atlay, op. cit. 25.   [2] Ed. Rev. cxxix 568; Atlay, op. cit. i 77, 79.
[3] Cited Martin, Life of Lord Lyndhurst 147 n. 1.   [4] Quart. Rev. cxxvi 15.
[5] Op. cit. i 25.   [6] Biographical Studies 326-327.

who in their eagerness and haste overdid their accusation. The true charge is that he had no principles, that he did not care to have opinions. If he had applied his splendid judicial faculties to the arguments for free trade or for Catholic emancipation, he would soon enough have discovered the truth.

It was this refusal of the Liberals to acknowledge that anything could be said against the articles of their creed which led them to brand those who refused to subscribe to them as fools, cynics or adventurers. But the historians should remember that, of the policy of Catholic emancipation, Melbourne said that all the fools were opposed to it, and the worst of it was that the fools were right; and that some of the evil results of adhering to the rigid creed of the free traders have been only too painfully brought home to our generation. If it be said that his opposition to some legal reforms, e.g. to Brougham's Local Courts Bill of 1833, was factious, the same charge can equally be made against his Whig opponents. Campbell admits that the Whig opposition to Lyndhurst's Charitable Trusts Bill of 1845 was quite as, if not more, factious.[1]

In my opinion Lyndhurst was a consistent Conservative statesman, ready like Peel to reform when convinced that reform was necessary, who, from the time that he entered Parliament to the end of his life, served both the party and the state well and faithfully. At any rate, as we shall now see, his services to the cause of law reform were considerable. Those services were both positive and negative. Sometimes he originated and supported reforms, and more often he criticized and helped to put into workable shape reforms proposed by others.

If we look at Lyndhurst's attitude to law reform, it would be true to say that the contemporary view that his political opinions moved from the advanced Whig or radical creed to the Tory creed is almost the reverse of the truth. In fact he moved from a Tory to a liberal attitude; and, as he became more and more converted to this attitude in the fourth decade of the nineteenth century, so his influence upon this type of legislation became more marked and more beneficial. Lyndhurst was never a Tory of the Eldon school. We have seen that before 1832 he supported the Dissenters' Marriage Bill and the repeal of the Corporation and Test Acts,[2] and that as attorney-general, as Master of the Rolls, and as Lord Chancellor he supported bills to give effect to the recommendations made by the Chancery Commission in 1826.[3] But, since these recommendations dealt most inadequately with the causes of the defects in the procedure of the

[1] Chancellors, viii 160.   [2] Above 7.   [3] Above 6, 7.

court,[1] it could not be expected that those bills would do much to cure them. It was suggested, for instance, in 1827 that the recommendations made by the Commissioners should be enacted, and that the Chancellor, the Master of the Rolls and the Vice-Chancellor should have power to alter them.[2] But these suggestions did not, as Brougham and M. A. Taylor pointed out, touch two of the main causes of the delays of the court—the procedure of the Masters' offices, and the addition of the jurisdiction in bankruptcy to the equitable jurisdiction.[3] The bill proposed in 1829 was also defective in these respects. Its main purpose was to expedite the hearing of the case after it had been set down,[4] and with that object it proposed to take away the equity jurisdiction of the Exchequer, to appoint an additional Vice-Chancellor, and to provide that the Master of the Rolls should sit in the mornings like the other judges.[5] Owing to the close of the session this bill did not reach the Commons; but in 1830 Lyndhurst introduced another bill which contained similar proposals, and outlined further measures for the reform of the judicial system.[6] But the dissolution of Parliament which followed the death of the King occasioned the loss of this bill.

After 1832 Lyndhurst's hostility to the Reform Act led him to oppose salutary measures of law reform.[7] His opposition in 1833 to Brougham's Local Courts Bill, though it was in fact to a large extent inspired by the fear of the legal profession that their profits would suffer,[8] was based on the theoretically tenable ground—a ground which had, Lyndhurst pointed out, the approval of Hale and Blackstone [9]—that, since the good quality of English justice was due to the centralization of the judicial system, a system of local courts would impair it. He said: [10]

Twelve or fifteen judges educated in the same manner, sitting together at one time and in one place, consulting each other daily and, if need be hourly, subject to the criticism of their compeers, subject also to the competition of an acute and vigilant Bar, kept constantly alive to the justice of the decisions of the judges and their own credit—ensure for suitors a certainty, a precision, a purity; and even a freedom from the suspicion of corruption, such as no other country in the world would ever boast of.

Lyndhurst thought mistakenly that the establishment of such

---

[1] Holdsworth, H.E.L. i 442-443.   [2] Hansard (2nd Ser.) 703-704.
[3] Ibid 712-714, 730, 734.   [4] Hansard (2nd Ser.) xxi 1289.
[5] Ibid 1281-1285.   [6] Ibid xxiii 674-693.
[7] Life of Lord Campbell ii 85-87.   [8] Atlay, op. cit. i 103.
[9] Hansard (3rd Ser.) xviii 872, 873; Hale, History of the Common Law (6th ed.) 340-341, cited vol. i 283-284; Bl. Comm. iii 355-356.
[10] Ibid xviii 871, cited Atlay, op. cit. i 104.

courts would degrade the bar.[1] On the other hand, he was right
when he foretold

the break-up of the circuit system, and the calling into existence of those
local Bars which, in spite of the ability and integrity that characterize
the majority of their members, have not, and never can, replace that old
united corporate Bar of England which was the pride of Copley and his
compeers.[2]

But such considerations as these were altogether outweighed by
the undoubted fact that, as Brougham pointed out, the result of
this centralization was a denial of justice to the poor man.[3] As
Atlay says,[4] Lyndhurst's abilities were on this occasion misdirected. In fact, it is probable that a similar bill had the approval
of Peel in 1830;[5] and though the bill of 1833 was badly drawn it
could have been amended. His abilities were equally misdirected
when he opposed the Municipal Corporations Bill.[6] Here again the
main principle of the Bill was approved by Peel.[7] But Lyndhurst
persisted in regarding it as a Whig job. Fortunately his opposition was not successful. In fact he almost admitted in other years
that his opposition had been factious.[8] However that may be,
there is no doubt that from the fourth decade of the nineteenth
century he acted very differently. In fact he applied to questions
of law reform the principles set out by Peel in his Tamworth
manifesto, with the result that he exercised a very considerable
influence upon the legislation of the middle years of the nineteenth century.

The extent of his influence was due to four main causes.
First, he judged proposals on their merits and was not afraid
to change his former opinions. Secondly, he was willing to promote
all reforms which could be proved to be reasonable. Thirdly, he
was both an effective advocate of reforms which he approved,
and an effective critic both of the principles of reforms of which
he did not approve, and of the details and draftsmanship of
reforms which he approved in principle. Fourthly, his qualities

---

[1] Hansard (3rd Ser.), xix 320-321.   [2] Atlay, op. cit. i 107.
[3] Hansard (3rd Ser.) xix 367-370; vol. i 188-191.
[4] Op. cit. i 106.
[5] Snagge, The Evolution of the County Court, cited Atlay, op. cit. i 102.
[6] Above 9.
[7] "The Whig historians have made the most of Peel's conduct in throwing over
Lyndhurst, as they term it, and Campbell glows with indignation when relating how
he told the ex-Chancellor that Peel had approved of certain clauses which the Lords
had struck out, and got for answer, 'Peel, d - - n Peel! What is Peel to me?' The true
inwardness of the remark, as Mr. Kebbel suggests, was d - - n Jack Campbell",
Atlay, op. cit. i 124.
[8] Greville, Memoirs iii 386, said that Lyndhurst had said to him on January 19,
1837, "I am sure I shall not go on in the House of Lords this year as I did last".

as a statesman and as a lawyer enabled him to persuade Parliament to give effect to his views.

(1) Lyndhurst judged proposals on their merits and was not afraid to change his former opinions. Thus in 1836 he actively supported the Prisoners' Counsel Bill which he had formerly opposed.[1] Though in 1833 he had opposed Brougham's Local Courts Bill,[2] in 1842 and 1845 he supported bills for the establishment of the new county courts. In 1842 there were three bills to establish these courts before the House—one sponsored by Brougham, the second by Cottenham, and the third by Lyndhurst.[3] Lyndhurst explained that his former objections were to a large extent removed by the establishment of a circuit system for the new county court judges, which diminished their number and prevented them from being tied to a particular locality, and by provisions for an appeal from their decisions.[4] But it was unfortunate that in 1845 Brougham's or Cottenham's bills, which would have given a jurisdiction in equity and bankruptcy to these courts, were preferred to Lyndhurst's bill, which, in effect, confined their jurisdiction to actions for breach of contract and tort when the amount at stake was £20 or less.[5] On another occasion, though he had opposed a bill introduced by Campbell to allow persons convicted for misdemeanours to be admitted to bail pending a writ of error, he introduced and carried a similar bill in the following year.[6]

(2) Lyndhurst was willing to promote all reforms which could be proved to be reasonable. The best evidence of this fact is the number of reforming statutes passed between 1841 and 1845 during his last Chancellorship. Important reforms were made in the land law—the mode of conveyancing was improved, feoffments ceased to have a tortious operation,[7] the enfranchisement of copyholds was facilitated,[8] the law of copyright was reformed.[9] The incapacity of witnesses on account of the commission of

---

[1] Atlay, op. cit. i 127.   [2] Above 8, 16, 17, 18.

[3] Hansard (3rd Ser.) lx 719, 1172, 1175; Cottenham had produced three bills—one dealing with the common law jurisdiction, the second with the bankruptcy jurisdiction, and the third with the equitable jurisdiction of those courts.

[4] Hansard (3rd Ser.) lxv 230-231, 255-256.

[5] Ibid 631; 9, 10 Victoria c. 95; vol. i 191-192.

[6] Campbell, Chancellors viii 153-155; 8, 9 Victoria c. 68, amended 16, 17 Victoria c. 32; Lyndhurst explained that his objection to Campbell's bill was founded on the fact that it was inexpedient to deal with the matter while O'Connell's case, to which it might apply, was pending, and he said that he had later taken the matter up at Campbell's request; Brougham agreed with Lyndhurst, and Campbell was so irritated by this agreement that he compared them to the Siamese twins, Hansard lxxviii 131-137.

[7] 7, 8 Victoria c. 76; 8, 9 Victoria c. 106.

[8] 4, 5 Victoria c. 35; 6, 7 Victoria c. 23.   [9] 5, 6 Victoria c. 45.

crime or on account of interest was abolished.[1] The Factors Act was extended;[2] and the formation of joint stock companies was facilitated and regulated by Act, which in effect begins the modern history of company law.[3] Extensive reforms were made in the judicial machinery of the state. Reforms were made in the offices of many of the courts.[4] The equitable jurisdiction of the court of Exchequer was transferred to the court of Chancery.[5] The practice and procedure of the Judicial Committee were reformed.[6] Lyndhurst supported Campbell's Act for the amendment of the criminal law of libel.[7] He was always a friend of religious toleration. He supported Acts to remove the religious disabilities of the Roman Catholics and the Jews,[8] and he was a consistent supporter of measures to allow Jews to hold municipal offices [9] and to sit in Parliament.[10] After he had ceased to be Chancellor he did not cease to promote the cause of law reform. He supported the Common Law Procedure Act [11] and the Chancery Procedure Act of 1852.[12] He supported the Act of 1857 [13] which reformed the law of divorce, and was prepared to allow greater freedom of divorce than the Act ultimately permitted.[14] In fact in this matter he was one of the protagonists of reform, as Gladstone was the protagonist of opposition to reform.[15] The last speech which he made in Parliament was, as we have seen,[16] a cogent and learned argument in support of Lord Kingsdown's Act.[17] Last, but not least, he was an advocate for the reform of legal education, and for a compulsory examination of students before they were called to the bar.[18]

(3) Lyndhurst was an effective advocate of the reforms of which he approved, and an effective critic both of the principles of reform of which he did not approve, and of the details and draftsmanship of reform of which he approved in principle. Lyndhurst's grasp of the principles of English law and his power

---

[1] 6, 7 Victoria c. 85. [2] 5, 6 Victoria, c. 39.

[3] 7, 8 Victoria c. 110 (formation and regulation); ibid c. 111 (winding up); see Formoy, Historical Foundations of Modern Company Law 67-83.

[4] 5, 6 Victoria c. 86 (revenue side of the Exchequer); c. 103 (court of Chancery); 6, 7 Victoria c. 20 (Crown side of the court of Queen's Bench); 8, 9 Victoria c. 34 (seal office of the courts of Queen's Bench and Common Pleas).

[5] 5 Victoria c. 5; vol. i 242. [6] 6, 7 Victoria c. 38.

[7] 6, 7 Victoria c. 96; Campbell, Chancellors, viii 150.

[8] 7, 8 Victoria c. 102 (repeal of twenty-four Acts against Roman Catholics); 9, 10 Victoria c. 59 (repeal of twenty-five Acts against Roman Catholics); ibid § 2 (Jews assimilated to Protestant dissenters with respect to schools, places of worship, and charitable trusts). [9] 8, 9 Victoria c. 52.

[10] Campbell, Chancellors viii 192, 196, 199-200, 204-206.

[11] 15, 16 Victoria c. 76. [12] 15, 16 Victoria c. 86; vol. ix 406-407.

[13] 20, 21 Victoria c. 85. [14] Campbell, Chancellors, viii, 194-196, 197, 199.

[15] Holdsworth, H.E.L. i 624. [16] Above 12.

[17] 24, 25 Victoria, c. 114. [18] Hansard (3rd Ser.) cxxii 1278.

to state them forcibly and lucidly enabled him to explain with equal force and lucidity, the reasons why they ought to be changed or amended. Two good instances of this power are his speech in support of his proposal to establish a body of Charity Commissioners to deal quickly and cheaply with the administration of small charities, and his speech in support of Lord Kingsdown's Act. In the former instance he summed up the reasons for his proposals as follows:[1]

The principle of the Bill is this—at present there is practically no judicial control over charities of the description to which I have referred. It is in my opinion a scandal that such a state of things should any longer exist. The object of my Bill is to establish another tribunal, constituted in the way I have described, with a power to administer the funds, and to protect the administration of these charities; and to avoid the heavy expenses of the present system, which is altogether inconsistent with the objects of these charities. This is the main foundation and principle of the measure. I have, however, grafted on it the power of making an enquiry; but an enquiry only into the amount and application of the funds of all charities; and, in addition to that, in consequence of the great expense attending the present mode of appointing the trustees of municipal charities, I propose that these Commissioners shall, in the first instance, exercise that power of appointment, and thereby avoid that course which involves an enormous expense on those charities, and a continual expense by the necessity that exists of renewing the trustees from time to time.

In the latter instance he explained the very doubtful state in which the law as to the form requisite for the execution of a will by a British subject living abroad had been left by the case of *Bremer v. Freeman*,[2] and pointed out that both continental and Scots law allowed such a testator a choice as to the forms which he might use.[3] At the same time he could foresee the difficulties which might arise from the changes in the law which he supported. Thus in the discussion on Campbell's Act for compensating the families of persons killed by accidents, he foresaw the difficulty which oppresses the courts of estimating compensation for the expectancy of life in particular cases. Campbell said that it had been objected to his Bill that, if the Lord Chancellor was killed by an accident, it would be difficult for a jury to estimate the loss to his family. How could they estimate the value of the tenure of his office? To this Lyndhurst, ever ready for a gibe at Campbell, replied

there is a much more difficult case to estimate for compensation than the one which my noble and learned friend has had the kindness to suggest.

[1] Hansard (3rd Ser.) lxxx 778-779.
[2] (1857) 10 Moo. P.C. 306; Cheshire, Private International Law, 5th ed. 537.
[3] Hansard (3rd Ser.) clxii 1638-1644.

If my noble and learned friend should unfortunately fall a sacrifice, how would any jury be able to estimate the value of his hopes.[1]

We have seen that, in the opinion of Hayward, Lyndhurst was an effective critic of the substance and draftsmanship of the bills in which suggested reforms in the law were embodied.[2] With this opinion Campbell concurs. Speaking of the year 1853 he says [3]

During this session of Parliament there were several Select Committees on bills for the amendment of the law.... I almost always found Lyndhurst at his post, rendering valuable service. This was very laudable conduct; for here he had no party or personal bias to follow, and there was no *éclat* to be obtained, for we sat *foribus clausis*.... Lyndhurst always showed admirable good sense, as well as acuteness and logical discrimination.

He said that Lyndhurst helped him to stop a bill for a partial codification of the criminal law, which if passed "would have thrown its administration into confusion"; and that he gave valuable help in improving a bill for the registration of deeds.[4]

(4) Lyndhurst's qualities as a statesman and as a lawyer enabled him to persuade Parliament to give effect to his views. He showed the same power as a statesman as he showed as a barrister and a judge—the power of so completely mastering all the facts and law of any given case or problem, that he could present its gist not only forcibly and clearly, but also tersely, and sometimes picturesquely. Arguments based on reasons, technical or non-technical, and on policy, were skilfully blended. "In making an introductory statement of any measure", says Campbell,[5] "he ever displayed powers unrivalled in either House of Parliament. Whatever the subject might be, no one could be within sound of his voice without earnestly listening, and warmly admiring, although he might remain unconvinced." And since he was a master of the weapons of ridicule and sarcasm he was able on occasion to make skilful use of them. A good illustration is the manner in which he dealt with Campbell's ill-drawn bill for the suppression of obscene literature. He said:[6]

My noble and learned friend's aim is to put down the sale of obscene books and prints; but what is the interpretation which is to be put on the word obscene? I can easily conceive that two men will come to entirely different conclusions as to its meaning. I have looked into *Johnson* to see what definition he gives of the word, and I find that he says that it is something "immodest; not agreeable to chastity of mind;

---

[1] Hansard (3rd Ser.) lxxxvi 174-175.   [2] Above 9.
[3] Campbell, Chancellors viii, 182.
[4] Ibid.   [5] Chancellors viii 155.
[6] Hansard (3rd Ser.) cxlvi 330-332.

causing lewd ideas. . . ." Suppose now a man following the trade of an informer or a policeman, sees in a window something which he conceives to be a licentious print. He goes to the magistrate and describes, according to his ideas, what he saw, the magistrate thereupon issues his warrant for the seizure of the disgusting print. The officer then goes to the shop, and says to the shop keeper, "Let me look at that picture of Jupiter and Antiope". "Jupiter and what?" says the shop-keeper. "Jupiter and Antiope", repeats the man. "Oh! Jupiter and Antiope you mean", says the shop-keeper; and hands him down the print. He sees the picture of a woman stark naked, lying down, and a satyr standing by her with an expression on his face which shows most distinctly what his feelings are and what is his object. The informer tells the man he is going to seize the print, and take him before a magistrate. "Under what authority?" he asks; and he is told "under the authority of Lord Campbell's Act". "But", says the man, "don't you know that it is a copy of one of the most celebrated masters in Europe?" That does not matter; the informer seizes it as an obscene print. . . . But this is not all. Our informant leaves the print shop and goes into the studio of some sculptor or some statuary, and sees there figures of nymphs, fauns, and satyrs, all perfectly naked, some of them in attitudes which I do not choose to describe. According to this bill they may every one be seized—

Nympharumque leves cum satyris chori.

. . . The informant next proceeds to the circulating libraries . . . Under the Bill a circulating library may be searched from one end to another. In the same way the dramatists of the Reformation, Wycherley, Congreve and the rest of them,—there is not a page in any one of them which might not be seized under this Bill. . . . Dryden, too, is as bad as any of them. . . . Take, too, the whole flight of French novelists, from Crebillon, *fils*, down to Paul de Kock; nothing can be more unchaste, nothing more immodest than they are; and when my noble and learned friend's Bill is passed, every copy of them may be committed to the bonfire with as little mercy as Don Quixote's chivalry books were.

These were the qualities which enabled Lyndhurst to leave a considerable mark upon the enacted law. The influence of his decisions as Chancellor, and as Chief Baron of the Exchequer, though by no means negligible, is less considerable. We have seen that he was as Bagehot said, essentially a judge for the parties.[1] He quickly mastered and clearly explained the essential facts; and then, having done so, he shortly stated the law applicable thereto—often without citing authorities. He was therefore an excellent judge of a case in which the facts were complicated. His gifts of clear statement and his marvellous memory enabled him to try such cases in a way which aroused the admiration of lawyers and laymen alike. The best illustration of these powers is the case of *Small v. Attwood* [2] of which Campbell gives the following account: [3]

It arose out of a contract for the sale of iron-mines in the County of Stafford; and the question was, whether the contract was not vitiated

<hr/>

[1] Above 10.   [2] (1833) 1 Younge 407.   [3] Chancellors viii 72-73.

by certain alleged fraudulent representations of the vendor. . . . Many days were occupied in reading the depositions, and weeks in the comments upon them. The Chief Baron paid unwearied attention to the evidence and the arguments, and at last delivered (by all accounts) the most wonderful judgment ever heard in Westminster Hall. It was entirely oral, and, without ever referring to any notes, he employed a long day in stating complicated facts, in entering into complex calculations, and in correcting the misrepresentations of counsel on both sides. Never once did he falter or hesitate, and never once was he mistaken in a name, a figure, or a date.

It is true that the House of Lords by a majority came to a different conclusion on the facts and reversed his decision. But,

Lyndhurst adhered to his original opinion, and defended it in a speech which again astounded all who heard it, by the unexampled power of memory and lucidness of arrangement by which it was distinguished.[1]

But though in ordinary cases his judgments were short, in important cases such as *Egerton v. Brownlow* [2] and *R. v. Millis* [3] his discussion and criticism of the authorities showed his great qualities as a lawyer. And as Chancellor, more especially in his last Chancellorship, he gave several important decisions.

During his first Chancellorship he decided important cases as to the circumstances in which a vendor of land retains a lien on it for unpaid purchase money,[4] as to the conditions under which a commission to review a decision of the Court of Delegates should be granted,[5] and as to the right of shareholders in a company to compel their directors to refund money of the company which they had improperly applied to their own use.[6] The best known of his decisions during this period is the case of *Dimes v. Scott*,[7] which deals with the liability of trustees, and the rights of tenants for life and remaindermen, where stock, bearing a high rate of interest, has, in breach of trust, been left unconverted.

During his last Chancellorship he decided several well-known cases. The cases of *Allen v. Macpherson* [8] and *Barrs v. Jackson* [9] settle important points as to the relation of the probate jurisdiction of the ecclesiastical courts to the jurisdiction of the court of Chancery. The former case decided that probate was conclusive to the validity of a will, so that it could not be impeached for fraud in the court of Chancery. The latter case decided that a decision of the ecclesiastical court, as to who is next of kin to an

---

[1] Campbell, Chancellors viii 73.　　　　[2] (1853) 4 H. L. C. 1 at pp. 155-164.
[3] (1843) 10 Cl. and Fin. 534 at pp. 831-873.
[4] *Winter v. Lord Anson* (1827) 4 Russ. 488, cited with approval in *In re Brentwood Brick and Coal Co.* (1876) 4 Ch.D. at p. 565.
[5] *Dew v. Clarke* (1828) 5 Russ. 163.
[6] *Hichens v. Congreve* (1828) 4 Russ. 562.
[7] (1828) 4 Russ. 195.　　　　[8] (1842) 1 Phil. 133.　　　　[9] (1845) 1 Phil. 582.

intestate is conclusive. In the case of *Mitford v. Reynolds* [1] there is a clear and learned exposition of the law as to charitable trusts; and in the case of *Jones v. Smith* [2] there is a discussion as to the limits of the unsatisfactory doctrine of constructive notice. The case of *Meek v. Kettlewell* [3] lays down the established principle that no effect can be given by equity to the voluntary assignment of a mere expectancy. The case of *Foley v. Hill* [4] elucidates the nature of the relation between banker and customer, and lays down the important principle that in the case of a purely legal demand courts of equity are bound by statutes of limitation. The case of *Re Plummer* [5] settles the rights of a creditor who has a claim against the separate estates of bankrupt partners and a security for his claim against the joint estates of the partnership. The case of *Baggett v. Meux* [6] decides that a restraint upon anticipation applies to real as well as to personal property, as to an estate in fee as well as to an estate for life. "The power of a married woman", he said,[7] "independent of the trust for separate use, may be different in real estate from what it is in personal: but a Court of Equity, having created in both a new species of estate, may in both cases, modify the incidents of that estate". In the many cases which turned upon the interpretation of wills and other documents his decisions are remarkable for their common sense and clarity of reasoning.

Other decisions of Lord Lyndhurst show that he was a very considerable common lawyer. He showed, in *Davies v. Lowndes* [8]—the last reported case of a writ of right, and in *Doe d. Thomas v. Jones*,[9] that he was well versed in the mysteries of the medieval land law; and his decision in *Viscount Canterbury v. The Attorney-General*,[10] though from some points of view unfortunate,[11] shows that he had mastered the medieval learning as to petitions of right. In the case of *Herring v. Clobery* he laid down the law as to what communications between solicitor and client are privileged in wider terms than did Lord Tenterden; and it is his opinion which has been followed.[12] The case of *Quarrier v. Colston* [13] decided that money won at play or lent for the purpose of gambling in a country where gambling is legal can be recovered in this country—a

---

[1] (1842) 1 Phil. 185.
[2] (1843) 1 Phil. 244; see *Patman v. Harland* (1881) 17 Ch.D. at p. 357.
[3] (1843) 1 Phil. 342; cf. *Re Ellenborough* [1903] 1 Ch. 697.
[4] (1844) 1 Phil. 399.   [5] (1841) 1 Phil. 56.
[6] (1846) 1 Phil. 627.   [7] At p. 628.
[8] (1843) 1 Phil. 328: vol. i 329.
[9] (1831) 1 Cr. and Jerv. 528.   [10] (1843) 4 S.T.N.S. 767; 1 Phil. 306.
[11] Vol. ix 43-44.
[12] (1842) 1 Phil. 91; cf. *Minet v. Morgan* (1873) L.R. 8 Ch. at pp. 367-369.
[13] (1842) 1 Phil. 147.

decision followed by the Court of Appeal in 1909.[1] His judgment in *Balme v. Hutton*,[2] that a sheriff was not liable for conversion, when by virtue of a writ of *fieri facias*, he had sold goods of a debtor after the commission of an act of bankruptcy of which he had no notice, was reversed, but it is both learned and clear. There are also important decisions on the law of evidence,[3] on common law liens,[4] on fixtures,[5] and on the question whether a person found guilty of a crime and fined, could recover compensation from a person who participated in the crime.[6] The law as to contempt of court was elucidated in the case of an attorney who, having been committed for a gross contempt of court, proceeded to sue the person who had got the order of commitment for false imprisonment.[7] International difficulties between France and Spain gave rise to proceedings by the King of Spain in which the right of a foreign sovereign to sue in an English court was established.[8]

Lyndhurst was great both as a statesman and as a lawyer. As a statesman he was one of the most distinguished representatives of that school of Tory statesmen who adopted the Conservative programme of adapting the Tory creed to the new political conditions created by the Reform Act of 1832, and to the new social and economic conditions created by the industrial revolution. It was because he belonged to this school that he was one of the most distinguished of the group of legal statesmen who undertook the task of adapting old law to new needs, and enacting new law, without breaking the continuity of its development. This work was perhaps his most important contribution as a lawyer to the development of English law. As a judge of the courts of Exchequer and Chancery, as a member of the Judicial Committee of the Privy Council and in the House of Lords, he did work both for the development of the common law and of equity. But though his grasp of principle and his quick mastery of the facts of a case made him an excellent judge, he was, as a rule, more intent on doing justice in each case according to law, than on the exposition of legal principles and the distinguishing of analogous cases, with the result that his work in these capacities, though not negligible, was less important. Notwithstanding this

---

[1] *Saxby v. Fulton* [1909] 2 K.B. at p. 221.   [2] (1831) 2 Cr. and Jerv. 19.
[3] *Morgan v. Morgan* (1832) 1 Cr. and Me. 235.
[4] *Judson v. Etheridge* (1833) 1 Cr. and Me. 743.
[5] *Trappes v. Harter* (1833) 2 Cr. and Me. 153.
[6] *Colburn v. Patmore* (1834) 1 Cromp. Me. and R. 73.
[7] *Ex pte. Van Sandau* (1844) 1 Phil. 445; (1846) ibid 605.
[8] *The King of Spain v. Machado* (1827) 4 Russ. 225; *Hullet v. King of Spain* (1828) 1 Dow and Cl. 169.

fact, I think that his qualities as a statesman, and his work for the reform of the law, make him one of the great Chancellors of the nineteenth century. And he was more than that. As Bagehot said, he both looked and was a great man. The distinction of his appearance, was a true index to the distinction of his moral and intellectual qualities—to his high-mindedness, to his grasp of principle in the spheres of politics and law, to his critical powers, to his skill in exposition at the bar, on the bench, and in the House of Lords, to his mastery of the weapons of sarcasm, epigram, and ridicule. In these qualities which made him a great statesman, a great Chancellor and a great man he has not been surpassed by any succeeding Lord Chancellor.

COTTENHAM
(1836-1841, 1846-1850)

Lyndhurst's successor, Charles Christopher Pepys, Lord Cottenham,[1] was a contrast to his predecessor in appearance, in manners, and in intellect. A Chancellor who was handsome and distinguished, an ornament of society, and a statesman who had many interests besides law, was succeeded by a short and thickset man, who was shy and unsociable, and interested only in equity.[2]

Pepys, the son of a Master in Chancery, was born on April 29, 1781. He was educated at Harrow and Trinity College, Cambridge. Like many other famous lawyers, he began his legal studies in Tidd's chambers.[3] He was a diligent student; for, as Atlay says,[4]

With him law was not merely the main, but an all absorbing, interest in life until politics embraced him in their vortex. . . . He was one of those thrice happy mortals who, by good fortune or by self knowledge, are guided to the one calling for which they are adapted by nature, and, secure in their arid fastnesses, cast no lingering looks behind to the green pastures of books, or art, or social pleasure.

He was called to the bar by Lincoln's Inn in 1804, and began his study of equity in Romilly's chambers. He soon got a practice, and took silk in 1826. In 1831, he entered Parliament. He was a thoroughgoing Whig; but he made no mark in the House of

[1] Atlay, Victorian Chancellors i 379-416; Foss, Judges ix 239-342; D.N.B.; Marchant, Memoir of Viscount Althorp 60-68.
[2] Selborne, Memorials, Family and Personal i 371-372.
[3] Holdsworth, H.E.L. vol. xiii. 450 et seq.   [4] Op. cit. i 384-385.

Commons—his practice always came first. The small number of good Whig lawyers available to the government, made him solicitor-general in 1834, and, to the disappointment of Campbell, Master of the Rolls in the same year. In 1835 he was appointed one of the commissioners of the Great Seal, and in 1836 Lord Chancellor with the title of Lord Cottenham. It was said by Greville that the Cabinet was divided as to whether Pepys or Bickersteth should be made Lord Chancellor. Some favoured Bickersteth on the ground that "he promised more as a law reformer".[1] But the party which favoured Pepys carried the day; and Greville with some justice said his promotion was "one of the most curious instances of elevation that ever occurred".

A good sound lawyer, in leading practice at the Bar, never heard of in politics, no orator, a plain undistinguished man, to whom expectation never pointed, and upon whom the Solicitor-Generalship fell as it were by accident, finds himself Master of the Rolls in a few months after his appointment, by the sudden death of Leach, and in little more than one year from that time a peer and a Chancellor.[2]

As a politician Cottenham was a failure.[3] But as a judge in the court of Chancery and in the House of Lords he was a great success; and he proved to be a useful member of the Cabinet. "In a body essentially deficient in backbone the presence of a sturdy obstinate Whig who knew his own mind, untroubled by qualms of hesitancy, was a distinct boon." [4] In fact his thoroughgoing preference for Whigs both in his appointments to the commission of the peace, and in the appointments of trustees to municipal charities within the Municipal Corporations Act aroused considerable criticism. The manner in which Master Brougham proposed to exercise this power in relation to the Ludlow charities aroused Lechmere Charlton, a barrister who represented Ludlow, to write so insulting a letter to him that a duel appeared to be imminent. But this danger blew over, the letter was handed to Cottenham, Charlton was committed for contempt, and the House of Commons refused to interfere.[5]

Cottenham was out of office from 1841 to 1846. When Russell took office in 1846 he again became Chancellor. He remained in office till ill-health forced him to resign in 1850. He died in the following year. His last year of office was embittered by the proceedings of an attorney named Dimes who, in the course of a long

---

[1] Greville, Memoirs iii 335 n.   [2] Ibid 335.
[3] Campbell says, Life ii 44, that he "hated the House of Commons, could with difficulty be made to attend, and only once while he was in his then office (Solicitor-General) was prevailed upon to speak".
[4] Atlay, op. cit. i 404.
[5] *Lechmere Charlton's Case* (1837) 2 My. and Cr. 316; Atlay, op. cit. i 403.

litigation against the Grand Junction Canal Company, had been committed by him for breach of an injunction. Dimes, thirsting for revenge, discovered that Cottenham had some shares in this Company, and induced the House of Lords to set aside his judgment on that ground.[1]—"it was a common belief that Dimes had killed Lord Cottenham".[2]

Cottenham ought to have resigned before. In the House of Lords and the Cabinet he was useless;[3] and his management of his judicial work in the court of Chancery tended to become more and more unsatisfactory. The growth of company law and the jurisdiction given to the court by the Winding Up Acts added enormously to its business. At the same time Cottenham's insistence on the strict observance of the often unreasonable rules of procedure [4]—a characteristic in which he resembled Parke B.;[5] his bad habit of constantly directing enquiries by the Masters; and his delay, caused by his growing ill-health, in giving judgment [6]—all caused a long arrear of causes. His dislike of Knight-Bruce V.-C., who was willing to relax rules of practice in order to do substantial justice,[7] and his growing irritability of temper,[8] did not make for either a smooth or an efficient administration of equity; and we shall see that the legislation which gave him and his colleagues power to make reforms in procedure, and the new Orders and the reforms made by new Orders issued under this power, failed to effect an adequate reform.[9] Atlay says [10] that in 1852, the year in which *Bleak House* appeared, "the existence in its full integrity of the historical office of Lord Chancellor was never in greater peril".

A competent observer declared that the most popular measure which could be introduced into the House of Commons would be one for the abolition *sans phrase* of the Court of Chancery; and the same authority expressed his belief that a determined effort would have swept it away as the Palace Court disappeared under the strokes of Jacob Omnium.[11]

But though Cottenham's last term of office cannot be accounted a success, his contribution during his two periods of office to

---

[1] *Dimes v. Grand Junction Canal Co.* (1852) 3 H.L.C. 759.
[2] Atlay, op. cit. i 415.   [3] Life of Lord Campbell ii 242.
[4] "He even upheld the hourly warrants which were one of the chief abominations of the Master's office." Atlay, op. cit. i 411; for this abomination, see vol. ix 360-361.
[5] See vol. ix 325-327; Vol. xv. 486-492.   [6] Atlay, op. cit. i 411.
[7] Ibid 412-413; Selborne, Memorials, Family and Personal i 375, says, "the seeds of dislike between him and Lord Cottenham were sown when that great lawyer, plain and dull of speech, had to endure what he regarded as daily affronts from his eloquent competitor. They bore fruit when one sat as Judge of Appeal over the other; for if Lord Cottenham did not approach his judgments with a disposition to reverse them, it was scarcely less an evil that Knight-Bruce thought he did."
[8] Atlay, op. cit. i 413-414.   [9] Below 31.   [10] Op.cit. i 450.   [11] Ibid.

the development of English law was considerable. In the first place, that contribution consisted to some extent in the reforms, legislative and otherwise, which he made in the practice and procedure of his Court and in other branches of the law. In the second place, it consisted more especially in the manner in which, by his decisions, he developed equitable doctrines.

(1) In spite of Brougham's efforts,[1] arrears in the business of the court of Chancery and the House of Lords continued to pile up. In 1836 Cottenham introduced a bill to deal with the situation.[2] It was proposed that the Lord Chancellor should be detached from the court of Chancery; that there should be a Chief Justice of the court of Chancery who should hear appeals from the Master of the Rolls and the Vice-Chancellor; and that the judicial duties of the Lord Chancellor should be confined to hearing appeals in the House of Lords and the Privy Council. It was also proposed that the House should sit to hear appeals during a prorogation or dissolution of Parliament, and that it should have the same power to summon the judges of the court of Chancery to assist it as it had to summon the judges of the court of Common Law. There was a good deal to be said for these proposals; and in another shape most of them have gradually materialized. The institution of a court of intermediate appeal for equity cases in 1851,[3] though it did not detach the Lord Chancellor from the court of Chancery, for he could sit to hear appeals either in the court of intermediate appeal or by himself concurrently with that court,[4] did induce him for the most part to confine his attention to the hearing of appeals in the House of Lords and the Privy Council;[5] and the Judicature Acts and the Appellate Jurisdiction Act brought some of the other suggested reforms into operation.[6] But Cottenham was an ineffective speaker in the House of Lords, and though his speech was clear, it did not produce a good impression.[7] His proposals were opposed by Lyndhurst,[8] and they were criticized by Bickersteth, now Lord Langdale M.R.,[9] who was a follower of Bentham, and, like him, wished to detach the ministerial from the judicial duties of the Chancellor.[10] He proposed to take from the Lord Chancellor the custody of the Great Seal, and to limit his functions to his judicial duties in the court of Chancery; to entrust the Great Seal to a Lord Keeper who should have no

---

[1] Above 17.   [2] Hansard (3rd Ser.) xxxiii 402-424.
[3] Vol. i 443-444; 14, 15 Victoria c. 83.
[4] Ibid § 11.   [5] Below 33.   [6] Vol. i 639, 644.
[7] Campbell said of his speech, Life ii 82, that it was "tame, confused, and *dissuassive*".
[8] Hansard (3rd Ser.) xxxiv 427-440.
[9] Ibid 410-477; for Lord Langdale, see below 115.   [10] See vol. xiii 89, 93.

judicial duties and should act as a Minister of Justice; and to entrust the hearing of appeals to a Lord President of the House of Lords who should be helped by lawyers to be styled "Lords Assistant" chosen by himself.

Neither of these proposals came to anything, and a proposal to increase the judicial strength of the court by the appointment of two additional Vice-Chancellors was abandoned.[1] But Acts were passed in 1840 [2] and 1841,[3] which gave the Chancellor, with the consent of the Master of the Rolls and the Vice-Chancellor power to alter rules of procedure. Under the powers given by these Acts reforms in procedure were made in 1841 by a set of fifty-one new Orders in Chancery, which made many detailed reforms,[4] but were quite inadequate to supply a remedy for the main defects in that procedure. Since, as we have seen, Cottenham was a stickler for the strict observance of all the rules of procedure,[5] it is not surprising that they afforded little relief, and that "ten years later the complaint rose loud that, as to the great bulk of Chancery grievances, the suitor and the practitioner were just as they had been in 1840".[6] For the rest, Cottenham gave his support to several Acts which effected much needed reforms in the law. Three important Acts were the Act which (1) abolished the right to arrest on mesne process for debts except in certain cases defined by the Act,[7] and (2) destroyed the chief argument for imprisonment for debt on final process by making it possible to to take in execution a debtor's choses in action;[8] the Wills Act;[9] and the Act which made a release sufficient for the conveyance of land held by a free tenure.[10] Another Act repealed an Act of 1817 [11] which had prohibited the clergy from all dealings in the way of trade. This Act had been interpreted to mean that if a clergyman was a partner or a shareholder in a joint stock company, the partnership or company was an illegal association and therefore could not recover money due to it.[12] Lastly an Act of 1847 provided facilities for the payment of trust money into court by trustees who wished to be relieved from the responsibility of administering the trust.[13]

(2) As a judge of the court of Chancery there is no doubt that Cottenham made the largest contribution to equity of any

[1] Atlay, op. cit. i 139; legal gossip said that it was abandoned because the government could not agree how the new judgeships were to be filled, ibid; this step was taken by Peel in 1842, vol. i 443.
[2] 3, 4 Victoria c. 94.   [3] 4, 5 Victoria c. 52.
[4] Sanders, Chancery Orders i Pt. ii 875-887.   [5] Above 29.
[6] Atlay, op. cit. i 408.   [7] 1, 2 Victoria c. 110 §§ 1-3.
[8] Ibid § 12; vol. xi 524-525, 600.   [9] 7 William IV and 1 Victoria c. 26.
[10] 4, 5 Victoria c. 21.   [11] 57 George III c. 99 § 3.
[12] 4, 5 Victoria c. 14.   [13] 10, 11 Victoria c. 96.

Chancellor since Eldon.[1] He was exclusively an equity practitioner; and it was to the study of the principles of equity that he had devoted all his talents. Though he was never a brilliant advocate, he was a very sound lawyer who could state and explain the facts of a case and the principles applicable thereto clearly and concisely. These qualities had made him a good advocate, and they made him an even better judge. The best appreciation of his qualities as a judge was written by his friend Sir Dennis Le Marchant. He says:[2]

He had an acute and logical understanding, in which the subtlety of discrimination was so nicely balanced by strong common sense, that it never betrayed him into over-refinement, or clouded his judgment. Hence his decision was prompt, and when once formed not easily shaken. In that point lay his superiority to Lord Eldon, whose turn for speculative disquisition, while it led him to scatter broad and vivid lights on all sides of the case which he had to decide, yet in the case itself perplexed his mind with doubts, and occasioned a vacillation of judgment, which was a fruitful source of delay to the suitors. . . . The genius of Lord Cottenham, on the other hand, lay rather in action than in speculation; when he indulged in disquisitions, and some of his judgments abound in them, it was always for the purpose of elucidating his view of the cases before him, not of starting incidental or extraneous questions. Hence, his judgments were at once businesslike and philosophical: sound determinations of the particular rights at issue, and, at the same time, treasures of legal knowledge and instruction to the general practitioner and the student. The style of them, like the character of the man, was perfectly free from all affectation and display; whether written or spoken, they were always simple, terse, and perspicuous; clear and condensed in their summary of facts, and in their exposition of law, comprehensive and vigorous, but at the same time cautious and precise. In those which he pronounced extempore, his delivery was too rapid to admit of much attention either to the choice of his words, or to the structure of his sentences; but his written judgments, though aspiring to none of the graces of composition, possessed all the highest attributes of the judicial style; not the least of which was a very sparing use of figurative or metaphorical language, which in subjects requiring logical precision is so fertile a source of fallacy and misconception. In all branches of his jurisdiction he exhibited the qualities of a consummate judge, but in none so conspicuously as upon questions relating to the Reformed Municipal Corporations, and to great Railway and other Companies,[3] which sprang up in such numbers during the period of his judicial career. The adjustment of the rights and obligations of those great bodies opened a new province of jurisprudence, in which he left a record of powers, which will bear comparison with those displayed by Lord Mansfield in the large domain of commercial law.

[1] Selborne, Memorials, Family and Personal i 371.
[2] Memoir of Viscount Althorp 63-65.
[3] Of his dealing with this class of case Sir John Rolt, Memoirs 78, says, "in these cases Cottenham was happy in his application of old principles to the new classes of transactions which the altered condition of society and affairs had introduced".

With this verdict Serjeant Manning,[1] Lord Kingsdown,[2] and Rolt L. J.[3] agreed. On the other hand Rolt complained that he was too apt "to crush the facts of any case so as to fit any principle upon which he professed to act". He said, truly enough, that his reputation was growing, and that it would grow as his contemporaries "who knew this weakness or wickedness" died off.[4]

His demeanour in court was harsh and unconciliatory. He was intolerant of mere declaration and repetition, but he listened patiently to arguments which pertained to the issue.[5] He was quick to detect a sophism—"He had a singularly disconcerting habit of condensing a specious train of reasoning into a sentence or two of his own, and presenting the result in all its naked deformity to the discomfited parent. 'It is very awkward, observed one of the counsel most frequently employed in his Court; he just puts it to you shortly, and asks, Is that your argument?, adding quietly, I only want to know, that is all, and then, when he sees he is right, he sinks back in his chair, and it is all over.'"[6] Once he had come to a conclusion he adhered to it with great obstinacy. He did occasionally recant; but "there was a certain Gladstonian twist in his mind, a burning desire to reconcile two incompatibles, and the task of recantation was marked by a laboured attempt to prove that his previous judgments did not carry the consequences that were imputed to them".[7] His capacity to perform this feat made him adept in the art of distinguishing cases which laid down rules of which he did not approve.[8]

Two branches of equity which were greatly developed by his decisions were the rules as to the issue of injunctions and some of the basic rules as to company law.

Two of Cottenham's decisions on the question whether the court will issue an injunction to enforce a negative stipulation in a contract which is not specifically enforceable, are not easy to reconcile. In the first of these cases—*Hills v. Croll*[9]—it was held that if the court cannot enforce specific performance of the whole of the contract it will not enforce part of it by an injunction, and an injunction was refused, although the contract had been executed in part. In the second of these cases—*Dietrichsen v.*

---

[1] Atlay, op. cit. i 402.   [2] Reminiscences 111, cited Atlay, op. cit. i 402.
[3] Memoirs 77-78.   [4] Memoirs of Sir John Rolt 90.
[5] Le Marchant, Memoir of Viscount Althorp 65.
[6] Atlay, op. cit. i 400.
[7] Ibid i 401; as Atlay points out, op. cit. i 401 n. 2, a good illustration of these characteristics is to be found in his decisions in *Massey v. Parker* (1834), 1 My. and K. 174, and *Tullett v. Armstrong* (1839) 4 My. and Cr. at pp. 397-407; see also the cases of *Hills v. Croll* and *Dietrichsen v. Cabburn* cited below.
[8] See *De Visme v. De Visme* (1849) 1 M. and G. 336, cited Atlay, op. cit. i 401.
[9] (1845) 2 Ph. 60.

Cabburn [1]—it was held that an express negative stipulation in a partly executed but not specifically enforceable contract could be enforced by injunction. This decision was followed by Lord St. Leonards in *Lumley v. Wagner*.[2] But later cases have shown that there are difficulties in the application of the rule in that case, which tend to show that there is much to be said for the stricter and clearer rule laid down in *Hills v. Croll* and other cases.[3] The case of *Tulk v. Moxhay*[4] in which Cottenham affirmed a decision of Lord Langdale M.R., began the series of cases which has made a large equitable addition to the legal rules which govern the running of covenants with an estate in the land.[5] Cottenham based his decision on a personal equity which affected the conscience of a purchaser who bought with notice of the covenant;[6] but in the later cases the inference has been drawn from the existence of this personal equity that such covenants are, like easements, annexed to the land, and therefore bind all who take the land with notice of them;[7] and it is upon this ground that they are now said to run with the land in equity.[8] In the case of *Spottiswoode v. Clarke*[9] Cottenham laid down the principle, which Eldon had in some cases overlooked,[10] that if an injunction is applied for to protect a legal right, the court must be certain that the legal right exists; for if its existence is not certain, "the court in granting the injunction is expressing a strong opinion upon the legal question, before that question is discussed in the proper tribunal", and might do great injustice if, after all, it turns out that the legal right does not exist.[11]

We have seen that Cottenham's decisions laid the foundations of our modern company law.[12] One of the most important of his decisions is the case of *Mozley v. Alston*,[13] in which he followed the decision of Wigram V.-C. in *Foss v. Harbottle*,[14] which laid it down that, as a rule,[15] it is the company and not the individual shareholders who must sue for redress for any illegal acts committed

---

[1] (1846) 2 Ph. 52.   [2] (1852) 1 De G.M. and G. 604; below 54.

[3] "I confess I look upon *Lumley v. Wagner* rather as an anomaly to be followed in cases like it, but an anomaly which it would be very dangerous to extend", *Whitwood Chemical Co. v. Hardman* [1891] 2 Ch. at p. 428, *per* Lindley L.J. See Hanbury, Modern Equity, 7th ed. 545-549.   [4] (1848) 2 Ph. 774.

[5] The decision had been forestalled by *Holmes v. Buckley* (1691) Eq. Cas. Abr. 27 (Eds.).   [6] At p. 778.

[7] *L.S.W.R. v. Gomm* (1882) 20 Ch.D. at p. 583 *per* Jessel, M.R.

[8] See *Rogers v. Hosegood* [1900] Ch. at p. 407.

[9] (1846) 2 Ph. 154; see also *Hilton v. Earl of Granville* (1841) Cr. and Ph. at p. 292.

[10] See vol. xiii 637, 638.   [11] *Spottiswoode v. Clarke* (1846) 2 Ph. at p. 157.

[12] Above 29, 32.   [13] (1847) 1 Ph. 790.   [14] (1843) 2 Hare 461.

[15] For cases to which the rule does not apply, see *Russell v. Wakefield Waterworks Co.* (1875), 20 Eq. at pp. 481-482 *per* Jessel M.R.

by its directors. In the case of *Ex parte Hall* [1] Cottenham laid down the principle, which was approved by the House of Lords in *Buchan's Case*, [2] that a trustee to whom shares had not been transferred, so that he was not a member of the company, could not be made liable as a contributory.

In all branches of the equitable jurisdiction of the court of Chancery Cottenham decided what may be fairly called leading cases in equity. The following are a few examples: *Tullett v. Armstrong* [3]—restraint upon anticipation; *Powys v. Mansfield* [4] and *Pym v. Lockyer* [5]—double portions; *Burrough v. Philcox* [6]—power in the nature of a trust; *Wedderburn v. Wedderburn* [7]—the position of surviving partners who are executors of a deceased partner and use their testator's capital in the business; *Cherry v. Boultbee* [8]—the equitable application of the rules of set off and retainer; *Jefferys v. Jefferys* [9]—the difference between the rights of a volunteer under an executed and under an executory trust; *Attorney-General v. Ironmongers Co.* [10]—the cy-près application of funds left upon a charitable trust; *Saunders v. Vautier* [11]—the power of a *cestui que trust* who is *sui juris* to put an end to the trust; *Styles v. Guy* [12]—the liability of executors and trustees for the acts of a co-executor or trustee; *Clough v. Bond* [13]—the liability of a trustee who permits the trust fund to remain under the control of his co-trustee who misapplies it; *Corporation of London v. Grainger* [14]—the application of the rule against perpetuities to charitable trusts; *Mason v. Bogg* [15]—the rights of a secured creditor against the estate of a deceased insolvent debtor; *Lassence v. Tierney* [16]—the rule applied where there is an absolute gift upon which trusts which fail are engrafted. On the other hand, in the case of *Hammersley v. De Biel*, [17] his somewhat loose expressions as to the duty to make good representations upon which another party has acted, [18] have been the source of doubts as to whether this is an equitable duty distinct from a duty arising from contract or estoppel. [19]

Besides these cases which settle important points of equitable doctrine there are one or two which are interesting on account of their facts. Prince Albert made a successful application to the

---

[1] (1849) 1 M. and G. 307.
[2] (1879) 4 App. Cas. 583 at pp. 590-592.
[3] (1839) 4 My. and Cr. 390.
[4] (1837) 3 My. and Cr. 359.
[5] (1841) 5 My. and Cr. 29.
[6] (1840) 5 My. and Cr. 72.
[7] (1838) 4 My. and Cr. 41.
[8] (1839) 4 My. and Cr. 442.
[9] (1841) Cr. and Ph. 138.
[10] (1841) Cr. and Ph. 208.
[11] (1841) Cr. and Ph. 240.
[12] (1849) 1 M. and G. 422.
[13] (1838) 3 My. and Cr. 490.
[14] (1849) 1 M. and G. 460.
[15] (1837) 2 My. and Cr. 443.
[16] (1849) 1 M. and G. 551.
[17] (1845) 12 Cl. and Fin. 45.
[18] Ibid at p. 62 *note*.
[19] Pollock, Contracts, Appendix 9.

court to protect his copyright in certain etchings, which the defendant had, in breach of his contract with the Prince, infringed.[1] The case of *Saunders v. Smith* [2] raised the question whether the defendant, the learned author of Smith's Leading Cases, had infringed the copyright of the plaintiff in certain of the cases which he had printed. Baron de Bode's petition of right, which went through all the courts, helped to elucidate many points relating to petitions of right. In one of its stages it came before Cottenham;[3] and Anstey's tract on the subject, which put forward an unorthodox view of the scope of a petition of right,[4] was addressed to him. Lyndhurst favoured de Bode's claim; and after the courts had turned it down,[5] though he was over eighty, he persuaded the House of Lords to appoint a committee to inquire into his claims by a speech which Campbell said was the most wonderful effort that he had ever witnessed.[6] But, though the committee reported in de Bode's favour,[7] cases of the nineteenth and twentieth century have proved the correctness of the decision that he had no legal claim.[8]

I think that these few illustrations show that Cottenham was one of the greatest of our purely legal Chancellors. His work did much to complete our modern system of equity. It supplemented and rendered more precise the principles laid down by his predecessors, and in some cases it inaugurated new developments of equitable principles.

[1] *Prince Albert v. Strange* (1849) 1 M. and G. 25.
[2] (1838) 3 My. and Cr. 711.
[3] (1840) 2 Ph. 85.   [4] Vol. ix. 39-40.
[5] *Baron de Bode v. The Queen* (1851) 3 H.L.C. 449.
[6] "He was now turned of eighty; he was obliged to support himself on a walking stick while he spoke, and he was nearly blind. But his voice was strong, articulate, and musical, his arrangement lucid, his reasoning ingenious and plausible, and he displayed a power of memory which at my age would have appeared almost miraculous. . . . He had a very bad case, yet he not only riveted the attention of all who heard him, but enlisted their sympathies on his side, and made all who had not before studied the facts convinced that he was pleading for a much injured and oppressed individual", Campbell, Chancellors viii 176-177.
[7] Lord Derby's government came to an end, and de Bode's claim was repudiated by Lord Aberdeen, whose action was approved by the House of Lords, ibid 177.
[8] *Rustomjee v. The Queen* (1876) 1 Q.B.D. 487, 2 Q.B.D. 69; *Civilian War Claimants Association v. The King* [1932] A.C. 14.

TRURO
(1850-1852)

After Cottenham's resignation the Great Seal was put into commission—with very bad results.[1] The government were obliged to find a Chancellor, and they selected Thomas Wilde, Lord Truro. Of his career I have already given an account.[2] He was essentially a common lawyer; but his services to equity were not inconsiderable. They consisted chiefly in the legislation which he promoted, and to a lesser extent in his decisions as Chancellor.

The Act of 1851,[3] which created a court of intermediate appeal for Chancery cases effected a real and effective reform, and, in Atlay's opinion, solved the problem of relieving the Chancellor without impairing, as Cottenham's and Langdale's proposals [4] would have impaired, his position. Atlay says:[5]

Under Lord Cottenham ... the Chancellor's Court had become little more than a court of appeal from the Master of the Rolls and the Vice-Chancellors. The new Act gave statutory sanction to the practice, and associated with the holder of the Great Seal two "Lords Justices" who were authorised to exercise the same judicial powers as the Lord Chancellor, either jointly with him or in his absence. At a single stroke the Gordian knot was cut. No more was heard of a minister of justice, or of a "chief judge in Chancery". The Chancellor was set free to attend to his duties in the House of Lords, and as a minister of State, without interruption to the business of his Court. And this was effected without impairing the dignity of the office and without divorcing the holder of the Great Seal from his connection with the practical administration of justice.

He took an active part in passing an Act which lowered the fees paid by the suitors, and abolished many sinecure offices.[6] He appointed the commission which recommended the first really effective reforms in the practice and procedure of the court of Chancery, and, before he left office, he had directed the preparation of a bill to give effect to some of their recommendations [7]— though he had been opposed to their principal recommendation, the abolition of the Masters and the procedure of their offices.[8]

---

[1] Rolfe was the only competent commissioner; Langdale was without vigour, and Shadwell was confined to his bed; the result was that the arrears of Chancery business continued to pile up, and Brougham was the only law lord available for hearing appeals to the House of Lords; the Chancery counsel sent a deputation to the Home Secretary to complain of the inadequacy of the judicial staff in their court; Life of Lord Campbell ii 281-282.

[2] Vol. xv 443-450.   [3] 14, 15 Victoria c. 83; vol. i 443-444.
[4] Above 30, 31.   [5] The Victorian Chancellors i 450-451.
[6] 15, 16 Victoria c. 87; vol. i 445.   [7] Atlay, op. cit. i 451 and n. 1, ii 40.
[8] Atlay, op. cit. i 452.

The bill was taken up by the succeeding conservative government, and passed in the Chancellorship of his successor, Lord St
Leonards,[1] who prepared and carried another measure for the reform of Chancery pleading and procedure[2]—though, like Truro,
he had with difficulty acquiesced in some of the reforms effected
by these Acts.[3] The latter Act is the counterpart of the Common
Law Procedure Act,[4] which was passed in the same year, and
carried out the recommendations of a commission appointed by
Cottenham. Both of these Acts were supported by Truro. On the
other hand he opposed, fortunately without success, the Act
which made parties to an action competent witnesses,[5] on the
ground that it would "open the flood gates of perjury".[6]

Truro, as attorney-general had argued equity cases;[7] and
though he was essentially a common lawyer he showed considerable capacity to master rapidly the principles of other bodies of
law. His very learned judgment in the *Braintree Case*,[8] which
decided that a church rate made by the minority of vestry was
invalid, showed that he could assimilate and apply the rules of
pleading in the ecclesiastical courts. In the same way some of his
decisions as Chancellor show that he had assimilated and could
apply correctly the principles of equity. In the case of *Briggs v.
Penny* [9] he showed that he had mastered the law as to precatory
trusts; and in the case of *Benyon v. Nettlefold* [10] there is a useful
discussion as to the rights of the parties to contracts founded
upon an illegal consideration. The case of *Rowland v. Witherden* [11]
asserted the liability of trustees to replace trust funds which had
been misapplied by their solicitor to whom they had been handed
over for investment. The case of *Staniland v. Willott* [12] is authority
for the proposition that if a *donatio mortis causa* has been made,
and the donor recovers from his illness, the donee holds the property as trustee for the donor till it is retransferred. The case of
ex parte Blakeley's Executors [13] explains the extent of the liability

---

[1] Atlay, op. cit. ii 41; 15, 16 Victoria, c. 80; vol. i 444-445; vol. ix 375.
[2] 15, 16 Victoria c. 86; vol. ix 375-376, 406-407.
[3] He had very reluctantly been converted to the idea that equity judges should
take over from the Masters the duty of working out their decrees, and he never
approved of the introduction into Chancery proceedings of *viva voce* evidence,
Atlay, op. cit. ii 41.   [4] 15, 16 Victoria, c. 76.
[5] 14, 15 Victoria c. 99.   [6] Atlay, op. cit. i 452.
[7] One illustration is the case of the *Corporation of Gloucester v. Osborn* (1847)
1 H.L.C. 272; see Truro's remarks in the case of *Briggs v. Penny* (1851) 3 M. and G.
at p. 554.
[8] *Gosling v. Veley* (1853) 4 H.L.C. at pp. 771-813.   [9] (1851) 3 M. and G. 546.
[10] (1850) 3 M. and G. 94; cf. Lord Selborne's remarks in *Ayerst v. Jenkins*
(1873) 16 Eq. at p. 282.
[11] (1851) 3 M. and G. 568.   [12] (1852) 3 M. and G. 664.
[13] (1852) 3 M. and G. 726; cf. *Baird's Case* (1870) L.R. and Ch. at p. 736 *per*
James L.J.

of the executors of a contributory in the winding up of a company. But since Truro was a common lawyer, it was in cases which involved questions of both law and equity that his decisions are most illuminating.[1] The following cases are illustrations: The case of *S.E.R. v. Brogden*[2] which raised the question of the conditions in which a case which involved the taking of accounts could be left to a court of law, and a case in which equity must assume jurisdiction; the case of *Stocker v. Brocklebank*[3] which raised the question when profit-sharing connoted partnership and when it did not; the case of *Owen v. Homan*[4] in which some of the incidents of the contract of suretyship were discussed. His judgments in all these cases are clear and well reasoned, so that it is not surprising that he soon gained "the confidence of all who practised before him".[5]

ST. LEONARDS
(1852)

Truro was succeeded by Edward Burtenshaw Sugden, Lord St. Leonards.[6] Sugden was born on February 12, 1781, and, like Abbott, Lord Tenterden,[7] was the son of a barber—but a barber in a larger way of business than was Abbott's father. He began his legal career as a clerk to a firm of solicitors. He had occasion to take some papers to Duval, the well-known conveyancer, who was so struck by his knowledge of the law relating to the matter in hand that he took him as his pupil without a fee. This episode illustrates the fact that, from his earliest years Sugden was interested in the study of the law of real property. It remained his principal interest throughout his life.

He became a student of Lincoln's Inn in 1802; and in the same year he published, when he was only twenty-one, a book entitled *A Brief Conversation with a Gentleman of Landed Property about to*

---

[1] Follett said that Rolt once argued a case before Truro in which he stressed the rule that equity followed the law which was in favour of his client; but that when he reargued it before St. Leonards that argument was dropped, and "not one word was said about equity following the law", Memoirs of Sir John Rolt 136.
[2] (1850) 3 M. and G. 8.   [3] (1851) 3 M. and G. 250.
[4] (1851) 3 M. and G. 378.   [5] Atlay, The Victorian Chancellors i 453.
[6] Ibid ii 1-52; Foss, Judges ix 267-270; D.N.B.; St. Leonard's tract on Misrepresentation in Campbell's Lives of Lyndhurst and Brougham supplies some details; Blackwood's Magazine lxxxi 243-264.   [7] Vol. xiii 516.

buy or sell Lands.[1] There is I think little doubt that Campbell's story that when he first met him he opened the conversation by asking his opinion of the doctrine of *scintilla juris*, is true.[2] He was then writing his book on *Vendors and Purchasers*,[3] and his mind was full of such topics. He began to practise as a conveyancer under the bar in 1805,[4] and in the same year he published the first edition of this book. It was the first book ever published on this subject, and it grouped together parts of the law which, though closely related, had never before been brought together in one book.[5] It was an immediate success, and two editions were published before his call to the bar in 1807. Sugden himself says that "it was certainly the foundation of my early success in life".[6] It was, as Atlay says,[7] "one of those rare books which not only attract the attention of the student and the practitioner, but bring business in their train. Young Sugden awoke to find himself famous, and his table loaded with abstracts and cases for opinion."

Immediately after his call he took rank as one of the leading conveyancing counsel; and at the same time he showed that he was equally effective in court. *Browne v. Like*,[8] heard by Grant M.R., was the first case which he argued.

Mr. Sugden's senior on that occasion was Sir Samuel Romilly, who left him to open the case. He has since said that when he first rose, at the corner of the back bench in that dusty little court, his knees shook under him; but if this were so, he disguised his nervousness, and spoke, as we have heard, with apparent calmness and self possession—so effectually arguing the first of the two points in dispute, and the main one, that, on his proceeding to the second, to his surprise, Mr. Richards, subsequently Chief Baron of the Exchequer, who led for the defendant, turned round and told him that they should abandon that point; thereby so encouraging the young counsel, that, in a more lively and confident frame of mind, he proceeded to his second point. His opponents were unable to answer his lucid argument; and after a few words in reply from Sir Samuel Romilly, the court decided in favour of the plaintiff.[9]

His practice became so large that he was obliged to abandon his conveyancing business, and confine himself to court work. Eldon thought so highly of his abilities that he gave him silk in 1822.

By that time he had become the leader of the Chancery bar, and in 1818 and 1826 he made two unsuccessful attempts to get

---

[1] Below 49, 50. [2] Vol. xiii 647. [3] Below 47.
[4] For this branch of the legal profession, see vol. vi 448; vol. xii 26-27, 71-72.
[5] Below 47.
[6] Vendors and Purchasers, Preface to the 13th ed.
[7] Victorian Chancellors ii 4. [8] (1807) 4 Ves. 302.
[9] Blackwood's Magazine lxxxi 246.

into Parliament. He succeeded in 1828. He was a Tory, but a Tory of the Peel rather than of the Eldon school. He was willing, as we shall see,[1] to support proposals for reforms in the law, provided that they were not "revolutionary"; and though he approved of Brougham's proposals for commissions on common law procedure and the law of real property, he was not prepared to support drastic reforms in the court of Chancery.[2] In fact he went so far as to say that those who found fault with the court were fraudulent trustees or persons of doubtful character.[3] But, like other distinguished equity lawyers,[4] he did not make a good impression either on the electors or the House of Commons. His delivery was monotonous, his voice was shrill, and his success in the courts had made him very vain of his own abilities and very supercilious in his manner towards his opponents. No doubt his vanity and defects of temper were aggravated by overwork.[5] But they were ingrained, and continued throughout his career, though his great legal abilities at the bar and on the bench were justly admired. The man himself never succeeded in making himself popular—Selborne said of him that he was "waspish, over-bearing, and impatient of contradiction";[6] and Rolt L.J. agreed with this verdict.[7]

In 1829 he was made solicitor-general. Lyndhurst admired his abilities, and was glad to have his assistance in the early days of his Chancellorship. The Tories resigned in 1830, and for the next four years Sugden was out of office. He did not find Brougham so easy a Chancellor to get on with as Lyndhurst. Brougham had on one occasion scored off him heavily in the House of Commons;[8] and Brougham's manners on the bench were resented by Sugden —more particularly his habit of writing letters while listening to the argument. Sugden, in order to stop this abuse, stopped dead in the middle of a sentence.

After a considerable pause the Chancellor, without raising his eyes from the papers, said, "Go on, Sir Edward; I am listening to you." *Sugden*—"I observe that your Lordship is engaged in writing, and not favouring me with your attention." *Chancellor*—"I am signing papers of mere form. You may as well say I am not to blow my nose or take snuff while you speak." [9]

---

[1] Below 52 *et seq.*   [2] Hansard (2nd Ser.) xix 85-89.   [3] Ibid 86.
[4] Atlay, op. cit. ii 12-13.   [5] Blackwood, op. cit. lxxxi 252.
[6] "A very clever man, profound in conveyancing and case law; waspish, over-bearing and impatient of contradiction. In Ireland, where everybody did homage to his superiority, he made a good Judge; but in England, both as Chancellor and in the House of Lords, the quality of his judgments suffered from his inability to endure a brother near the throne", Memorials, Family and Personal i 374-375.
[7] Memoirs of Sir John Rolt 133-134.
[8] Atlay, op. cit. ii 13.   [9] Campbell, Chancellors viii 386.

Sugden denies Campbell's allegation that he sat down in a huff and was laughed at. But he admits the substantial truth of the story, and says that henceforth Brougham did not dare openly to pursue this practice.[1] Naturally the relations between the two men continued to be strained. Sugden was reported to have said that if Brougham had known a little law he would have known a little about everything; and he took advantage of Brougham's appointment of his brother to one of the sinecure offices in his court, which had been marked for abolition, to attack him in the House of Commons. Brougham replied in so offensive a speech that Sugden called attention to it in the House of Commons,[2] and all friendly relations between them were broken off. But Brougham showed his usual genius for healing the enmities which his indiscretions had caused, and friendly relations were restored.[3]

In 1834 Sugden was made Lord Chancellor of Ireland. Though he only held office for a few months his abilities as a judge won the admiration of the Irish bar.[4] The loss of his office on the return of the Whigs to power left him unemployed. He employed his leisure in writing new, and re-editing his old, legal treatises, and in criticizing in the House of Commons, sometimes unjustly, the government's proposals for law reform.[5] His criticisms of the Wills Act was particularly misplaced.[6] It caused an irritation between him and Campbell which left its traces in some serious misrepresentations in Campbell's posthumous volume, to which Sugden made an effective reply.

When Peel took office in 1841 Sugden returned to Ireland as Chancellor. His term of office lasted for five years, and during that term he performed its various duties admirably. Of the way in which he performed his judicial duties Atlay says:[7]

He was equally at home in delivering a weighty and considered judgment, or in coping with the daily emergencies of Court work. Unsparing of time and labour where he entertained any doubt, his vast experience and his habits of literary composition generally enabled him to give judgment as soon as counsel had sat down. His memory was as retentive as that of Lord Lyndhurst; he hardly ever took a note, and the form of his decisions was as perfect as their matter.

His achievements in his other spheres of action were equally impressive. He reformed the administration of the law relating to lunatics, and personally visited asylums to see that his orders were obeyed—a malicious story was circulated that he was once

---

[1] Misrepresentation in Campbell's Lives 5-9.   [2] Ibid 827-849.
[3] Ibid 16-29; Atlay, op. cit. ii 20-25; Hansard (3rd Ser.) xiv 721-724, 735-737.
[4] Cited Atlay, op. cit. ii 26-27.   [5] Ibid 29.
[6] Ibid 30; Hansard (3rd Ser.) xxxix 521-553.
[7] Victorian Chancellors ii 32.

detained by the officials of an asylum who had been told that they
were to expect a gentleman who was under the delusion that he
was Chancellor of Ireland.[1] To the indignation of some of the
Whigs he removed from the commissioners of the peace all
persons who belonged to the Repeal Association—an action
successfully defended by Brougham and Lyndhurst; and it was
his and the Lord Lieutenant's action in proclaiming the Clontarf
meeting in 1843 which gave a decisive blow to O'Connell's
reputation.[2] The Encumbered Estates Court set up by Peel was
based on a scheme which Sugden had drawn up.[3] That the
Irish appreciated his qualities and his achievements is clear from
a summary of them which appeared at the end of his period of
office. The writer said:[4]

He never mixed himself up in the party politics of the country; he had
no followers or connections there; was ruled by no clique, and earwigged
by no favourites. He was distinguished as a great Chancery Reformer
as well as a great Chancery Judge. He reformed the Master's offices and
established a tribunal for the taxation of costs. In matters of lunacy and
in the Accountant-General's Department he introduced large and
sweeping changes, some of which have been followed in England by
Lord Cottenham.

From 1846 to 1852 Sugden was out of office. He employed his
leisure in the revision of his books, and the writing of his book on
The Law of Property as Administered in the House of Lords,[5] of
which Brougham said that, like Bentley's Phalaris, it was "a
book no scholar can lay down when he has once taken it up, and
exercising an almost equal fascination over those who are no
scholars".[6] It was during this period that he had a controversy
with Dickens who, in preparation for the writing of *Bleak House*,
was studying the court of Chancery. In 1850 Dickens wrote in
Household Words an article entitled *The Martyrs of Chancery*, in
which he asserted that persons imprisoned for contempt of the
court of Chancery were forgotten and left to die in prison "on
account of Chancery proceedings of the very existence of which
they were almost in ignorance before they somehow or other
were found in contempt". Sugden replied in a long letter to *The
Times* in which he had no difficulty in showing that this abuse had
been put an end to by an Act of 1830 which he had proposed and
carried.[7] In fact Dickens's statement in the Preface to *Bleak*

[1] He denied the truth of this story, but suspected Sir P. Crampton, an Irish
surgeon, who had once accompanied him on these visits, of having invented it;
Life of Lord Campbell ii 231-232.   [2] Ibid ii 34.   [3] Ibid ii 33.
    [4] Cited Blackwood's Magazine lxxxi 257.   [5] Below 48.
    [6] Misrepresentation in Campbell's Lives 33, citing a letter from Brougham of
February 5, 1857.   [7] Below 50, 53.

House that "everything set forth in these pages concerning the Court of Chancery is substantially true and within the truth", though true of 1827 when the action of the story takes place, was not wholly true of 1850.[1]

On February 27, 1852 he became Lord Chancellor in Lord Derby's government and was raised to the peerage with the title of Lord St. Leonards of Slaugham. In England, as in Ireland, he was a very successful judge of the court of Chancery.[2]

Long experience had prepared him for every possible complication of facts; his vast memory and piercing intelligence provided him with a solution for every conceivable problem of law. His manner, though dry and disconcerting, was full of judicial dignity. He was patient enough, so long as counsel, whatever their standing, eschewed redundancy and irrelevance. But undoubtedly those fared best before him who recognised the intuitive celerity with which he grasped the real issue, and who indulged in the least superfluous adornment of their cases. He was especially intolerant of those adjournments which were largely responsible for the block in Chancery. And by his own habit of giving judgment at the conclusion of the argument without delay or "further consideration", he did much during his tenure of office to stimulate a healthy flow.[3]

But his term of office was very short. The Government was defeated, and on December 28, 1852, he was succeeded by Cranworth.[4] St. Leonards went back to the task of rewriting and re-editing his books. When Lord Derby regained office in 1858 he refused to become Chancellor a second time—much to the disappointment of the legal profession in general and of Brougham in particular.[5] He continued to hear appeals in the House of Lords. Brougham's frequent absences, and the way in which, when present, he performed his judicial duties,[6] and the bad relations existing between St. Leonards and Cranworth, made the House of Lords so unsatisfactory a tribunal that the project of creating life peers to strengthen its judicial strength was mooted;[7] and it was attempted without success to create a life peer by an act of the prerogative.[8] It would seem that at the close of his life his arrogant temper and great reputation as a real property and equity lawyer made him so intolerant of opposition to his

[1] Holdsworth, Charles Dickens as a Legal Historian 80-81; Atlay, op. cit. ii 35-37.
[2] "He is undoubtedly a great master of his judicial work", Life of Lord Campbell ii 308.
[3] Atlay, op. cit. ii 39.   [4] Below 57.
[5] He says, Misrepresentation in Campbell's Lives 29, that Brougham, "when he heard that I had declined to accept the Great Seal a second time, he laid hold of my two arms in the House of Lords . . . and with tears in his eyes, urged me to retract my refusal".
[6] Life of Lord Granville i 171, cited Atlay, op. cit. ii 73.
[7] Ibid ii 47, 73; below 60.   [8] Below 51.

view of the law that he would not listen to any argument against it.[1]

He continued to criticize changes in the law of which he did not approve, and thus, he had some hard things to say of the Act of 1853 [2] which imposed a succession duty on the devolution of real property.[3] He also continued to take part in debates on projects of law reform. To the end of his life he opposed projects for the fusion either of law and equity or of the jurisdiction of the courts administering law and equity. Thus, he opposed a proposal of Campbell's to give common law judges the power to grant equitable relief;[4] and, "when in 1870 Lord Hatherley introduced the first phantasmal sketch of The Judicature Act the veteran of eighty-eight subjected 'the fusion—or, as he should prefer to call it the confusion—of law and equity' to a vigorous criticism. He especially objected to the proposed removal of the Law Courts from Westminster." [5]

It was in this year that Cockburn C.J. referred to him as "the Nestor of the profession, who has done more to teach the law and improve the law then any man of his age".[6] He died in 1875 in his ninety-third year.

Appropriately enough he left as a legacy to the legal profession a leading case on the law as to lost wills.[7] He had executed his will in 1870, and eight codicils to it between 1870 and 1873. They were prepared with great care, as became so distinguished a convevancer. In 1873 his daughter Miss Sugden, who had acted

---

[1] "I would give as an instance of his unjust way of hearing Causes, the way in which he heard, in the House of Lords the appeals of *The Duke of Portland v. Topham* ((1864) 11 H.L.C. 32). The subject of the appeals relating, chiefly if not exclusively, to the execution of Powers, he soon let his Brother Peers, and the Bar, know that in this subject he was the great Master. . . . He was against the Appellant; I, for the Respondent, had nothing to do but to sit still. *Giffard*, who was for the Appellant, had no fair hearing. I was not called on, and the appeal was dismissed, substantially without any Argument. In my opinion the Case was by no means without difficulty, was certainly arguable, and ought to have been deliberately heard. I could mention other instances in which by some sudden and arrogant crotchet he has forced Counsel to fold up their Briefs, and sit down unheard. Like other Oracles he was frequently oracular, that is, mysterious, and not very intelligible", Memoirs of Sir John Rolt 133-134; Campbell, Life ii 375, said that it was impossible "to act comfortably with him".

[2] 16, 17 Victoria c. 51.

[3] The Act, he said, "has deprived property of half its charms; it is as if a blight had fallen on the fair fields of England. Every man had the right to keep his parchments—his sheepskins—in his own box in his own house; no one had a right to pry into the contents of his settlements. Now every man's settlement must be open to the tax office and to the Government of the day, ever on the watch for a new succession, in order to levy a new duty", A Handy Book of Property Law 129.

[4] Misrepresentation in Campbell's Lives 51–53.

[5] Atlay, op. cit. ii 47; see his speech on the housing of the courts in 1865, Hansard (3rd Ser.) clxxviii 1181-1188.

[6] Letter on "Our Judicial System" (1870) 7 n.   [7] Atlay, op. cit. ii 49-52.

as secretary and amanuensis and who was appointed his executrix, removed the box containing the will and codicils from an escritoire in a sitting room to her bedroom. When the box was opened after his death the will was missing. But Miss Sugden in her capacity as secretary had become so well acquainted with its contents, and so learned in property law through her work on the different editions of her father's treatises, that she could repeat the substance of the will. It was clear on the evidence that St. Leonards had not destroyed his will *animo revocandi*. But would the court accept the secondary evidence of its contents given by Miss Sugden, who was an interested witness? Though some great lawyers thought that the court would not grant probate to a will thus proved, Hannen P. held that the contents of a lost will could be proved, like the contents of any other lost document, by secondary evidence; and

Miss Sugden's remarkable display in the witness box, aided by a minute examination of the wording of the codicils and the co-ordination of some parol evidence, prevailed with the judge who decreed that the contents of the will of 1870 were, with a single exception, what Miss Sugden had represented them to be.[1]

This decision was upheld on appeal.[2] Both courts refused to speculate upon the manner in which the will had disappeared; and the mystery of its disappearance has never been finally cleared up. But it is generally believed that it was taken from the box by a servant when it was in the escritoire, with the object of seeing if any legacies had been given to the servants. It was easy to do this since it was proved that no less than five keys of the escritoire were in existence. When the box was moved to Miss Sugden's bedroom the servant found it impossible to replace the will, and so he destroyed it.

St. Leonards is unique amongst Chancellors from the fact that he left his mark upon English law not only as a legislator and a judge, but as an author. We must now consider his work in these three capacities.

The author

St. Leonard's two principal works are his treatises on Vendors and Purchasers and on Powers. Of them I shall speak in the first place. Secondly, there are books on subjects cognate thereto— his editions of Gilbert on Uses, his account of the decisions of the House of Lords on the law of property, and his summary and

---

[1] *Sugden v. Lord St. Leonards* (1876) 1 P.D. 155, at pp. 175-205.
[2] Ibid at pp. 217-252.

account of the new statutes relating to property. Thirdly, there is an elementary book on the law of property. Lastly, there are pamphlets upon current legal topics.

(1) St. Leonards himself in the Preface to the thirteenth edition of his *Law of Vendors and Purchasers of Estates* has related the history of that book. Here is his account of its genesis:

Determined at my outset in life to write a book, I was delighted when I hit upon the subject now before the reader—The Law of Vendors and Purchasers. The title promised well, and many portions of the law had not previously been embodied in any treatise. . . . When this work was announced for publication, nearly the universal opinion was that it would be a failure, as the subjects to be considered were too multifarious for one treatise. Nothing dismayed, I laboured diligently, and, with the aid of Lincoln's Inn Library, in which a considerable portion of the book was written—for my own shelves were but scantily furnished —I at length finished the work in its original shape. My courage then failed me. The expense of publication was certain; and success, I thought, more than doubtful; and it was not without some difficulty that I could be persuaded to refrain from committing the manuscript to the flames, and to join with a bookseller in incurring the risk of publishing it on half profits, as it is termed. As soon as the book was printed, another bookseller bought my interest in the Edition, and thus relieved me from my obligations. The amount I received as the price of the Edition was small, but I have never since received any sum with anything approaching the same satisfaction.

Edition followed edition;[1] and in spite of the demands of an immense practice he kept it up to date. After his return from Ireland in 1835 he had abundant leisure, which he used to produce in 1839 a much enlarged tenth edition of the book in three volumes. In 1846 an eleventh edition of the book was compressed into two volumes; but even with this compression the book was becoming unwieldly. The twelfth edition was still further compressed into one volume. The commentary on real property statutes was published in a separate volume, and lengthy discussions were omitted. In the thirteenth edition, which was published in 1857, he endeavoured to combine the virtues of the twelfth and the preceding editions. It was to be a treatise on the subject and at the same time a concise view of it. The fourteenth edition, the last to be edited by the author, was published in 1862. Every edition was carefully revised, and all the relevant cases and statutes were added and discussed. In its final form the book consisted of twenty-five chapters which cover completely the many disparate legal problems which may arise out of dealings in land.

[1] The dates of these editions are 1805, 1806, 1809, 1813, 1818, 1822, 1826, 1830, 1834, 1839, 1846, 1851, 1857, 1862.

St. Leonard's *Practical Treatise on Powers*,[1] did not, like his book on Vendors and Purchasers, break new ground, We have seen that J. J. Powell published a book on that subject in 1787.[2] Because the subject was intimately related to very many branches of the law of real property, and to the practice of the conveyancer's art, St. Leonards was eminently competent to deal with it. In the eighth and last edition, which was published in 1861, he inserted, by way of introduction, his introduction to his edition of Gilbert on Uses, and added the substance of many of his notes to that edition.[3] Though it was not the first book on this topic, it was by far the most comprehensive and the most learned. In its nineteen chapters all the cases old and new and all the relevant statutes are fully stated, discussed and criticized. It had no rival till the publication of Lord Justice Farwell's treatise in 1874, and it is still a useful authority.

(2) Of Gilbert's book on *Uses and Trusts* I have already spoken. We have seen that it was an unfinished book which dealt mainly with the medieval use.[4] St. Leonards greatly added to its value by completing it and bringing it up to date. We have seen that much of the additional information which he supplied he used in his introductory chapter to his treatise on *Powers*.[5] His *Treatise on the Law of Property as Administered in the House of Lords*, which was published in 1849, comprises a discussion of all cases on the law of property decided during the preceding thirty-five years. The book begins with an introductory chapter in which the history of the jurisdiction of the House of Lords is clearly related, and a useful account is given of the various projects for the reform of its appellate jurisdiction from the author's own project in 1830 to a plan suggested by him in 1841. The cases are dealt with in the following six chapters: I, Contracts, Deeds and Settlements; II, Wills; III, Powers; IV, Leases; V, Mortgages; VI, Purchases. The cases discussed include some not reported and are taken from the printed cases presented on appeals to the House, and other materials, and include many in which he was counsel. The cases are clearly stated and the discussion and criticism of them is acute and very learned. We have seen that the book won high praise from Brougham.[6] His *Treatise on the New Statutes Relating to Property* [7] is a summary and a discussion in the light of decided cases of some seventeen statutes passed between 1833 and 1862. His account of the Real Property Limitation Act, 1833, the

---

[1] The dates of the editions of this book are 1808, 1815, 1821, 1826, 1831, 1836, 1845, 1861.   [2] Vol. xii 382.
[3] Preface to the eighth ed.   [4] Vol. xii 187.
[5] Vol. xv 292, 293.   [6] Above 43.   [7] First ed. 1852, 2nd ed. 1862.

Prescription Act, 1832, and the Wills Act, 1837 are particularly full and learned. The preface to the book tells us something of the author's attitude to law reform. His view was that the advantages of large changes, which disturbed old principles and introduced fundamental changes, were very uncertain whilst the cost of working them out was certain. On the other hand he favoured changes in detail which removed anomalies in substantive and adjective law, and decreased the expense of dealings with property. He said:

It was said long ago by a great man that every line of the Statute of Frauds was worth a subsidy. We know that every line of it has cost a subsidy. This conviction may reconcile us to our old laws, the operation of which has been long settled, and may deter us from hasty and ill-considered changes. We are, perhaps, too apt to think every alteration an improvement, and we do not sufficiently consider that a long period must elapse before our new laws will obtain that ready, cheerful obedience which is accorded to our time honoured institutes. Still there is room for improvement; but this is a point upon which few men agree. The tendency of the age seems to be in favour of some striking and extensive scheme, regardless of expense—the necessity of which may not be obvious and the operation of which none can foretell—whilst little favour is extended to measures which would clear up doubts and remove obstructions, and thus, at no expense, invigorate our system, prevent litigation, and lessen the expenses of our daily transactions with our property.

We shall see that it was this policy which Sugden pursued in the legislative reforms of the law which he effected.[1]

(3) In 1809 St. Leonards published *A Series of Letters to a Man of Property on the Sale, Purchase, Leasing, Settlement, and Devising of Estates*. Their object is thus explained by the author:

You complain to me, my dear Sir, that though utterly ignorant of Law, you are constantly compelled to exercise your own judgment on legal points: that you cannot always have your solicitor at your elbow; and yet contracts for sale, purchase, or lease of an estate, or, perhaps, even an agreement to make a settlement on a child's marriage, must be entered into off-hand; and it is not until you have gone too far to retreat that you learn what errors you have committed; that you are even at a loss in giving instructions for your will, and wholly incapable of making the most simple one for yourself; that, in a word, you have been plunged into a law-suit, which a slight previous knowledge might happily have prevented. . . . You ask me to remove the cause of your complaint. This I may undertake as a *friend*, without any violation of professional etiquette; and I shall, therefore, readily comply with your wishes.

The ten letters expanded to the number of twenty-five were reissued in 1858 under the title of *A Handy Book of Property in a*

[1] Below 52 *et seq.*

Series of Letters. In both books the advice given on points of law is so excellent and so clearly and simply expressed that Campbell said from the bench that if it were proposed to pass an Act to declare that everything in the book was law he would support it, and in a letter that the formality of passing such an Act was quite unnecessary. And the book is valuable not only on matters of law but on matters of conduct and policy. Of the latter aspect of these letters one instance will suffice. St. Leonards gives the following piece of advice to a man about to make his will:

No hatred is more intense than that which arises in a man's family after his death, when, under his will, the rights of each member of it are not separately and strictly defined. None is more afflicting or degrading to our common nature. We weep over the loss of our relative, and we quarrel over the division of his property. Be careful not to make an unwise or ill-considered disposition, particularly of your residue, upon which the contest generally arises. As you love your family pity them—throw not the apple of discord amongst them. If you leave to every one *separately* what you desire each to have, and give nothing amongst them which requires division, and therefore selection and choice, peace and goodwill will continue to reign amongst them.[1]

(4) Throughout his life St. Leonards wrote letters or tracts on legal problems or on topics of current interest. In 1819 he wrote a learned tract in the form of a letter to Charles Butler,[2] in which he discussed the question when the court could presume the surrender of terms assigned to attend the inheritance, and questioned the correctness of a case decided by Abbott C. J. in that year.[3] In 1825 he replied to John Williams's strictures on the court of Chancery.[4] It is not a very convincing reply since it consists partly of a *tu quoque* statement of the defects of the common law courts, and does not grapple with the deep-seated defects of the procedure of the court of Chancery. In 1825 he wrote a very able letter to Lord Melbourne in which he pointed out the inconveniences of continuing to keep the Great Seal in commission,[5] and criticized the schemes of Cottenham and others [6] for dividing the functions of the Chancellor. His letter of 1850 in reply to Dickens I have already mentioned.[7] In 1852 he criticized very ably Cranworth's schemes for the registration of deeds,[8] and distinguished them from the registration of

---

[1] Handy Book 154-155.   [2] For Butler, see vol. xii 372-373.
[3] *Doe d. Putland v. Hilder* 2 B. and Ald. 782.
[4] For these strictures, see vol. xiii 289, 291, 292.
[5] His view was that the decisions of the commissioners carried no weight; he also pointed out that there was a question relating to the separate property of married women on which the two equity commissioners—the Vice-Chancellor and the Master of the Rolls—differed; the result was that each in turn could reverse the other in the House of Lords.   [6] Above 37.   [7] Above 43.
[8] Shall we Register our Deeds? by Sir Edward Sugden; cf. Atlay, The Victorian Chancellors ii 72-73.

judgments and other similar incumbrances on land which an Act promoted by him had made compulsory.[1] In 1856 he published his speech on *The Wensleydale Peerage Case*,[2] which contains an argument against the policy and the legality of life peerages. It succeeds in proving that, whether or not a life peerage can be legally created, such a peerage can carry with it no right to sit in the House of Lords. In 1861 he published his speech on the *Berkeley Peerage Case*,[3] which demonstrated finally that baronies by tenure, if they ever existed, were things of the past. He argued that whether or not they had once existed, they had been made impossible by Charles II's Statute of Tenures. In 1869 the sarcastic references made to St. Leonards by Campbell in his Lives of Lyndhurst and Brougham produced what Atlay calls "a rather pathetic tract" which is "a valuable exposé of Lord Campbell's methods, and of his views as to the obligations of friendship".[4] We have seen that it supplies some valuable autobiographical details.

The merits of St. Leonards's books are considerable. His enthusiasm for law and for its correct ascertainment and exposition are equalled only by that of Coke. As with Coke[5] so with him, his books were in many cases produced whilst their author was conducting a leading practice at the bar, and in later life, was filling an important position on the bench; and, unlike Coke, he found time while at the bar and on the bench to re-edit and in many cases to rewrite them. The books covered the whole of the subjects treated by them. All the cases were read and considered and critically discussed, and all the relevant statutes were similarly treated. Both the decisions on points of law and equity, and the decisions on the construction of the relevant statutes, were stated clearly and either supported by additional reasoning or criticized acutely. The main defect of these books was the consequence of their repeated re-editing by their author, and the addition to them of new cases and discussions of those cases. Sugden himself admitted in the preface to the fourth edition of his *Vendors and Purchasers* that "the grafts upon the original stock, if they added to its value, were not likely to improve its symmetry". It became a little difficult to see the wood for the trees. This is the element of truth contained in Bryce's unduly harsh criticism of his books. Bryce,[6] from this point of view,

---

[1] 2, 3 Victoria c. 11; for the distinction between these two very different kinds of registers which was not clearly grasped till the latter part of the nineteenth century, see vol. xii 379-380.   [2] Vol. xiv 146.   [3] Vol. xiv 145.
[4] The Victorian Chancellors ii 48.   [5] Vol. v 426, 456.
[6] "His treatises show the same acuteness and ingenuity in arguing from cases which his forensic career displayed. But these treatises are a mere accumulation of

compares them unfavourably with the works of the great Roman jurists. But his comparison is unjust to St. Leonards. St. Leonards's power of discussing legal problems in the light of the concrete facts of the case is not unlike the power displayed by the Roman jurists. No doubt St. Leonards's discussions are fuller and more exhaustive—but we only have fragments of the Roman juristic writings. However that may be, there is no doubt that St. Leonards's books do show a great grasp of principles and considerable power of stating them. That power is perhaps most conspicuously displayed in his short book on property law to which, as we have seen, Campbell gave deservedly high praise.[1] In fact very learned men such as Coke, St. Leonards, and Vinogradoff have often been most successful when they have been compelled to be brief, for their grasp of the subject enables them to select the essential principles and to state them briefly, clearly, and accurately.[2]

It was these qualities which in his own day made Sugden's books almost books of authority. We shall now see that the mastery of legal principle which they gave him made him able to propose, and in many cases to induce Parliament to enact, important reforms in the law.

The legislator

St. Leonards's views as to the reform of the law by legislation were very consistent. In 1828, speaking on Brougham's motion for the reform of the law, he said,[3]

No one was more desirous than he was to see the abuses which may have gradually crept into the administration of the law effectually reformed; but he confessed he looked with no little alarm at the disposition which he saw beginning to prevail, of attempting rash innovation, and striking, under the vain hope of amendment, at the root of that system, under which the country had flourished for ages. Laws, he considered, not to be so much made by the wisdom of man as to have been formed and improved by time; and he thought that nothing was more absurd in that point of view, than to suppose that any individual, however profound his wisdom or extensive his knowledge, could form a code of laws, for the purpose of governing the property and rights of the people, and thereby supersede all the wisdom of the ages which were past. He hoped therefore that the House would not sanction too large or too extensive

details, unillumined and unrelieved by any statement of general principles. In literary style, and no less in the cast and quality of his intellect, he is harsh and crabbed, but his frequent obscurity must be due less to a want of clear thinking than to the fact that our legal text-books have so rarely arrived at excellence of literary form that this famous case-lawyer had no ideal of lucidity or finish before him"; Studies in History and Jurisprudence, ii 199-200.

[1] Above 50.   [2] Vol. v 460.   [3] Hansard (2nd Ser.) xviii 898-899.

an enquiry, which might have the effect of setting men's minds afloat upon points which the experience of time had sanctioned, although the reasons which supported them or the principles upon which they were founded, might not be immediately apparent.

We have seen that he expressed the same views in 1862. They were in substance the same views as those expressed by Hale,[1] and he gave effect to them by proposing or supporting a considerable number of useful reforms.

The first reported case which St. Leonards argued involved a consideration of the Act of 1777 which required the enrolment of grants of annuities and prescribed the form which deeds granting them must take:[2] the first piece of legislation for which he was responsible was the repeal of this Act by an Act which substituted other not very dissimilar provisions.[3] The other statutes for which he was responsible deal with the practice of the court of Chancery, the rules of equity, lunatics, and some of the rules of the law of property.

The most important of the statutes dealing with *the practice of the Court of Chancery* is the statute of 1830 which reformed the law as to commitments for contempt by the court of Chancery.[4] I have already given some account of this statute,[5] to which, as we have seen,[6] St. Leonards successfully appealed in his controversy with Dickens on this subject. The Act of 1852, which abolished the Masters and made great and salutary changes in the procedure of the court of Chancery,[7] was passed during his Chancellorship; but it was the work of his predecessors. In 1853, he promoted an Act which effected improvements in the suitors fee fund of the court of Chancery.[8] Amongst the Acts which he promoted for improving *the rules of equity* are the following: Acts of 1825 and 1830[9] consolidated and amended the law as to conveyances by trustees who were infants or lunatics or who could not be compelled or who refused to act and as to stock belonging to infants or lunatics, and gave new powers to the court to render effective decrees for specific performance where the vendor had died and to appoint new trustees; a second Act of 1830 amended the law as to illusory appointments;[10] a third Act of 1830[11] consolidated and amended the statutes of Fraudulent Devises and

---

[1] Vol. vi 592-594.   [2] 17 George III c. 26; vol. xi 604-606.
[3] 53 George III c. 141; this Act was repealed by the Act which abolished the usury laws, 17, 18 Victoria c. 90; vol. viii 112; vol. xv 13.
[4] 11 George IV and 1 William IV c. 36.   [5] Vol. xiii 412.   [6] Above 43.
[7] 15, 16 Victoria c. 80; above 38.   [8] 16, 17 Victoria c. 98.
[9] 6 George IV c. 74; repealed and re-enacted with amendments by 11 George IV and 1 William IV c. 60.
[10] 11 George IV and 1 William IV c. 46; vol. vii 175.
[11] 11 George IV and 1 William IV c. 47; vol. vi 397-398; vol. xiii 266, 408, 414.

the law as to the payment of the debts of deceased persons and of their real property; a fourth Act of 1830 consolidated and amended the law as to the property of infants, married women, and lunatics.[1] Throughout his career St. Leonards was interested in the laws as to *lunatics*, and it was mainly by his efforts that the law as to many aspects of this subject was effectually reformed. In 1842 [2] he carried an Act for the reform of private lunatic asylums in Ireland. In 1845 and 1853 [3] he supported Acts to regulate the care and treatment of lunatics; and in 1853 Acts to regulate proceedings under commissions of lunacy and the management of their property,[4] and as to the provision of lunatic asylums by counties and boroughs and the case of pauper lunatics.[5] St. Leonards's contributions to *the law of property* are contained in an Act of 1839 for protecting purchasers by requiring the registration of judgments, *lis pendens*, and fiats in bankruptcy;[6] in an Act which made a very useful amendment to the Wills Act 1837 as to the position of a testator's signature to his will;[7] in an Act of 1860 [8] which made further reforms in the law of property, including the abolition of the doctrine of *scintilla juris*; and more especially in an Act of 1859, which is generally called by his name, [9] which effected valuable reforms in the law *inter alia* of landlord and tenant, the execution of powers, powers of sale where land is charged with the payment of debts or legacies, inheritance, fraudulent concealment of title deeds, and the powers and liabilities of trustees and executors. Lastly, in 1854 St. Leonards carried an Act for the extension of the laws against cruelty to animals.[10]

The judge

Lumley v. Wagner[11] is perhaps the best known of St. Leonards's decisions. We have seen [12] that he followed a decision of Cottenham's, and enforced by injunction a negative stipulation in a contract of service. We have seen, too, that though the decision

---

[1] 11 George IV and 1 William IV c. 65, amended 15, 16 Victoria c. 48.
[2] 5, 6 Victoria c. 123.　　　　[3] 8, 9 Victoria c. 100; 16, 17 Victoria c. 96.
[4] 16, 17 Victoria c. 70.　　　　[5] 16, 17 Victoria c. 97.
[6] 2, 3 Victoria c. 11, amended by 18, 19 Victoria c. 15.
[7] 15, 16 Victoria c. 24; the Wills Act required the testator's signature to be placed "at the foot or end of the will"; it was, says St. Leonards, "decided that if there was somewhat more room than enough for the signature between the end of the will and the actual signature, the will was void, so that at last it rather required a carpenter to measure the distance in each case than a judge to decide upon the application of the Act. The sad result was that this law made hundreds of wills void", Misrepresentations in Campbell's Lives 40-41.
[8] 23, 24 Victoria c. 38; vol. vii 141.　　　　[9] 22, 23 Victoria c. 35.
[10] 17, 18 Victoria c. 60; for these laws, see vol. xv 152, 153.
[11] 1 De G.M. and G. 604.　　　　[12] Above 34.

is well reasoned and supported by weighty technical arguments, it has given rise to considerable difficulties.[1]

As we might expect from his books, some of his decisions on different points in the law of property were very important. As Lord Chancellor of Ireland he laid it down in the case of *Cole v. Sewell* [2] that the rule against perpetuities does not apply to legal contingent remainders; and in the case of *Allen v. Allen* [3] he gave a clear account of the position of a person holding an estate *pur autre vie* in quasi-entail. As Lord Chancellor of England he defined the scope of the *cy-près* doctrine in the case of *Monypenny v. Dering*.[4] In the case of *Dyke v. Rendall* [5] he explained clearly the difference between a legal and an equitable bar to dower. In the case of *Egerton v. Brownlow* he discussed more thoroughly than any of the other Lords the nature and validity of the limitations contained in the settlement of the Earl of Bridgewater, from the point of view of a conveyance, and apart from the question of public policy which they raised.[6]

On other matters falling within the jurisdiction of the court of Chancery the following cases are good illustrations of the breadth of his learning and his powers of exposition. In the case of *Maunsell v. Hedges* [7] he repudiated the supposed equitable doctrine that a person must make good his representations upon which another had acted, and said that to create liability the representation which had been acted on must amount to a contract.[8] On the other hand, in his dissenting opinion in the case of *Jorden v. Money* he differed from the majority of the House as to the existence of a contract in that case,[9] and committed himself to the erroneous opinion that a statement of intention might give rise to an estoppel.[10] In the case of *Stroughill v. Anstey* [11] he discussed the powers of trustees where a trust for sale, and out of the proceeds a trust for the payment of debts and legacies, had been created, and the position of purchasers from the trustees. Many questions relating to companies came before him. In the

---

[1] Above 34.
[2] (1843) 4 Dru. and War. at pp. 28-29, cited vol. vii 98 n. 6; on this question, see ibid 234-23 7.
[3] (1842) 2 Dru. and War. at pp. 325-327.
[4] (1852) 2 De G.M. and G. 145; for this doctrine, see vol. vii 211.
[5] (1852) 2 De G.M. and G. 209; for this distinction, see vol. iii 196-197.
[6] (1853) 4 H.L.C. at pp. 205-230. [7] (1854) 4 H.L.C. 1039.
[8] At pp. 1051, 1059-1060; see also his Treatise on the Law of Real Property as apministered in the House of Lords 54, there cited; later cases have shown that this is the law, see *Maddison v. Alderson* (1883) 8 App. Cas. at p. 473; *Farina v. Fickus* [1900] 1 Ch. at p. 335, and see Pollock's note on the latter case, L.Q.R. xvi 114.
[9] (1854) 5 H.L.C. at p. 254.
[10] Ibid at pp. 249-251; cf. *Maddison v. Alderson* (1883) 8 App. Cas. at p. 473.
[11] (1852) 1 De G.M. and G. 635.

Eastern Counties Railway v. Hawkes he laid down the important principle that a corporation has "all the powers incident to a corporation except so far as they are restrained by their Act of Incorporation";[1] in the case of *In Re St. James's Club* [2] he defined the rights and duties of the members of a club, and distinguished a club from other associations; and in the case of *Myers v. Perigal* he held that shares in companies, even though their assets consisted of land, were personalty, and so did not come within the Charitable Uses Act.[3] In the last mentioned case he gave an interesting account of the fluctuations of judicial opinion on this matter.[4] In the case of *Re Cumming* [5] he discussed with much learning the obscure question of the conditions in which the findings of a commission of lunacy could be traversed. One of his decisions in the House of Lords in the case of *Navulshaw v. Brownrigg* [6] illustrates his knowledge of the common law. In that case he gave a very clear account of the Factors Acts, and of the conditions in which a pledge of goods by a factor is valid as against the principal.[7] In the case of *Jeffreys v. Boosey* [8] he gave a very learned judgment on the subject of copyright, in which he adhered to the established view that after publication copyright depended solely on statute law. In the case of *Brook v. Brook* [9] he took the view, which was not acceded to by the other law lords, that a marriage with a deceased's wife's sister was contrary to the law of God and therefore could not be recognized by English law, even though the parties were domiciled in a country where such marriages were legal.[10]

Though considerable reforms had been made in the practice and procedure of the court of Chancery the old defects of expense and delays were by no means completely cured. That St. Leonards was not blind to some of these defects his remarks in *Re Cumming* show. He said: [11]

This lady's property is of small amount, and without care and caution it will be swallowed up in litigation, and the person whom both sides are professing to protect, will, at the age of seventy-six, be stripped of her whole means of subsistence, and this by the operation of law brought

[1] (1855) 5 H.L.C. at p. 373.
[2] (1852) 2 De G.M. and G. 383.
[3] (1852) 2 De G.M. and G. 599.
[4] At pp. 619-620.
[5] (1852) 1 De G.M. and G. 537.
[6] (1852) 2 De G.M. and G. 441.
[7] Ibid at pp. 444-452; for these Acts, see vol. xv 94.
[8] (1854) 4 H.L.C. at pp. 976-996; vol. vi 378-379; vol. xii 484, 559.
[9] (1868) 9 H.L.C. at pp. 230-239.
[10] "The grounds upon which, in my opinion, this marriage in Denmark is void by our law, depend upon our Act of Parliament, and upon the rule that we do not admit any foreign law to be of force here where it is opposed to God's law, according to our view of the law", at p. 231; below 63.
[11] (1852) 1 De G.M. and G. at p. 556.

in to protect her. Let the parties on both sides seriously consider this. Upon the present occasion eight counsel have appeared, three on the part of Mrs. Cumming and five on the other side. I now make an order that no more costs shall be allowed than for two counsel on each side; and I will make an order that in whatever further steps are taken on either side, the expenditure shall be restricted to the lowest possible point, so as to preserve to this lady, if it is in the power of the Great Seal to do so, some remnant of her fortune for the remainder of her days.

CRANWORTH

(1852-1858, 1865-1866)

St. Leonards's successor was Robert Monsey Rolfe, Lord Cranworth.[1] Rolfe was born on December 18, 1790 at Cranworth near Thetford. He was educated at Winchester and Trinity College, Cambridge, and graduated seventeenth wrangler in 1812. In 1815 he was elected a fellow of Downing College. He was called to the bar by Lincoln's Inn in 1816, and practised in the court of Chancery and on the Norfolk circuit. From the first his manners and conversation made him popular;[2] and his abilities of the solid, safe and practical kind enabled him slowly to build up a Chancery practice. At the same time the fact that he had been appointed recorder of Bury St. Edmunds kept him in touch with the common law. In 1831 he became a member of the House of Commons. There he was not a success. His appearance was not impressive, and he was no debater. He took silk in 1832, with the result that he lost a large part of his practice. Therefore his appointment as solicitor-general in 1834 caused considerable surprise. That appointment he owed to Campbell, then attorney-general, who was attracted both by his social qualities and his solid fund of legal knowledge.[3] Campbell says that he had no cause to repent his choice, "for I afterwards acted with him for five years most harmoniously, and always received from him most effectual assistance".[4] In fact he did most of the work of writing opinions on cases submitted by the Government, and Campbell felt his loss when Rolfe was succeeded by Wilde in 1839.[5] One of his opinions on martial law, given in 1838, lays down clearly the now

---

[1] Atlay, The Victorian Chancellors ii 53-78; Foss, Judges ix 251-253; D.N.B.
[2] "Our new junior, Mr. Rolfe, made his appearance. His manners are genteel; his conversation easy and sensible. He is a very acceptable companion, but I fear a dangerous rival", Crabb Robinson, Diary ii 41, cited Atlay, op. cit. ii 55.
[3] Life of Lord Campbell ii 53, 312.
[4] Life of Lord Campbell ii 53.   [5] Ibid. 135.

accepted view of the meaning which the common law attaches to this term.[1]

In 1839 he became a Baron of the Exchequer. His experience as solicitor-general had familiarized him with revenue cases, his experience as recorder of Bury St. Edmunds had familiarized him with the administration of the criminal law, and his Chancery practice had familiarized him with the principles and practice of equity. He was therefore well fitted to deal with all the different kinds of jurisdiction which a Baron of the Exchequer might be called upon to exercise. Apparently there were some doubts as to his qualifications; but, as in the case of his appointment as solicitor-general, and indeed of all his other later appointments, he soon silenced all doubts. Pollock, writing from the Northern Circuit in 1840,[2] says:

Baron Rolfe has most agreeably disappointed every one. There was great and universal wailing and lamentation when it was first known that he would come to this circuit. No one supposed that a chancery man, of no great practice, and in no ways distinguished, except in the opinion of his private friends, would make a good common law judge; but the event has reversed all expectations, and stamps with a higher value the sort of limited reputation which he enjoyed, and which is not in general worth much. He is singularly clear-headed, by no means deficient in knowledge of law, and has a ready straightforward way of getting through business which saves much time; besides he is a perfect gentleman, and is courteous to every one, without showing fear or favour to counsel or shrinking from his duty on any account whatever. Every one is now speaking well of him.

His greatest success as a common law judge was the trial of Rush for murder in 1848. Since this was a *cause célèbre* Rolfe's qualities were advertised.[3]

When Cottenham resigned in 1850 Rolfe was one of the commissioners of the Great Seal, and his claims to be made Chancellor were advocated. We have seen that Wilde was appointed;[4] but in August 1850 Rolfe was made a Vice-Chancellor *vice* Shadwell, and raised to the peerage with the title of Baron Cranworth. This was an unprecedented honour for a Vice-Chancellor. But the social qualities, which all through his life had stood him in such good stead, silenced objectors. In 1845 the critical Greville had written of him:[5]

Nobody is so agreeable as Rolfe: a clear head, vivacity, information, an extraordinary pleasantness of manner without being either soft or affected, extreme good humour, cheerfulness, and tact make his society on the whole as attractive as that of anybody I ever met.

[1] Forsyth, Leading Cases 198-199; vol. x 711-713.
[2] Personal Remembrances of Sir F. Pollock i 161.
[3] Atlay, op. cit. ii 61-64.   [4] Above 37.   [5] Memoirs, v 270-271.

In 1851 he and Knight-Bruce were appointed the two first Lords
Justices in Chancery. In the following year, on the fall of Derby's
government, he was made Lord Chancellor. "His promotion",
says Atlay,[1] "was universally applauded, and he had gained
greatly in reputation during his short apprenticeship as Vice
Chancellor and Lord Justice."

We shall see that as a judge of the court of Chancery he did
much for the development of equitable principles.[2] His judgments
are clear and accurate; and "his manner on the bench was considered to fall not far short of perfection".[3] Selborne said that he
was one of the best Chancellors he had known;[4] Campbell
testifies to his legal knowledge, his conscientiousness, and his
industry;[5] and Rolt, though he thought that he was "slow in
approaching facts and arguments", admitted that he was a
master of the principles of equity and "in the main right".[6] He
was not so successful in the House of Lords. It is true that he
supported or promoted several very important legislative
reforms;[7] but his achievements in this sphere were considerably
less than those of St. Leonards.[8] He was ineffective in debate; he
and his law officers, Cockburn and Bethell, did not see eye to eye;[9]
and in the exercise of the appellate jurisdiction the disputes
between him and St. Leonards, and the inefficiency of Brougham,
when he was present, made the House of Lords a very unsatisfactory tribunal. Lord Granville, writing on March 7, 1855,
says:[10]

The Solicitor-General was examined yesterday as to the defects of the
Appellate Jurisdiction. He, with his most mincing manner and perfect
aplomb, supposed the case of two learned lords, one of whom gave
judgments without hearing the arguments, ran about the House,
conversed with lay lords, and wrote notes and letters; the other who
made declamatory speeches, thumped the table, asked whether any one
would venture to say that was law which had just been laid down by the
Lord Chancellor, and who in short entirely forgot the dignity of a judge
of the highest Court of Appeal. Brougham and St. Leonards were furious
—tried to bully him, but were completely foiled. Derby and Lyndhurst
laughing fit to kill themselves.

[1] Victorian Chancellors ii 66.   [2] Below 62.
[3] Atlay, op. cit. ii 66-67.   [4] Memorials, Family and Personal ii 494.
[5] "Cranworth is Chancellor. His life must some day be written, and I should
delight to do justice to his unsullied honour, his warmth of heart, his instinctive
rectitude of feeling, his legal acquirements, his patient industry, and his devoted
desire to do his duty", Life of Lord Campbell ii 312.
[6] Memoirs 133.   [7] Below 60.   [8] Above 52 et seq.
[9] Life of Lord Campbell ii 314, 315, 330-331; below 60.
[10] Life of Lord Granville, i 171; as Campbell said, Life of Lord Campbell ii 332,
the result was that the judgment was always affirmed—"pretty comfort for the
appellant, who is thus for ever barred, perhaps, of an estate of £10,000 a year".

It was to remedy these defects that it was proposed to create Baron Parke a life peer.[1] Cranworth had no doubt of the power of the Crown to make such a creation. But his reputation suffered when the House resolved that it had no such power.

He ceased to be Chancellor when Palmerston's government fell in 1858; and when Palmerston returned to power in 1859, Cranworth, to the astonishment of many, including Selborne, was not made Chancellor. The reasons probably were his weakness as a debater in the House of Lords, and his bad relations with Bethell who was now Attorney-General,[2] upon the evil effects of which Campbell had remarked three years before in a letter to Palmerston.[3] Bethell was more valuable to the government than Cranworth, and so Cranworth was sacrificed. But he continued to do useful work in the House of Lords as a legislator and a judge; and when Bethell, now become Lord Westbury, resigned in 1865, he again became Chancellor. "Well Cranny", some one is said to have remarked, "Kingsley is right, it *is* better to be good than clever".[4] He ceased to be Chancellor when Russell resigned in 1866. He made his last speech in the House of Lords on July 20, 1868, and died on the 26th of the same month.

As a legislator his achievement is not inconsiderable. He and Bethell supported the measures taken to revise the statute book, which have resulted in the Statute Law Revision Acts.[5] In 1853 he promoted an Act for the better administration of charitable trusts,[6] and supported the Act which made penal servitude a substitute for transportation and instituted the ticket-of-leave system.[7] In 1854 he supported the reforms made by the Common Law Procedure Act of that year,[8] some of which are a step in the direction of the fusion of the jurisdiction of the courts of law and equity.[9] In 1856 he promoted an Act to facilitate the sale and leasing of settled estates, which is one of the forerunners of the Settled Land Acts.[10] In 1860 he promoted an Act to enable children to get the benefit of the education provided by endowed

---

[1] "I asked the Chancellor what was the real history of the Life Peerage last year, and he told me that it originated in his finding great inconvenience from himself and Lord St. Leonards frequently sitting together in the House of Lords without any third, and as St. Leonards invariably opposed his view of every case great injustice was often done to suitors, and he urged on Palmerston the expediency of giving them some assistance. Palmerston said it would be a good opportunity for making some Life Peers", Greville, Memoirs viii 123.

[2] Life of Lord Campbell ii 368.   [3] Ibid ii 343-344.

[4] There is authority for saying that Queen Victoria was the author of this *mot*, but Atlay is sceptical, Victorian Chancellors ii 77 n. 3.

[5] Vol. xi 315; Atlay, op. cit. ii 69.   [6] 16, 17 Victoria c. 137.

[7] 16, 17 Victoria c. 99.   [8] 17, 18 Victoria c. 125.

[9] Vol. i 636-637; Life of Lord Campbell ii 324-325.

[10] 19, 20 Victoria c. 120.

schools, although they did not belong to the religious denomination which the school was founded to support;[1] and in the same year he promoted the Act, which is called by his name, to shorten conveyances by giving to trustees, mortgagees, and executors the powers which were usually inserted in settlements, wills, or conveyances;[2] but, as Atlay says,[3] "his constitutional timidity induced him to render its adoption optional instead of compulsory, and the intolerable verbosity of legal instruments was maintained in riotous profusion until the Conveyancing Act of 1881". In 1862 he promoted an Act to enable persons interested in land to get a judicial declaration of title.[4]

In 1854 he advocated a Testamentary Jurisdiction Bill, in which it was proposed to take away the jurisdiction of the ecclesiastical courts to make grants of probate and letters of administration, and to vest it in the Court of Chancery.[5] He pointed out that a similar scheme had been recommended by the Real Property Commissioners in 1833, and that bills had been prepared to give effect to their recommendation in 1834, 1836, 1842, and 1845.[6] In order to avoid conflicting decisions sometimes given by the ecclesiastical courts as to the validity of wills of personalty and the common law courts as to wills of realty, it was proposed that wills both of realty and personalty should be proved in the court of Chancery. There is much to be said for this proposal, which vests the jurisdiction to determine both the validity of a will, and its construction, in the same tribunal; and it was for this reason that he opposed the proposal to create a separate court of probate. He summed up his proposals as follows:[7]

We propose to abolish at once all existing jurisdictions relating to the probate of wills and the grant of letters of administration; to transfer to the Court of Chancery jurisdiction in all contentious matters, and in non-contentious business transacted in London; we propose that the subject matter of the jurisdiction shall be all property left by will, whether it be real or personal estate; that in non-contentious business for cases where the deceased persons have left a small amount of property which can be properly managed in the country, there shall be district registrars appointed, who shall be little more than persons who will examine the apparent accuracy of the instruments, and to see that they are regular, and to transmit them to the central registry, whether they are proved in London or in the country, so that the benefit of the system should be extended throughout the whole of the kingdom, whether the property be large or small.

---

[1] 23, 24 Victoria c. 11.   [2] 23, 24 Victoria c. 145.
[3] The Victorian Chancellors ii 69.   [4] 25, 26 Victoria c. 67.
[5] Hansard (3rd Ser.) cxxx 702-720; he pointed out, ibid 703, that "the question whether an instrument which a deceased person has left behind him is or is not a will, may be entertained and decided by no less than 386 tribunals scattered over the kingdom".   [6] Ibid 709-710.   [7] Ibid 720.

But the bill was opposed by Cockburn, the Attorney-General; and it aroused so much opposition that it was dropped. Nor was his proposal, also made in 1854, to create a divorce court any more successful.[1] Both these reforms were made in another way by the Acts of 1857;[2] and Cranworth showed much "tact and pertinacity" in getting the Act which reformed the law of divorce through the House of Lords. The patronage which the Act gave to the Chancellor "he placed unreservedly at the disposition of Sir Cresswell Cresswell the first judge ordinary of the courts of probate and divorce".[3]

Cranworth's services as a judge both to equity and to other branches of English law were more considerable than his services as a legislator.

Equity

One of the most notable of Cranworth's decisions is his judgment in the case of *Cox v. Hickman*[4] in which, in a classic passage, he defined the test to determine whether or not the relation of partnership exists between two or more persons, and inferred from that test that partnership in the profits, though "cogent and often conclusive evidence" of a partnership, is nothing more than evidence.[5] In the case of *Money v. Jorden*[6] his dissentient judgment was upheld by the House of Lords.[7] The case of *Reynell v. Sprye*[8] is a valuable decision upon the kind of conduct which equity will regard as fraudulent. The case of *Attorney-General v. Alford*[9] is a leading case upon the question where trustees who have committed breaches of trust are chargeable with compound interest. In the case of *Underwood v. Wing*[10]

---

[1] Hansard (3rd Ser.) cxxxiv 1-12, 935-947, 1436-1440; there was to be a divorce court with jurisdiction to grant divorces *a vinculo*, and when other relief was sought the court of Chancery was to have jurisdiction.   [2] Above 20.

[3] Atlay, op. cit. ii 74-75.   [4] (1860) 8 H.L.C. at pp. 303-311.

[5] "It is often said that the test, or one of the tests, whether a person not ostensibly a partner, is nevertheless, in contemplation of law, a partner, is, whether he is entitled to partnership in the profits. This, no doubt, is, in general, a sufficiently accurate test; for a right to participate in profits affords cogent, often conclusive evidence, that the trade in which the profits have been made, was carried on for or on behalf of the person setting up such a claim. But the real ground of the liability is, that the trade has been carried on by persons acting on his behalf. . . . It is not strictly correct to say that his right to share in the profits makes him liable to the debts of the trade. The correct mode of stating the proposition is to say that the same thing which entitles him to the one makes him liable to the other, namely, the fact that the trade has been carried on on his behalf", at p. 306.

[6] (1852) 2 De G.M. and G. 318.   [7] (1854) 5 H.L.C. 185; above 55.

[8] (1852) 1 De G.M. and G. 660.   [9] (1855) 4 De G.M. and G. 843.

[10] (1855) 4 De G.M. and G. 633. (It is provided by the Law of Property Act, 1925, section 184, that where two or more persons die in circumstances rendering it uncertain in what order the deaths occurred, they shall be deemed to have died in order of seniority. But where the dead persons are husband and wife and the elder is intestate,

he, assisted by Wightman J. and Martin B., held that when a husband and wife perished together in a shipwreck and no evidence as to which perished first, there was no presumption as to which of the two was the survivor. The consequence was that the person who was entitled to the husband's property if the wife died in the husband's lifetime, could not claim it. In the case of *Jones v. Lock* [1] he explained in a short and clear judgment the distinction between a gift and a declaration of trust, and held that from an imperfect attempt to give no intention to declare a trust could be inferred. In the sphere of company law he gave the very important decision in the case of *Oakes v. Turquand,* [2] to the effect that a contract voidable for fraud cannot be rescinded when, by reason of a winding up, the creditors have acquired new rights as against the company. His judgment contains a valuable account of the history of the Companies Acts. [3] In the case of *Hopkinson v. Rolt* [4] he dissented from the judgment of the majority of the House of Lords, partly because he thought that authority was contrary to it, which was arguable, and partly on grounds of public policy, which is less arguable. [5]

Other branches of law

Cranworth was a party to two important cases in *private international law*. In the case of *Brook v. Brook* [6] he laid it down that though the forms of contracting a marriage are regulated by the *lex loci contractus*, capacity to contract it is regulated by the *lex domicilii* of the parties to it; so that when two persons domiciled in Great Britain contracted a marriage in Denmark, lawful by Danish law, but unlawful by English law, the marriage was illegal and void. [7] The decision in this case has been criticized; [8] but whatever view may be held as to the correctness of the decision, there is no doubt that Cranworth's judgment was a clear and

the rules of intestacy, under the Administration of Estates Act, 1925, as amended by the Intestates' Estates Act, 1952, take effect as if there had been no presumed survivorship by the younger spouse. Eds.)

[1] (1865) L.R. 1 Ch. 25.   [2] (1867) L.R. 2 H.L. 3250.
[3] Ibid at pp. 358-366.   [4] (1861) 9 H.L.C. at pp. 539-548.
[5] But the Law of Property Act, 1925 (15, 16 George V c. 20 § 94, as amended by Law of Property (Amendment) Act, 1926. Schedule (2)) has to some extent given effect to Cranworth's view on this matter; see Cheshire, Modern Law of Real Property (8th ed.), 613.
[6] (1861) 9 H.L.C. 193.
[7] Cranworth pointed out, at p. 226, that such a marriage between two persons domiciled in Denmark would be held to be valid by English law; for St. Leonards's different view, see above 56 n. 10.
[8] See Cheshire, Private International Law (5th ed.), 313, who thinks that the test of the capacity of the parties is not the law of their pre-marriage domicil, but the law of the matrimonial domicil.

logical statement of the law. In the case of *Shaw v. Gould* [1] he and
the other law lords held that a divorce in Scotland, when the
divorced husband was domiciled in England, was invalid, and
that therefore the children of a second marriage contracted by
the woman were illegitimate, although the matrimonial domicil of
this second marriage was Scottish. Though the correctness of this
premise—the invalidity of the divorce—cannot be questioned, the
correctness of the conclusion—the illegitimacy of the children—
has been questioned. [2]

Cranworth's experience as a Baron of the Exchequer had made
him a respectable *common lawyer*. Though his judgment in
Rylands v. Fletcher is thin, [3] and though he adhered to his opinion
in the court below, and dissented from the majority decision of
the House of Lords in *Egerton v. Brownlow*, [4] some of his decisions
show a considerable command of the principles of the common
law. Illustrations are his judgments in *Jeffreys v. Boosey* [5] and
Startup v. Macdonald. [6] In the case of *Ranger v. G.W.R.* [7] he
dealt with the much debated question whether a corporation can
be held liable for fraud. He came to the conclusion that though
"strictly speaking" a corporation could not be guilty of fraud,
there was nothing to prevent a commercial corporation from
being liable for the fraud of its agents. [8] Though his view that it
is impossible to impute malice or fraud to a corporation has not
prevailed, his view that it is liable for the acts of its agents, like
any other employer, is now the established rule of the common
law. [9]

---

[1] (1868) L.R. 3 H.L. 55.
[2] Cheshire, op. cit. 398. [The children of a voidable marriage which has been
annulled, were made legitimate by section 9 of the Matrimonial Causes Act, 1950, and
the same benefit was conferred, by section 2 of the Legitimacy Act, 1959, on the
children of a void marriage, if at the time of conception one or both parents reason-
ably believed it to be valid.] Eds.
[3] (1868) L.R. 3 H.L. at pp. 340-342.
[4] (1853) 4 H.L.C. at pp. 247-255; but he said that he was glad that the decision
would have the effect of making it difficult to carry into effect "these extraordinary
wills", at p. 255.
[5] (1854) 4 H.L.C. at pp. 952-960, at pp. 608-613.
[6] (1843) 6 Man. and Gr. 593 (Tender of goods.)   [7] (1854) 5 H.L.C. 78.
[8] At pp. 86-87; he expressed the same view in *Western Bank of Scotland v.
Addie* (1867) L.R. 1 Sc. and Div. App. at p. 167.
[9] *Citizens Life Ass. Co. v. Brown* [1904] A.C. at p. 426 *per* Lord Lindley.

CHELMSFORD

(1858-1859, 1866-1868)

In 1858 Palmerston's government fell. In Derby's government Cranworth's successor as Chancellor was Frederick Thesiger, Lord Chelmsford.[1]

Thesiger was born on July 15, 1794. His early years were spent in the West Indies where his father held a post as secretary to the Governor of St. Vincent. He entered the navy in 1806; but the death of his elder brother caused him to leave the service and join his father in the West Indies, in 1811. His father was collector of customs at St. Vincent, and had a flourishing sugar plantation. It was intended that Thesiger should manage this plantation and practise at the West Indian bar. But in 1812 an eruption of La Sanfrien submerged the plantation, so that he was thrown back upon the bar. He returned to England and became a student at Gray's Inn in 1813. He read in the chambers of Walker, a conveyancer, of Heald, an equity draftsman, and of Sykes, a special pleader, and read diligently the leading text books. He made so good an impression on Sykes that he persuaded him not to return to the West Indies. He was called to the bar in 1818, soon got a practice at the Surrey Sessions and in the Palace Court,[2] where he bought a place as one of the four counsel who were allowed to practise there. Two cases helped to establish his reputation—his defence of Hunt,[3] and an ejectment action tried at the Chelmsford Assizes in 1832, and twice again in 1833. By this time Thesiger was showing that he had the qualities of a leading counsel. Foss tells us that he was "present on two occasions when Chief Justice Abbott highly complimented him to the jury on his management of cases which he had been called upon to lead in the absence of his senior".[4] He took silk in 1834, and in 1840 he entered parliament, where he showed himself to be a very competent debater. In 1844 he became Solicitor-General, and, on the death of Follett in 1845, Attorney-General. He ceased to be Attorney-General when Peel was defeated in 1846.

Before he had become a law officer he was recognized as one of the leaders of the common law bar; for his appearance, his legal abilities, and his forensic gifts made him a consummate advocate.

Standing over six feet high, of a muscular and manly build, his handsome and vivacious countenance and his animated gestures gave juries

---

[1] Atlay, The Victorian Chancellors ii 79-126; Foss, Judges ix 274-281; D.N.B.
[2] For this court, see vol. i 209.
[3] Indicted with Murtell for the murder of Wheare.   [4] Judges, ix 277.

an early prepossession in favour of his client. Carefully eschewing any pretence of eloquence, he would put his points plainly and forcibly to the Court, or talk to the jury in a sort of homely chit-chat which robbed them of all suspicion. He possessed a gift of narration which seemed to render comment superfluous, and he was particularly adroit in examination in chief, taking the witness by the hand and conducting him through his story without allowing him to drop anything by the way. Long experience had given him a full insight into the mental processes of the varying types of humanity with whom he had, day by day, to deal.[1]

And he had a ready wit which made him popular with his brother barristers. Of his speech for the defendant in the breach of promise action which a Miss Smith brought against Earl Ferrers, Cockburn said that he would rather have made it than any he had ever heard at the bar.[2]

In 1852 he again became Attorney-General for a few months. In 1858 he was entrusted by the government with the prosecution of the directors of the Royal British Bank. It was a most complicated case to which Thesiger devoted all his time, and Serjeant Ballantine, who was with him, said that his four and a half hours opening was one of the finest speeches he had ever heard. Before the case was concluded Palmerston's government fell, and Derby made Thesiger Lord Chancellor. He took the title of Chelmsford— from the town where he had won one of the earliest and most decisive of his successes at the bar. The Derby government fell in 1859. Chelmsford occupied himself with his judicial duties in the House of Lords and the Privy Council, where he was in constant conflict with Westbury. "Each", it was said,[3] "had the faculty of rousing what have been happily termed the travelling acids in the system of the other." In 1866 the Conservatives again returned to power, and Chelmsford again became Chancellor; but he had not been a success as a debater in the House of Lords, and there was an undertaking that, if requested, he would give way to Cairns. Disraeli disliked Chelmsford on account of his opposition to the removal of Jewish disabilities. It is not surprising, therefore, that when he succeeded Derby, he made the request to Chelmsford, and made it in terms which offended him.[4] Unfortunately he advertised his grievance. The public took sides:

Society and the clubs were entertained by stories of his bitter jokes and of Disraeli's pungent retort. It was said that the ex-Chancellor talked of premature elevation making some people *dizzy*, and that he distinguished the old and the new administrators as the "Derby" and the "Hoax"; while the Prime Minister was declared to have curtly summed up his former colleague in the biting words, "useless in council, feeble in debate, and—a jester".[5]

[1] Atlay, op. cit. ii 96-97.   [2] Ibid 105.   [3] Nash, Life of Westbury ii 37.
[4] Atlay, op. cit. ii 123-125; Monypenny and Buckle, Life of Disraeli iv 595.
[5] Ibid 329.

His many friends at the bar and elsewhere thought that he had been hardly used. But he did not let his grievances interfere with the performance of his judicial duties. For several years to come he continued to hear cases in the House of Lords and the Privy Council.

Not long before the end the late Mr. H. G. Rothery, who had recently been appointed Wreck Commissioner, met him walking down Whitehall in company with another aged judge. "Are you going to sit on us?" said the ex-Chancellor, with a flash of his old jocose humour.[1]

He died on October 5, 1878.

Chelmsford's decisions are always clearly expressed, and generally contain a careful review of the authorities. As a rule they have been followed, and they show him rather as a learned lawyer than as a very profound lawyer, and that he had an acute rather than a full mind. He was conscious of his ignorance of equity,[2] and worked hard to remedy it.[3] His industry, his ability, and the help of the Lords Justices enabled him, as Selborne said, to play his part in the court of Chancery "as well as most common law Chancellors", and he added that his "tact, kindliness, and courtesy made him popular".[4] Since some of his decisions are leading cases it cannot be denied that he left his mark upon the development of the law. These and other decisions can be grouped under three heads—equity, mixed law and equity, and common law.

Equity

Two of his decisions—*Hopkinson v. Rolt* [5] and *De Mattos v. Gibson* [6]—have attained the rank of leading cases. In the first of these cases he held that a mortgagee who makes further advances to the mortgagor, with notice of a second mortgage, cannot tack those further advances to his first mortgage. In the second of these cases he in effect applied the rule in *Tulk v. Moxhay* [7] to the sale of a chattel; and that decision was followed in 1926 by the Judicial Committee of the Privy Council in *Lord Strathcona Steamship Co. v. Dominion Coal Co.*[8] In both cases the subject matter of the sale was a ship, but in both the rule was said to apply to chattels generally [9]—though it is clear that

---

[1] Atlay, op. cit. ii 125.   [2] Selborne, Memorials, Family and Personal ii 334.
[3] Atlay, op. cit. ii 119.   [4] Selborne, op. cit. ii 334.
[5] (1858) 3 De G. and J. 177, affirmed on appeal 9 H.L.C. 514.
[6] (1858) 4 De G. and J. 276.
[7] (1848) 2 Phill. 774; above 34.   [8] [1926] A.C. 108.
[9] (1859) 4 De G. and J. at p. 282 *per* Knight-Bruce L.J.; [1926] A.C. at p. 117. [Diplock J. did not follow it in *Port Line v. Ben Line Steamers* [1958] 2 Q.B. 146. Eds.]

physical differences between land and chattels, are differences in the rules of law applicable to them, must result in differences in the application of the rule. Other less important cases are *Austen v. Boys* [1] which deals with the valuation of goodwill when a partnership has been entered into for a fixed term; *Parker v. Taswell* [2] in which it was held that an instrument void as a lease because not under seal, might be valid as an agreement to lease; and *Vansittart v. Vansittart* [3] in which it was held that a term in a separation deed which deprived the father of the control of the children, was void because it was contrary to public policy to interfere with a father's control.

Mixed law and equity

In the case of *In re Royal British Bank* [4] and *Peek v. Gurney* [5] Chelmsford elucidated the rights of persons induced by fraud to take shares in companies. In the case of *Wythes v. Labouchère* [6] he decided that a contract of suretyship is not, like a contract of insurance, a contract *uberrimae fidei*. In the case of *Bain v. Fothergill* [7] he decided that, on a contract for the sale of realty, if the vendor, without fraud, cannot make a good title, the purchaser cannot recover damages for the loss of his bargain—a rule the justice of which is not very obvious.[8] *Chasemore v. Richards,* [9] in which he made a notable speech, is the leading case as to rights to water percolating underground in undefined channels; and in the case of *Attorney-General v. Chambers* [10] he investigated the obscure topic of title by *alluvio*.

Common law

Two leading cases on doctrines of the common law which Chelmsford decided are *Lister v. Perryman* [11] in which he explained the functions of judge and jury in an action for malicious prosecution; and *Hollins v. Fowler* [12] in which the law as to conversion was explained and settled.

[1] (1858) 2 De G. and J. 626.   [2] (1858) 2 De G. and J. 559.
[3] (1858) 2 De G. and J. 249; the law on this matter is changed by 36, 37 Victoria c. 12 § 2; see *Hart v. Hart* (1881) 18 Ch.D. at pp. 681-682.
[4] (1859) 3 De G. and J. 387.   [5] (1873) L.R. 6 H.L. 377.
[6] (1859) 3 De G. and J. 593.   [7] (1873) L.R. 7 H.L. 158.
[8] Fry, Specific Performance (6th ed.) 607.
[9] (1859) 7 H.L.C. 349.   [10] (1859) 4 De G. and J. 55.
[11] (1870) L.R. 4 H.L. 521.   [12] (1874) L.R. 7 H.L. 757.

CAMPBELL
(1859-1861)

Of the career and character of Chelmsford's successor Lord Campbell I have already spoken.[1] He was essentially a common lawyer. It is true that he had been Lord Chancellor of Ireland for a few months; but the shortness of his tenure of that office had made his experience as an equity judge negligible. He was eighty years of age when he became Lord Chancellor, and he only held office for two years. Therefore although his great legal ability, his judicial experience, and the help of his colleagues enabled him to perform his judicial duties adequately, his contribution to the development of equity is slight.

The most remarkable of the cases which came before Campbell was *The Emperor of Austria v. Day* [2] in which the plaintiff sued for an injunction to prevent Kossuth, an Hungarian refugee, from causing to be manufactured in England notes purporting to be legal currency in Hungary. Campbell granted the injunction and, in granting it, he laid down a principle which is as much a constitutional as an equitable principle. He said that a foreign sovereign cannot sue in an English court "merely to support his political power and prerogatives, or for any alleged wrong sanctioned by the Government of England", but that he can sue "for a wrong done to him by an English subject unauthorized by the English Government, in respect of property belonging to the foreign sovereign, either in his individual or his corporate capacity".[3] In the case of *Norris v. Chambres* [4] he pointed out that the principle of *Penn v. Lord Baltimore* [5] cannot be applied to a case where there is no privity, by reason of contract or otherwise, between the person in possession of foreign land and a person to whom his vendor had previously agreed to sell it. Two cases illustrate the principle that the rule as to the need for certainty, and the rule against perpetuities, apply to trusts for public purposes which are not charitable.[6] The rules which he laid down in the case of *Slim v. Croucher*,[7] as to the conditions in which equity would give relief against a person who had made a material misrepresentation, have been held to be inconsistent with the rule laid down in *Derry v. Peek*;[8] but Campbell's

---

[1] See vol. xv 405-429.　　　[2] (1861) 3 De G.F. and J. 217.
[3] At p. 238.　　　[4] (1861) 3 De G.F. and J. 583.
[5] (1750) 1 Ves. Sen. 444; vol. xii 264-265.
[6] *Thomson v. Shakespear* (1860) 1 De G.F. and J. 399; *Carne v. Long* (1860) 2 De G.F. and J. 75.　　　[7] (1860) 1 De G.F. and J. at pp. 523-526.
[8] (1889) 14 App. Cas. 337; *Low v. Bouverie* [1891] 3 Ch. 82.

exposition of the extent of the equitable jurisdiction in cases of fraud was approved by Lord Haldane in the case of *Nocton v. Ashburton*.[1] In the case of *Montefiore v. Guedalla* [2] he explained the rules as to the ademption of a legacy by a portion; and in the case of *Evans v. Carrington* [3] he laid down the rule that non-disclosure by a woman that she had committed adultery before marriage was no ground for setting aside an ante-nuptial settlement. In the case of *Walters v. Morgan* [4] his exposition of the duties of persons negotiating a sale and purchase of land has been approved.[5] His decision in *Fraser v. Thompson* [6] illustrates the rule that an ante-nuptial settlement, if made in bad faith, is voidable under the Bankruptcy Act. His decision in the case of *Jenner v. Morris* [7] reasserted the important principle that, though at law money advanced to a deserted wife cannot be recovered from the husband, in equity the lenders can sue him for the money actually expended in the purchase of necessaries. His enforcement of a restrictive covenant in the case of *Piggott v. Stratton*,[8] notwithstanding the surrender of the lease imposing the restriction, has caused some difficulty; but has been defended on the ground that it was a case of a building scheme, and depended on the doctrine of estoppel by representation.[9]

WESTBURY

(1861-1865)

Campbell's successor was Richard Bethell, Lord Westbury—intellectually one of the greatest of our Chancellors, but by reason of his deficiency in manners, temper and moral sense one of the least admirable.

Richard Bethell, Lord Westbury [10] was born on June 30, 1800. Though his father was very poor, he recognized the genius of his son, and gave him the best education that he could afford. That

---

[1] [1914] A.C. at p. 953.   [2] (1859) 1 De G.F. and J. 93.
[3] (1860) 2 De G.F. and J. 481.   [4] (1861) 3 De G.F. and J. 718.
[5] *Turner v. Green* [1895] 2 Ch. at p. 209 *per* Chitty J.
[6] (1859) 4 De G. and J. 659.
[7] (1861) 3 De G.F. and J. 45; *Harris v. Lee* (1718) 1 P. Wms. 482; the principle was the same as that applied to an infant, *Marlow v. Pitfeild* (1719) 1 P. Wms. 559; vol. xii 235.   [8] (1859) 1 De G.F. and J. 33.
[9] *Wilkes v. Spooner* [1911] 2 K.B. at p. 483 *per* Farwell L.J.; cf. Lord Macnaghten's remarks in *Spicer v. Martin* (1888) 14 App. Cas. at p. 23.
[10] T. A. Nash, The Life of Lord Westbury; Atlay, Victorian Chancellors ii 219-91; Foss, Judges ix 134-136; D.N.B.

he might compete for a scholarship at Wadham College, Oxford, he was matriculated as a member of that college at the early age of fourteen.[1] At the end of his first year he won a scholarship and an exhibition which paid the greater part of his expenses. In later life he said that after he was seventeen he had never cost his father a penny. At the age of eighteen he took a first class in classics. For the next four years he stayed at Oxford and supported himself and helped his parents by taking pupils; he won the Vinerian law scholarship; and in 1822 he was elected a Fellow of his college. To his college he was always grateful for giving him the chance of beginning his prosperous career, as a tablet in the ante-chapel of the college records; and he never lost his love for the classics.

A bishop who could cap Horace and Aeschylus with him, as they sat waiting for the Lords to make a House, found the old Erastian a delightful companion, while the Queen's Counsel whose sense of quantity was deficient, and who failed to appreciate a classical allusion, had more than usual cause for complaining of his bitter tongue.[2]

In 1822 he went to London and was called to the bar by the Middle Temple in 1823. He read in the chambers of Lee, an equity draftsman. In his first year after his call he made a hundred guineas, and his practice steadily increased. His brief in his first big case he owed to his classical attainments. Brasenose found itself involved in a Chancery suit, and the Principal had been so struck by his ability in his examination for his degree that he caused him to be retained for the college. Though several counsel advised a compromise, Bethell advised the college to fight, and he won his case in the court of Chancery and the House of Lords.[3] He said that this success trebled his practice. In 1834-5 the leaders of the Chancery bar—Sugden,[4] Pepys,[5] and Bickersteth[6]—were promoted to the bench, and Bethell, Knight Bruce,[7] and Pemberton Leigh[8] succeeded to their places. In 1840 Bethell took silk. In 1841 Knight Bruce became a Vice-Chancellor, and in 1844 Pemberton Leigh retired from the bar. From that time till he became Chancellor he was the undisputed head of the Chancery bar. It is said that just before that event he was making an income of some £30,000 a year.

Such a career of uninterrupted success at the bar denotes

---

[1] In 1863 he said that the University authorities considered that he was old enough to subscribe the thirty-nine articles, but not old enough to take the oath of obedience to the university statutes, and that he did not take this oath till he was sixteen, Hansard (3rd Ser.) clxxii 163.   [2] Atlay, op. cit. ii 221.

[3] *Attorney-General v. Brasenose College* (1834) 2 Cl. and Fin. 295.

[4] Above 39 *et seq.*   [5] Above 27 *et seq.*   [6] Below 115 *et seq.*

[7] Below 129 *et seq.*   [8] Below 159 *et seq.*

the possession of extraordinary intellectual qualities. Bethell's intellectual qualities as an advocate and a man were extraordinary, and in some respects contradictory.

From the first he was supremely confident in his own abilities. Writing to a friend who had congratulated him on his appointment as Chancellor, he said truly that from his youth up he had "truckled to no man, sought no man's favour, but both at the Bar and in politics had been independent to a fault".[1] That confidence was justified. Great industry and subtlety of mind [2] were united to powers of quickly grasping the essential facts of a case, and of stating and applying to them the principle or principles of equity by which in his view they ought to be governed. His argument, it has been said, seemed to lift his subject on to a higher level, and to bring a theory to the test of original principles.[3] To these powers he added the gift of a "finished diction". His arguments were concise and clear, packed with matter, fluent, and perfectly expressed.

His voice was clear and musical, and as he warmed to his argument, it gained a volume, and there was a touch of sympathy which, coupled with the quaint wit of his illustrations, gave intellectual entertainment to his audience. When he was replying in any great case the Court was usually crowded with the ablest young men fresh from the University, who considered that to hear Bethell was a liberal education in advocacy.[4]

Bethell's effectiveness as an advocate was due in no small degree to the way in which he used his gifts as an orator to expound lucidly the underlying principle or principles which he contended should govern the case in hand. It is not surprising therefore, that throughout his life he condemned the ignorance displayed by English lawyers of jurisprudential principles, which he rightly ascribed to the absence of adequate legal education; [5] and we have seen that he played no inconsiderable part in inducing the Inns of Court to provide it.[6] But this search for broad and simple principles, and the manner in which he brushed aside cases which did not square with them as the product of pedantic technicality, prevented him from becoming a very learned or a very profound lawyer;[7] and his training as an advocate caused

---

[1] Nash, Life of Westbury ii 7.
[2] Gladstone said that in subtlety of mind, and in ability to express subtle shades of thought in clear language, he was equalled only by Cardinal Newman.
[3] Ibid i 71.　　　　　　　　　[4] Nash, Life of Westbury i 72-73.
[5] Below 82.　　　　　　　　　[6] See vol. xv 237 et seq.
[7] Selborne, Memorials, Family and Personal ii 491, said, "not very profound as a lawyer, nor serious or earnest as a politician, his independence of mind, and quick mastery of all questions which he had to decide, won for him a judicial reputation, greater than that of his rivals and contemporaries, and certainly greater than the quality of his performance as a Judge can explain".

considerable versatility in his views as to what the true legal principle or principles really were.[1] Two stories illustrate this failing. On one occasion he drew a bill against a client for whom he had a standing retainer.

At the hearing of the suit his services were claimed by the defendant, and it was Bethell's painful duty to demolish his own handiwork. "Your Honour", he said, "of all the cobwebs that were ever spun in a Court this is the flimsiest: it will dissolve at a touch." And it did. By way of reparation and consolation, he whispered as he went out of Court, in the ear of the solicitor who had first instructed him, "the bill is as good a bill as was ever filed".[2]

These contradictory qualities as an advocate and a lawyer, which made him unpopular with his brother lawyers, were paralleled by equally contradictory qualities as a man. His gifts as an advocate were, says Atlay,[3]

rendered all the more formidable by a sarcasm and an irony which he exercised without pity or remorse, and the sting of which he scarcely appreciated. If they were true, he could not see why the subject of his observations should resent them, and there were few with whom he was brought into contact who came away unscathed. The epigrams which seemed to come by instinct, his ingenuity in touching the raw spot, the exquisite appropriateness of the gibe to the victim, were allied with an unconcealed contempt for the world at large which rendered him superior to any attempt at repartee or interruption.

His "mincing manner and refinement of intonation", which procured for him the nickname of "Miss Fanny", "lent an especial quality to his bitter sayings".[4]

All fell under the lash of his tongue, solicitors, juniors, and even the Court. Here is a story of Bethell and Knight-Bruce:

Bethell was conducting a case before Lord Justice Knight-Bruce, whom he did not love and who did not love him. Knight-Bruce was of Welsh extraction, and disliked any allusion to it; he was also a scholar, and fond of quoting classical authors. Knight-Bruce interrupted the argument with a classical quotation. Bethell's opponent was at that moment in conversation with his junior, and becoming aware that the Lord Justice had said something, looked up and said, "I did not catch his Lordship's remark". "Neither did I", said Bethell, "it was an observation couched, I believe, in the Welsh language."[5]

On another occasion, he provoked a scene in court when he protested, very rightly, at some observations made by Knight-Bruce

[1] "His opinions expressed as if they had been the strongest and best settled in the world, in reality sat loosely upon him; and those who knew him well were surprised at the facility with which he could shift from one opinion to another", ibid.
[2] Atlay, Victorian Chancellors ii 226.   [3] Victorian Chancellors ii 226-227.
[4] Ibid 223.   [5] Mr. Gladstone at Oxford by C.R.L.F. 60-61.

about the conduct of the defendant, his client, before he had heard
the defendant's case.[1] "As he became more eminent this habit of
venting bitter sarcasms, like his habit of laying down principles
which he could not support, grew upon him, and betrayed him
into excesses of speech and conduct which neither their wit nor
their appositeness could excuse".[2] And yet he was a model son, a
too indulgent father, and, as the events which led to his fall
showed, too trustful of, and too kind to, his subordinate
officials.[3] Beneath his haughty manner there was "a natural
kindness of disposition", which few realized, because he had few
intimate friends.[4] We shall see that it was due both to the enmities which his bitter tongue created, and to this kindness of
disposition, that his fall was due.

Bethell had no great love for politics in his early days. His
political views were vague. If anything he was a Peelite.[5] In
1847 he had unsuccessfully contested Shaftesbury as a liberal-
conservative. But his genuine desire to reform the law, his dislike
of all forms of sacerdotalism, and his opposition to the law which
excluded the Jews from Parliament,[6] finally led him to throw in
his lot with the liberals. In 1851 he was elected for Aylesbury in
the liberal interest.

Just before this election he had refused the offer of a Vice-
Chancellorship; but he had accepted the office of Vice-Chancellorship of the County Palatine of Lancaster, which did not involve a
cessation of practice at the bar. But this office he resigned when,
on the defeat of the conservatives, he became Solicitor-General
in 1852.

During the session of 1851-52 he established his position in
the House by the part which he played in the Chancery Procedure

---

[1] Atlay, op. cit. ii 249; Nash, op. cit. i 290-292; this scene in court produced
articles in *The Times* approving Bethell's conduct, and a poem in *Punch*, March 26,
1859, "The Battle of the Big Wigs", the first verse of which runs as follows:

Sing, O, Punch the quick wrath, the soon-put-up "Monkey" of Knight-Bruce:
Knight-Bruce the active of mind, the jumper to hasty conclusions:
Knight-Bruce the feared of the Bar, the bully of junior counsel:
Sing of the hot anger of Bruce and the cool encounter of Bethell:
Bethell the feared of the Bench, the Rarey, the tamer of Horse hair,
Tamer of legal Big Wigs, subduer of Lords and Vice-Chancellors:
Twister of Courts round his thumb with his silvery voice of persuasion.

[2] Atlay, op. cit. ii 250-261.   [3] Below 79 *et seq.*
[4] Nash, op. cit. i 79-80, ii 262-263; for an instance of a case where he gave his
services and so saved an acquaintance from ruin, see ibid, i 270.
[5] Nash, op. cit. i 103-104.
[6] In 1853 in a debate on Jewish disabilities the existence of Easter and Whitsun
had been used to prove that Christianity was part of the constitution—it might just
as well be contended, said Bethell, "that the use of the word Wednesday, which was
derived from Woden, was a proof of the country being heathen", Hansard (3rd Ser.)
cxxv 1246.

Act. "His mincing speech, his trim precision of manner, and the unexpected turn of his mordant humour amused instead of irritating the House"[1]—though his sarcasms made enemies there as they did in the courts. As Solicitor-General he was a success in the House. He tried with some success to be conciliatory, and Gladstone acknowledged gratefully his help in piloting the Succession Duty Act through the House.[2] When Cockburn became Chief Justice of the Common Pleas in 1856 Bethell succeeded him as Attorney-General. His conduct in that office added to his fame. His speech in defence of the government in the Chinese difficulties which arose out of the *lorcha* Arrow, though it did not avert a vote of censure, was "long regarded among the classics of Parliamentary oratory".[3] He carried Acts to punish fraudulent trustees,[4] to make important amendments in the Companies Act,[5] to establish a court of Probate;[6] and in the debates on the Act which reformed the law of divorce [7] he and Gladstone were the protagonists.[8] He refused the offer of the judgeship of the Probate and Divorce court on the ground that it was due to his exertions in the House that considerable additions had been made to the salary and patronage of the judge, so that if he accepted the post it might be said that he had been working for his own aggrandisement.[9]

The Orsini plot, and the Conspiracy to Murder Bill which followed it, caused the fall of the government. The attack made by Campbell on Bethell's statement of the law produced from Bethell a personal explanation in which he rebuked Campbell in a speech of polished and sarcastic invective. If a judge, he said, declared what the law was in a case in which he might hereafter be called upon to adjudicate, he was disqualified from sitting to hear it as a judge. In fact, there was "nothing more to be deprecated in the judges of the land than that they should be incontinent of tongue".[10]

---

[1] Atlay, op. cit. ii 232.

[2] Gladstone wrote to Bethell: "The memory of the Succession Duty Bill is to me something like what Inkerman may be to a private of the Guards: you were the sergeant from whom I got my drill and whose hand and voice carried me through", Morley, Life of Gladstone (Shilling Ed.) i 350 n. 2.

[3] Atlay, op. cit. ii 237; Hansard (3rd Ser.) cxliv 1564-1585.

[4] 20, 21 Victoria c. 54.

[5] 20, 21 Victoria c. 14; he helped also to pass another Act in 1862, 25, 26 Victoria c. 89.　　　　[6] 20, 21 Victoria c. 77.　　　　[7] 20, 21 Victoria c. 85.

[8] "In the hundred encounters between Mr. Gladstone and Bethell polished phrase barely hid unchristian desire to retaliate and provoke. Bethell boldly taunted Mr. Gladstone with insincerity. Mr. Gladstone, with a vivacity very like downright anger, reproached Bethell with being a mere hewer of wood and drawer of water to the cabinet", Morley, Life of Gladstone i 425.　　　　[9] Nash, op. cit. i 236.

[10] Hansard (3rd Ser.) cxlix 4-13; Nash, op. cit. i 254-258.

On the defeat of Disraeli's government in 1859 Bethell expected to be made Chancellor. But the government could not afford to lose his services in the House of Commons. Much to his disappointment the difficulty was tided over by making Campbell Chancellor. Here is his account of the matter:[1]

I should wish the circumstances relative to my appointment as Chancellor to be known. Pam.[2] came to me to talk about the Chancellorship. . . . He said, "We cannot do without you in the House of Commons. Campbell is your senior both in years and at the bar. Considering his advanced age, it is not likely that he will continue Chancellor long, after which you would succeed as a matter of course." I said, "I am, personally, utterly indifferent about the Great Seal; but I am bound to support the claim of the Equity bar. No Equity barrister has been Chancellor for a long time, and if I waive this occasion, there is no saying when the Equity bar may have another opportunity, so that if I give way now the rights of the Equity bar might suffer." But Pam pressed the matter. At length I said, "This not being a personal matter with me, I will agree to submit to four law lords the point whether, if I allow Campbell to be Chancellor, the rights of the Equity bar will suffer." Pam agreed to that. Suggested Brougham, Kingsdown, Wensleydale, and Cranworth. . . . I went to the House of Lords, got out the four, and they agreed decidedly that the appointment of Campbell would not in any way be injurious to the rights of the Equity bar; so I waived my personal right, but made it clearly understood and admitted that I had the right and waived it. It is a singular thing that as I came out from seeing the law lords I met Campbell, and saluted him with "How do you do, my Lord Chancellor"?

When he was Chancellor he animadverted on the conduct of certain trustees. Their counsel handed up to him an opinion signed "R. Bethell" which had recommended them to take the course of conduct which they had pursued. He read the paper and said: "It is a mystery to me how the gentleman capable of penning such an opinion can have risen to the eminence which he now has the honour to enjoy." [3] Rolt, between whom and Bethell no love was lost,[4] says that on a second consultation he always expressed a confident opinion different from that which he had expressed equally confidently on the first.[5] So, too, in court, as his fame increased, he would lay down a principle which he thought ought to be law or wished to be law for the purposes of his case; and if asked for authority was unable to produce it.[6] It is not surprising

---

[1] Nash, Life of Westbury i 275.   [2] Palmerston.
[3] Ibid ii 259-260; for another illustration of a change of opinion which led him to contradict one of his own decisions, see Nash, op. cit. ii 30.
[4] Atlay, op. cit. ii 252.   [5] Memoirs of Sir John Rolt 147-148.
[6] "During his argument one day in the House of Lords, Lord Campbell stopped him and asked for an authority for the proposition which Sir Richard had laid down with such confidence. 'My Lord', replied Bethell, 'such is the law.' 'But as I have to be elsewhere in a few minutes, my friend, Mr. Archibald, will produce to your Lordship abundance of authority in support of it.' Mr. Archibald anticipated his leader in retiring from the Court as soon as he heard this assurance", Nash, Life of

that his opponents sometimes doubted his honesty.[1] The fact was that, as Jowett said,[2] "his mind was so plastic, and he represented things to himself and others in so graphic a manner, that he may not have known at the moment whether he was feigning or not". The new Chancellor and the Attorney-General, somewhat to the surprise of the former, got on well together;[3] but, as Atlay says, when Bethell succeeded him, "he was never happier than in applying the test of a 'few elementary rules of law' to the decisions of his predecessor".[4] One of the last cases which Bethell argued was the appeal of certain Fellows of All Souls' College, Oxford, to the Visitor against the procedure adopted by the College in their elections to fellowships, which, it was alleged, was contrary to the Ordinance of 1857.[5] He appeared for the appellants and succeeded. Coleridge was his junior, and he said of his argument in reply that it was

the finest and greatest thing I have ever heard at the Bar. He sat all day taking elaborate notes, and there was a good deal to answer. He spoke less than two hours, never touched or looked at a paper, did not leave one point unnoticed, and poured out a flood of powerful invective besides which electrified us. The whole speech too was so beautifully clear, so balanced, so well proportioned, that it seemed as if it must have been composed beforehand, and yet we knew it could not have been. With all his affectation he has *a very great intellect*—the greatest I ever came near or have any belief of in our profession at our time. Bovill and Cairns were *babes* to him.[6]

Campbell died in 1861, and Bethell succeeded him, taking his title from Westbury in the county of Wilts.

Westbury never succeeded so well in the House of Lords as he had succeeded in the House of Commons. He began badly. The Lords had mutilated his Bankruptcy Bill, and he made a personal attack on Cranworth and Chelmsford, the two law lords responsible for this mutilation.[7] But though he was disappointed by his

Westbury i 240; As Atlay says, op. cit. ii 253, "A counsel whom the judges cannot trust implicitly in the statement of a fact or the citation of a case is not usually regarded in the profession with either admiration or respect".
  [1] Bethell ruled Shadwell (vol. xiii 667, 668). Rolt, op. cit. 99, tells the following tale: "Sometime before 1846 . . . I was entering Shadwell's Court, and met Roundell Palmer coming out, visibly boiling with rage. I stopped him to ask what ailed him: his answer was, 'I have been arguing before a Fool, and against a Knave'. My rejoinder was, 'Is that all? I thought you were used to that.'"
  [2] Nash, Life of Westbury ii 292.   [3] Life of Campbell ii 387.
  [4] Victorian Chancellors ii 245.   [5] Ibid 246-248.
  [6] Life of Lord Coleridge i 265, cited Atlay, op. cit. ii 247.
  [7] "If the Select Committee (of the House of Lords) had no further information before them as to the contents of the bill than the knowledge of the subject and of the subject of bankruptcy generally which has been exhibited by my two noble and learned friends, I was not right to be at all surprised at that conclusion. From beginning to end not one word is correct of all you have heard from these two noble and learned lords", Hansard, clxiv 1606, cited Atlay, op. cit. ii 255.

failure to carry his reform of the law of bankruptcy in its entirety, he did not relax his efforts in the cause of law reform. We shall see that he carried an Act for the registration of title to land which, like a later Act of Lord Cairns,[1] failed to effect is purpose,[2] and that he attempted an ambitious scheme for a digest of English law which also failed,[3] but that he succeeded in his efforts to promote the cause of the revision of the statute law,[4] and in amending the lunacy laws.[5] But his brother peers, though they recognized his legal abilities, were never reconciled to his sarcastic manner, and his intellectual arrogance.

He added materially to his unpopularity by his conflict with the bishops, which arose out of his sturdy Erastianism. His chief opponent on the episcopal bench was Wilberforce, the Bishop of Oxford—known by the nickname of "Soapy Sam" which he explained by saying that he was always in hot water and always came out with clean hands. His first bout with him was over a bill to establish bishoprics in heathen countries without the licence of the Crown, which Westbury regarded as an attack on the royal supremacy.[6] But he had, to say the least, overstated his case, and in the opinion of many had the worst of the encounter. His most serious contest was over the book entitled *Essays and Reviews*. Two of the authors, Williams and Wilson, had been condemned by Lushington, the Dean of the Arches, on the ground that their essays had thrown doubts on the inspiration of the Bible, and on the doctrine of everlasting punishment. They appealed successfully to the Privy Council.[7] The effect of that decision was summarized in a witty epitaph on the Chancellor which runs as follows:[8]

RICHARD BARON WESTBURY

Lord High Chancellor of England
He was an eminent Christian,
An energetic and merciful statesman,
And a still more eminent and merciful Judge.

During his three years' tenure of office
He abolished the ancient method of conveying land,
The time-honoured institution of the Insolvents' Court,
And
The Eternity of Punishment.

---

[1] Below 109, 110.   [2] Below 110.   [3] Below 84.
[4] Below 84.   [5] Below 85.   [6] Hansard (3rd Ser.) clxviii 226.
[7] *Williams v. Bishop of Salisbury, Wilson v. Fendall* (1863), 2 Moo. P.C. N.S. 375.

[8] Cited Atlay, op. cit. ii 264; the epitaph is attributed to Sir Philip Rose, "though the most pungent line in it is said to have been endorsed on his brief by Charles Bowen *currente calamo*", ibid.

Towards the close of his earthly career
In the Judicial Committee of the Privy Council
He dismissed Hell with costs,
And took away from orthodox members of the Church of England
Their last hope of everlasting damnation.

Most churchmen were indignant at the decision,[1] and Convocation passed a "symbolical judgment" condemning the essays.
When the question of this judgment was raised in the House of
Lords Westbury, in a speech full of sarcastic raillery, said that
Convocation might have incurred the penalties of a *praemunire*
but for the fact that such a judgment was merely "a well
lubricated set of words so oily and saponaceous that no one could
grasp it".[2] His law was, to say the least, dubious; and Wilberforce
rebuked Westbury's ribaldry, and carried the House with him.[3]

Westbury's sarcastic tongue had made for him many enemies
amongst the lawyers and in both Houses of Parliament. It was
due to this enmity that two cases in which he had shown considerable negligence in the performance of his duties were made
the occasion of an attack upon him which caused his downfall. The
facts of these cases were as follows:[4]

The first case concerned one Edmunds who was reading
clerk in the House of Lords and clerk to the Commissioners of
Patents. In the latter capacity he had converted some £18,000 of
public money to his own use. Proceedings against him were
stayed by Westbury provided that he repaid the money and
resigned his office. He offered to resign also his clerkship in the
House of Lords if the usual retiring pension was granted to him.
Westbury accepted this resignation, and presented his petition
for a pension to a committee of the Lords without disclosing all
the facts. These happenings aroused considerable scandal, which
was aggravated by the not very relevant fact that Westbury
had appointed his son Slingsby to the vacant office in the House
of Lords. To allay the scandal Westbury moved for a select
committee to enquire into the matter. It reported that the
Chancellor had failed in his duty in not informing the committee
of the House of all the facts about Edmunds before it granted the

---

[1] Gladstone said that "the spirit of this judgment has but to be consistently and
cautiously followed up, in order to establish, as far as the court case established it, a
complete indifference between the Christian faith and the denial of it"; and "I feel
that the most vital lay interests are at stake in the definite teaching and profession of
the Christian faith, and the general tendency and effect of the judgments has been
and is likely to be hostile to that definite teaching", Morley, Life of Gladstone ii 125,
126.   [2] Hansard (3rd Ser.) clxxvi 1544-1549.
[3] Atlay, op. cit. ii 265-267; the action of Convocation had been taken under the
advice of Cairns and Rolt.
[4] Nash, op. cit. ii 112-145; Atlay, op. cit. ii 268-278.

pension. Westbury then wished to resign, but Palmerston would not accept his resignation.

The second case was connected with the scandals in the administration of the law of bankruptcy into which Westbury had instituted an enquiry. Wilde, the Leeds registrar in bankruptcy, was told that, unless he resigned, he would be called on to show cause why he should not be dismissed. Nevertheless he was allowed to retire with a pension on the ground of ill health. The vacant office was given to a barrister named Walsh who, unknown to Westbury, had lent large sums of money to the Chancellor's son Richard, who had represented that he could influence the disposal of the Chancellor's patronage. Richard's extravagance was notorious; he had recently been compelled to resign a bankruptcy registrarship in London; and he was an undischarged bankrupt. Westbury had refused to give his son another appointment, but it was rumoured that Walsh was only holding the Leeds registrarship till Westbury could be persuaded to appoint his son to it. A select committee of the House of Commons was appointed to enquire into the affair of the Leeds registrarship, which reported that the pension to Wilde should not have been granted; and that, though no corruption could be imputed to the Chancellor, the appointment of Walsh indicated corruption in his officials. Again Westbury's offer to resign was refused. But when, on the report of this committee, a vote of censure was passed upon him, his resignation became inevitable.[1] In his last speech from the Woolsack he announced his resignation in a dignified speech of apology and regret which went far to redeem his faults.

Westbury's fall suggested and invited a comparison between him and Bacon. As Frederic Harrison truly said,[2] "his mind had something of the qualities of Lord Bacon's, both on the stronger and the weaker side. The restless desire to bring order out of disorder, to classify, group, and harmonize ideas, out-stripped in both the knowledge of details and the stubborn reality of facts." And there was another similarity. Just as Bacon's unemotional temperament led to a weakening of the sense of personal honour, and caused him to take his tone from the corrupt society of James I's court,[3] so Westbury's deficiency in moral sense led him to an insensitiveness to the consequences of acts which men of far less ability would have realized. As Roundell Palmer, who defended him in the House of Commons'[4] said,[5]

---

[1] Hansard (3rd Ser.) clxxx 1445 *et seq.*   [2] Cited by Nash, op. cit. ii 165-166
[3] Vol. v 243-245.   [4] Hansard (3rd Ser.) clxxx 1120-1129.
[5] Memorials, Family and Personal ii 491-492.

Strange as it may seem, there was in him, mixed with all that was artificial, an element of extraordinary simplicity (what the Greeks called εὐήθεια), a want of tact and practical good sense, in which may be found the explanation of the errors and oversights which produced his fall. His mind was not sufficiently in touch with the minds of other men.

The gist of the matter is contained in an Imaginary Conversation between Bacon and Westbury which was published by *Punch* at the time of his fall.[1] Here are the concluding sentences

Lord Bacon: Your country is the scrutineer. Your countrymen know that the Vote of Censure was a Party Move.[2] You are hated by the Tories for the reforms you have wrought, and still more for those you threaten. The vermin of the Bankruptcy Court have been rudely brushed by you, and you would have brushed them out entirely, had you remained in office. You have given the Divorce Court to the people. You have simplified conveyancing. This and more will be remembered, when your errors shall be forgotten.

Lord Bethell: I admit the errors.

Lord Bacon: They were two, and *non licet in bello bis peccare.* But Englishmen do not hate a man much because he has been too lenient, or because he has been wrongly tolerant of the evil deeds of his children. You have been punished, my Lord, and will live to serve the State. *Non ignarus mali.* I give you this consolation. I add that much of your trouble is from another fault.

Lord Bethell: I wish to hear it.

Lord Bacon: Intolerant of fools and knaves, you made yourself, by virtue of a bitter tongue, the least popular man in England. My gracious manners and flowing eloquence made friends out of enemies.

Lord Bethell: It may be so. But it is very hard to bear a knave talking what he knows to be folly, and yet not to give him a back-hander. However, I will mend. You would not have me retire from public life?

Lord Bacon: Minime. The nation can ill spare such a brain. Go to the House of Lords and do your duty. A Bishop or so may be spiteful, but the Peers are gentlemen, and will remember that *nemo bis vexari debet pro eadem causa.* It is from your country that you have your retaining fee, my Lord.

Westbury took this advice. In 1866 he began again to hear appeals in the House of Lords and the Judicial Committee of the Privy Council; and in 1867, after the death of Lord Kingsdown, he generally presided over the Privy Council. In 1868 he might have had a Lord Justiceship of Appeal if he had cared to take it. After Cranworth's death he presided over the Commission set up to examine into one of his favourite projects—a digest of English law. Frederic Harrison, the secretary, said that though he realized that the Commission could do little more than preparatory work, he applied himself to the work with "freshness and

---

[1] July 15, 1865.

[2] In 1868 Gladstone said, "Lord Westbury suffered heavily in 1865. He became to a great extent a scapegoat. The vials of public virtue, a very acrid composition, were discharged upon him", cited Nash, op. cit. ii 186.

versatility", and showed all his old wit and ingenuity.[1] From 1868 onwards he was a friendly critic of the measures of Gladstone's government. He did not wholly approve of the provisions of the Act which disestablished the Irish Church, because they meant a weakening of the royal supremacy, and they confiscated its revenues; and he was a strong critic of the negotiations which led up to the Geneva arbitration on the Alabama case. He lived long enough to criticize privately Lord Selborne's first draft of the Judicature Act, but he was unable to attend the debates upon'it. His last public work was as the arbitrator appointed by a private Act of Parliament in 1872 to wind up the affairs of the European Assurance Society.[2] In that complicated arbitration he showed all his old powers of unravelling complicated transactions and getting to the bottom of fraudulent proceedings. In spite of a most painful illness he carried on the'arbitration. But at his last session of the court which was held only a few weeks before his death, he was obviously a dying man.[3] He died on July 20, 1873.

Westbury is remarkable amongst the English Chancellors in that he was not only a legislator and a judge, but also a jurist who was dissatisfied with many of the principles of English law, and was prepared to go to Roman law and foreign systems of law to get suggestions for reform. I shall consider his work first as a jurist and legislator, and, secondly, as a judge.

The jurist and legislator

Westbury was as dissatisfied with the condition of English law as were Brougham and Bentham. The technicalities and complexities of Chancery practice and conveyancing; the different and sometimes contradictory principles and rules applied by the common law courts, the court of Chancery, and the courts held by the civilians and Doctors' Commons; the chaos of the statutes; the bulk and uncertainty of case law; the want of a proper system of legal education which left English lawyers in ignorance of Roman law, foreign law, and jurisprudential principles; and the consequent inferiority of English legal literature—aroused in him scorn and anger, and a determination to do something to remedy these crying defects.

It was his keen sense of the intellectual deficiencies of English law and English lawyers which, as we have seen,[4] led him to take so great an interest in legal education. It was for the same reason that he stressed the importance of the teaching of Roman law.

---

[1] Nash, op. cit. ii 166.   [2] 35, 36 Victoria c. cxlv.
[3] He did not live long enough to finish the arbitration, which was conducted by Lord Romilly, D.N.B.   [4] Above 72.

His advice to his pupils was "read the Pandects";[1] in 1846 he
induced the Middle Temple to appoint a reader in jurisprudence
and the civil law.[2] In 1854, on a motion for the commission to
enquire into the arrangements made by the Inns of Court to
promote the study of the law, he urged the government to
consider the project of converting the Inns of Court into a legal
university;[3] and in his inaugural address to the Juridical Society
in 1855 he ascribed "our inferiority in jurisprudence" and the
poverty of English literature upon the philosophy of law to "the
antipathy which the English lawyer has always felt to the study
of the civil law".[4] He considered that the principal reason for
this antipathy was the divergence between law and equity and
the law administered by the civilians. That divergence prevented
English lawyers from acquiring a mastery of the whole field of
English law;[5] and it made English lawyers averse to the construction of a code or a digest of the whole law, and led them to
prefer the chaos of the statute book and the reports.[6] In 1859,
in his valedictory address to the same Society he stressed the need
for a Ministry of Justice, to watch the working of the law enacted
and unenacted, make suggestions for its reform, or restatement,
and express in compact form the results of the cases.[7] The need
for such a Ministry was, he pointed out, the more pressing by
reason of the changing conditions of the age. The law had been
unable to deal satisfactorily with the new conditions. It had,[8]

ebbed and flowed sometimes in one direction and then in the opposite . . .
the reason of that was, that there was not in our constitution a body of
men armed with authority to take the different cases as they arise, and
see if, owing to peculiar circumstances, it has become requisite to lay
down some new principle by authority, and with that view to take some
case to the highest tribunal, and there have it settled once for all. For, in
England, although society has the greatest possible interest in the
results of particular cases, yet, whether from those cases shall accrue
benefit to society, depends entirely on the litigant parties to them.

Such a ministry would help the executive to assert control over
the drafting of statutes, which in too many cases was grossly
defective.[9] Like Blackstone before him,[10] he ascribed these evils
largely to the defects of the existing system of legal education.[11]

[1] Nash, op. cit. i 61.   [2] Ibid 91-94.
[3] Hansard (3rd Ser.) cxxxi 163-166.   [4] Papers of the Juridical Society, i 2, 6.
[5] Ibid 5.   [6] Ibid.   [7] Ibid ii 132 *et seq*.   [8] Ibid ii 135.
   [9] He said, ibid 136-137, "You will not wonder at the present state of things, when
I tell you that, while in the House of Commons, I have been compelled to draw upon
the instant, and write on the back of my hat, clauses of proposed enactments which
have afterwards been put on the statute book"; for the history of this topic, see vol.
xi 364-383, and for the evil effect of hastily drawn amendments, see ibid 385-386.
   [10] Vol. xii 97-99.   [11] Papers of the Juridical Society ii 137-139.

In 1863 he repeated and amplified these suggestions in the greatest speech which he ever made on a purely legal topic. It was delivered on the motion for the first reading of a bill for the revision of the statute law.[1] In it he dwelt upon the defects of case law, recalled Bacon's project for its revisions[2] and suggested the appointment of a commission,

to revise and to expurgate the Reports, to weed them of decisions which are in contradiction with one another; where there are opposing decisions, to settle those which ought to remain; and to cleanse out and get rid of all matters that are not warranted by the present state of the law, or applicable to the existing conditions of society. I divide the Reports into three classes. The first class would include all the old Reports to the end of the 17th century; the second would include the Reports of the 18th century and down to the death of George III; and the third would include the Reports to the present time. . . . As to the old Reports, I propose that we should preserve only the conclusions properly come to; that in the second period we should weed the Reports of what is useless, and retain only those cases which are fit to be used as precedents; and to perform a similar work in respect of cases of the present time. The result will be a body of recorded precedents, brought into a moderate compass, and occupying, we may estimate, but a tenth of the bulk of the present Reports.[3]

Similarly the statutes must be revised and expurgated. The bill proposed to get rid of obsolete statutes from 20 Henry III (1235) to the end of the eighteenth century, yet taking care that no constitutional or private rights should be impaired. When this work had been done, he proposed that the rules laid down both by the statutes and by the cases be classified and digested. All this ought, he thought, to be preparatory to the construction of a code, which was not yet possible, largely because of the division of the law between common law and equity.[4] He ended his speech with a plea for the creation of a Ministry of Justice which should keep a constant survey of the results of the cases, and subject them to a process of annual revision, "with power to determine which is to be regarded as entitled to authority, and which ought not to be quoted hereafter for the purpose of determining the law".[5] In 1866 a commission was appointed to enquire into the expediency of preparing a digest of the law, of which Westbury was chairman after Cranworth's death. But it effected nothing, and five years later came to an end.[6]

[1] Hansard (3rd Ser.) clxxi 775-791.　　　[2] Vol. v 487.
[3] Hansard (3rd Ser.) clxxi 785.
[4] Hansard (3rd Ser.) clxxi 788-789.　　　[5] Ibid 791.
[6] Atlay, op. cit. ii 283-285; an account of some of the aspects of this movement for the reform of the law enacted and unenacted will be found in T. E. Holland, Essays on the Form of the Law; there is a useful chronological table of the principal events in the Appendix.

To these large projects for improving the education of English lawyers, for improving the machinery for making and developing the enacted and the unenacted law, and for reshaping the form of English law, Westbury added proposals for simplifying the working of the land law by a scheme for the registration of titles. We have seen that, from the latter part of the seventeenth century onwards, many lawyers had advocated the registration of titles to, or conveyances of, land,[1] and that in the age of reform which came after 1832 many such projects had been discussed.[2] In 1862 no less than six bills to effect this object were before the House of Lords.[3] A select committee reported in favour of Westbury's scheme for the registration of titles. It passed into law,[4] in spite of the protests of Lord St. Leonards.[5] Westbury was confident that its effect would be to make land "as easily transferable as consols";[6] and he said that of all the law reforms which he had promoted this was the reform by which he would be hereafter remembered.[7] We have seen that he was mistaken. The Act did not make registration compulsory; the legal profession and the landowners were hostile; and the machinery provided by the Act was so complex that the trouble and expense of registration were greater than the trouble and expense of a sale under the old system.[8]

Westbury failed to carry his larger plans of law reform. His scheme for the registration of titles to land was a failure. A university of law was not established by the Inns of Court. There was no revision of the reports and no restatement of the rules of English law. But his work was not altogether in vain. He did persuade the Inns to institute a scheme of education and examination for their students;[9] and he helped forward the work of the revision of the statute law.[10] Though his bankruptcy bill was mutilated, it effected useful reforms, and it got rid of the absurd distinction between bankruptcy and insolvency.[11] He helped to pass the Chancery Procedure Acts of 1852,[12] he passed an Act to facilitate dealings with settled estates,[13] he succeeded in amending the lunacy laws,[14] he played a large part in securing the passing of the Acts which set up the Probate and Divorce Courts,[15] and the Acts which consolidated large parts of the criminal law.[16] His Act for the sale of small livings in the Chancellor's gift was very

[1] Vol. vi 532, 594, 610; vol. xi 586-588; vol. xii 378-380.
[2] Vol. xv 182.   [3] Nash, op. cit. ii 17.   [4] 25, 26 Victoria c. 53.
[5] Nash, op. cit. ii 20.
[6] Ibid citing a letter from Westbury to the Prime Minister.
[7] Ibid ii 24.   [8] Vol. xv 186.   [9] Vol. xv 237.
[10] Vol. xi 314-315.   [11] Vol. xv 98, 99, 100; 24, 25 Victoria c. 134.
[12] Vol. i 444; vol. ix 375-376; 15, 16 Victoria cc. 80, 86.
[13] 19, 20 Victoria c. 120; above 60.   [14] 25, 26 Victoria c. 86; above 78.
[15] Above 75.   [16] 24, 25 Victoria cc. 95-100.

beneficial to the incumbents.[1] His Act which gave an equitable jurisdiction to the county courts was equally and more generally beneficial.[2] He supported the Act for the concentration of the courts on their present site,[3] an Act to improve the law as to copyright in works of art,[4] and an Act to increase the judicial strength of the Judicial Committee of the Privy Council.[5] A statement made by one of the newspapers in 1865 that in him "the nation has for the first time a law reformer who is terribly in earnest", was the simple truth;[6] and Fitzjames Stephen once lamented the national incapacity to make use of a great legal reformer, such as Westbury, when we get him.[7]

Westbury's successes and his failures as a law reformer illustrate the strong and the weak sides of his intellect. The reforms in the law which he succeeded in effecting illustrate his keen eye for abuses and anomalies, and his skill in suggesting suitable remedies. His failure to effect his larger schemes illustrate his tendency to over-simplify problems, and to brush aside objections and difficulties, which, whether well founded or not, made his solution impossible to carry into effect. Just as in his work as counsel and judge his main failing was a tendency to rely on broad and simple principles for which it was sometimes impossible to find authority,[8] so as a jurist and a legislator his failing was to put forward a large and simple principle as the foundation of a sweeping reform, without considering the strength of the opposition to so extensive a change, or the real merits in some of the rules or institutions which he wished to sweep away. His scheme for the registration of titles to land would, if it had succeeded, have substituted a new set of technicalities for the old. It would not have been for the advantage of the legal profession or the law if the Inns of Court had been turned into a university of law. There were more merits in the system of case law than he imagined; and the revision of the reports would have been a work of far greater difficulty and delicacy than he seems to have imagined. Like Starkey in the sixteenth century,[9] he exaggerated the extent of the divergence between the rules of law and the rules of equity.[10] We shall now see that as a judge he showed the same strength and the same weaknesses as he showed as a counsel and as a jurist and legislator.

[1] 26, 27 Victoria c. 120; Nash, op. cit. ii 51-55. [2] 28, 29 Victoria c. 99.
[3] 28, 29 Victoria c. 49. [4] 25, 26 Victoria c. 68. [5] 34, 35 Victoria c. 91.
[6] Nash, op. cit. ii 99. [7] Life of Fitzjames Stephen 225.
[8] Above 72.
[9] Vol. iv, 259-261; he was quite wrong when he said, Papers of the Juridical Society i 2, that English law at the time of the Conquest "was in great measure derived from the jurisprudence that had been introduced and administered by the Romans during the 300 years of their dominion in Britain".
[10] Ibid i 4, cited vol. xii 602 n. 4.

The judge

Westbury's judgments are remarkable for their clear polished style, their clarity and their conciseness. The defect of some of them is the same defect as he showed in his arguments at the bar —an over-simplification of principles was attained by a neglect of relevant authority, and a consequently inaccurate statement of the law. As E. P. Macdonald said,[1]

His habit was to brush aside, or pass by unnoticed, the crowd of cases which had accumulated during the argument, to treat with scant respect judicial opinions which might stand in his way and to come to his decision by the light of "a few elementary rules of law"—a phrase which he had a malicious fondness for using when about to reverse Lord Campbell.

Westbury said of Roundell Palmer, Lord Selborne, that if he "could get rid of the habit of pursuing a fine train of reasoning on a matter collateral to the main route of his argument, he would be perfect".[2] But it is probable that his arguments on these matters were not wholly collateral, but introduced considerations needed to ensure the accuracy of the principle which should have guided the decisions. This was probably Selborne's opinion; for, as we have seen,[3] he said of Westbury that he was not profound as a lawyer, and that his capacity for mastering quickly the essential facts of a case gave him "a judicial reputation . . . greater than the quality of his performances as a judge can explain". But Jessel, whom he did not love and to whom he had once refused a silk gown,[4] said of him that he was "a man of genius who had gone to the Bar".[5] It is therefore not surprising to find that some of his statements of principle, more especially on such matters as the law of domicile, where authority was scanty, did enable him to elucidate and develop many branches of equity and some branches of law. Let us look at one or two examples.

In many cases Westbury's judgments give illuminating surveys of the *principles of equity*. The following are a few examples: the case of *Taylor v. Meads*,[6] which established the right of the married woman, not restrained from anticipation, to alienate her separate property *inter vivos* or by will, contains a very

---

[1] D.N.B. [2] Nash, op. cit. ii 9.

[3] A good illustration is the case of *Enohin v. Wylie* (1862) 10 H.L.C. 1, in which, as Selborne pointed out in *Ewing v. Orr Ewing* (1883) 9 App. Cas. at p. 39, Westbury laid down the principle that it is only the courts of the country in which a testator dies domiciled which can administer his estate, is laid down too absolutely.

[4] Atlay, Victorian Chancellors ii 252 n. 1; but Selborne persuaded him to relent, Memorials Personal and Political ii 93.

[5] Nash, Life of Westbury ii 293. [6] (1865) 4 De G.J. and S. 597.

lucid exposition of the equitable doctrine of the separate use, and its divergence from "the principles and policy of the common law as to the status of the wife during coverture".[1] In the case of *Forrest v. Manchester, Sheffield and Lincolnshire Railway* [2] he laid down the principle that a plaintiff in equity, who pretends to sue in one character and is in reality acting in another, has no *locus standi* in court, so that the bill of a person purporting to sue on behalf of Company A who is acting in reality on behalf of a rival Company B must be dismissed. In the case of *Willes v. Greenhill* [3] he followed a decision of Lord Lyndhurst's,[4] and held that notice of an incumbrance to one of several trustees was sufficient to preserve priority. In the case of *Phillips v. Phillips* [5] he explained the meaning of the maxim *qui prior est tempore potior est jure,* and gave a clear exposition of the limitations of the defence of purchase for value without notice of an equitable claim. In his judgment in the case of *Hunt v. Hunt* [6] there is an interesting account of the history of the way in which the law treated agreements between husband and wife to separate—though the correctness of the actual decision in that case, that a covenant by a husband to allow his wife to live apart from him would entitle her to an injunction to prevent her husband suing in the divorce court for restitution of conjugal rights, has been questioned.[7] In the case of *Dillwyn v. Llewelyn* [8] he discussed the conditions of the application of the rule that equity will not, in favour of a volunteer, perfect an imperfect gift. In the case of *Isenberg v. East India House Estate Co.*[9] he discussed the principles upon which the court will grant or refuse to grant a mandatory injunction.

Many of his decisions discuss various aspects of the *law of property*. There are several important cases upon easements. In the case of *Jackson v. Duke of Newcastle* [10] he discussed the question when the court will issue an injunction to stop an interference with ancient lights; in the case of *Suffield v. Brown* [11] he explained the conditions in which the law will imply the grant or reservation of an easement; and in the case of *Hanmer v. Chance* [12] he distinguished a claim to an easement by custom which comes within the Prescription Act, 1832, from a claim by a

---

[1] At p. 605.
[2] (1861) 4 De G.F. and J. 126; for a case where this principle was distinguished and held not to apply, see *Mutter v. Eastern and Midlands Rly. Co.* (1888) 38 Ch.D. 92.   [3] (1861) 4 De G.F. and J. 147.
[4] (1835) *Smith v. Smith* 1 Y. and C. Exch. 338.
[5] (1861) 4 De G.F. and J. 208.   [6] (1862) 4 De G.F. and J. at pp. 226-230.
[7] *Cahill v. Cahill* (1883) 8 App. Cas. at p. 421 *per* Lord Selborne L.C.
[8] (1862) 4 De G.F. and J. 517.   [9] (1863) 3 De G.J. and S. 263.
[10] (1864) 3 De G.J. and S. 275.   [11] (1864) 4 De G.J. and S. 185.
[12] (1865) 4 De G.J. and S. 626.

copyholder by virtue of the custom of the manor. The case of *Spirett v. Willows* [1] discusses the circumstances in which a voluntary settlement will be held to be void because it is made with the intention of defeating or delaying creditors. In the case of *Wyllie v. Pollen* [2] he said that he agreed with those judges who had said that the doctrine of constructive notice ought not to be extended. One of the most important of his decisions on this branch of the law is *Holroyd v. Marshall*, [3] in which he laid down the principle that a contract for a valuable consideration, by which it is agreed to make a present transfer of property, passes the property in equity. [4] It is true that some little confusion has been caused by his statement that the contract must be specifically enforceable. As Lord Macnaghten explained, he was thinking, not of the specific performance of an executory contract—specific performance properly so called, but of cases in which equity would give some sort of specific relief. [5] The fact that the protection given by the court to trademarks is based upon property, [6] and the conditions under which the owner will be protected by injunction, were elucidated in several of his decisions. [7]

In the *law of trusts* one of the most important of his decisions is his exposition, in the case of *McCormick v. Grogan*, [8] of the principle upon which equity enforces secret trusts. But his remarks should be taken with the caution that when he says that the equitable jurisdiction is based on fraud, it is equitable and not legal fraud that he is referring to [9]—though this is somewhat obscured by his insistence on *malus animus*. Other cases deal with the question when a trustee can be made liable for a breach of trust committed by a co-trustee; [10] and with the liability of third persons who have received trust property from a trustee with notice that the trustee has transferred it to him in breach of trust. [11]

Westbury made some contribution to *Private International Law*. In the case of *Udny v. Udny* [12] he explained in a classic passage the distinction between political and civil status, that is, the difference between the conceptions of nationality and domicil.

---

[1] (1865) 3 De G.J. and S. 293.   [2] (1863) 3 De G.J. and S. at p. 601.
[3] (1862) 10 H.L.C. 191.   [4] At p. 209.
[5] *Tailby v. Official Receiver* (1888) 13 App. Cas. at p. 547.
[6] *Leather Cloth Co. v. American Leather Cloth Co.* (1863) 4 De G.J. and S. 137; *Hall v. Barrows* (1863) ibid 150.
[7] *Edelston v. Edelston* (1863) 1 De G.J. and S. 185.
[8] (1869) L.R. 4 H.L. at pp. 97-98.
[9] *Blackwell v. Blackwell* [1929] A.C. at pp. 334-335 *per* Lord Sumner.
[10] *Barnard v. Bagshaw* (1862) De G.J. and S. 355.
[11] *Rolfe v. Gregory* (1865) 4 De G.J. and S. 576.
[12] (1869) L.R. 1 Sc. and D. 441.

In the case of *Cookney v. Anderson* [1] he explained the reason why the jurisdiction of municipal courts is, as a rule, limited to persons within the territorial limits of the state, and the reason why, by statute or by the rules of private international law, that limitation is sometimes transcended. [2] As law officer, Westbury had advised the government upon many difficult questions of *international law*. [3] His command of its principles is illustrated by the case of *Ex parte Chavasse*, [4] in which he explained the position of the neutral merchant who transports contraband of war. Though the trade is not unlawful he carries it on subject to the risk that the cargo will be captured and condemned. He held that the sale by a neutral to a belligerent of a ship of war built *bona fide* on the neutral's own account, is not an infringement of the Foreign Enlistment Act of 1819. [5] This would seem to be the law. [6] But the Alabama Arbitration [7] showed the need for the amendment of the law made by the Foreign Enlistment Act of 1870, [8] when it gave the state a larger control over the building and sale of such ships, by making it an offence to build, commission, equip or despatch a ship with intent, or with reasonable cause to believe, that it will be employed in the military or naval service of a foreign state at war with a friendly state. [9]

Lastly, we have seen that Westbury played a large part in the reform of the law of bankruptcy. He made an almost equally notable addition to this branch of the law by his very numerous decisions on the interpretation of the statute law.

HATHERLEY
(1868-1872)

With Westbury's two immediate successors—Cranworth and Chelmsford—I have already dealt. Chelmsford's successor was Cairns. But Cairns's first Chancellorship only lasted for a few months. It was not till after the Chancellorship of Lord Hatherley and the first Chancellorship of Lord Selborne that he became Chancellor for a considerable period. Therefore I shall sketch the career of Lords Hatherley and Selborne before that of Lord Cairns.

[1] (1863) 1 D.G.J. and S. 365.　　[2] At pp. 379-381.
[3] Above 75.　　[4] (1865) 4 De G.J. and S. 655.
[5] At p. 662; 59 George III c 69; vol. xiv 77 *et seq.*
[6] Halsbury, Laws of England (2nd ed.), vi 524 n. (5).
[7] Vol. xv 433, 434.　　[8] 33, 34 Victoria c. 90.　　[9] § 8.

William Page Wood, Lord Hatherley,[1] was born on November 29, 1801. He was the son of the Alderman Wood, nicknamed by Brougham "Absolute-Wisdom", who brought Queen Caroline to England.[2] He was educated at Winchester, where he attained to the position of second prefect; but in 1817 he, together with the other prefects, were sent down for the part which they played in a "barring out". The next two years he spent at Geneva, where he made himself master of the French and Italian languages, and met many famous scholars, among whom were Dumont and Sismondi. In 1820 he attended Queen Caroline from Geneva to St. Omer and England, and later in the year was employed by her to interpret for her agents, who were sent to Italy to collect evidence on her behalf. To the end of his life he was convinced of her innocence. In October of this year he took up his residence at Trinity College, Cambridge. He graduated 24th Wrangler in 1824, and in 1825 was elected to a fellowship at Trinity. He became a member of Lincoln's Inn in 1824, and read first in the chambers of Roupell, an equity draftsman, and then in the chambers of Tyrrel, the well known conveyancer, who, unlike most counsel, took considerable pains to teach his pupils. During these years his social and literary gifts earned him the friendship of Basil Montagu. He translated the *Novum Organum* for Montagu's edition of Bacon's works; and at his house at Highgate "he made acquaintance with the literary lions of London, with Edward Irving, with Carlyle, with Barry Cornwall, with the Kembles, and, above all, with Coleridge, at whose feet he sat through many a summer evening".

He was called to the bar on November 27, 1827, and soon got a good practice at the Parliamentary bar, which was then beginning to be a very separate bar,[3] and in the court of Chancery. In 1841 his father had a great accession of fortune. "Jiminy Wood" of Gloucester, "banker, draper, and miser", who was no relation, left a fortune to his father because he admired his championship of Queen Caroline. In the Prerogative Court, probate of the will and a codicil thereto was refused, but, owing to the exertions of Sir John Campbell and Pemberton Leigh, the judgment was, to

[1] W. R. W. Stephens, Memoir of Lord Hatherley—from the point of view of legal history the most valuable part of the book is the fragment of autobiography, vol. i 1-99; the rest of the book tells us more of his religious and political activities than of his legal career; from the point of view of legal history the best account is in Atlay, Victorian Chancellors, ii 334-376; D.N.B.

[2] Vol. xiii 219.

[3] Vol. xi 336-33 ; Wood says (Stephens, op. cit. 61-62), that in 1828 the new business, consequent on the passing of the Liverpool and Manchester Railway Bill in 1827, had much increased the size of the parliamentary work; at the time it only numbered two or three—Harrison and Adams being the two leaders.

the surprise of many, reversed by the Privy Council.[1] Alderman Wood found himself richer by some £150,000 and the estate of Hatherley in Gloucestershire. Therefore, on his father's death, in 1843 Wood found himself independent of his profession.

Since he was now independent, he gave up the Parliamentary Bar in order that he might be qualified to stand for Parliament. His Chancery practice so increased that he took silk in 1845 when he attached himself to the court of Wigram V.-C. In 1846 he was elected a member for the City of Oxford in the liberal interest. Wood was both a moderately high Anglican and an advanced liberal. On the one hand, he was always ready to defend the church, and to promote measures for increasing the efficiency of its work. In conformity with what he believed to be its teaching he was a strong opponent of the deceased wife's sister bill; and he supported the Ecclesiastical Titles Bill because he regarded it as "a most becoming declaration of national adherence to the faith".[2] In fact no more sincere Christian than Wood ever lived. His charitable gifts to individuals and for public objects were beyond count.[3] He and his wife taught at the Sunday schools of his parish of St. John's, Westminster till 1877, they never failed to attend the early morning service at Westminster Abbey,[4] and in 1875 he said that they had read the Bible through forty-four times.[5] On the other hand, he opposed all political disabilities on religious grounds,[6] and he supported the ballot, an extension of the franchise,[7] a proposal to abolish the game laws,[8] and all measures of law reform, including the reform of the law of divorce and the establishment of a legal University of which the Inns of Court were to be the colleges.[9]

He soon made his mark in the House of Commons, and in 1849 he became Vice-Chancellor of the County Palatine of Lancaster. Up to that date the post had been somewhat of a sinecure. He got a bill through Parliament which reformed its procedure and made it an efficient court.[10] In 1851 he became solicitor-general, and in that capacity he had a considerable share in drafting and supporting in Parliament the Chancery Reform Acts of 1852.[11] He was offered a Vice-Chancellorship in 1851; but the government

---

[1] Greville, Memoirs v 29; Greville thought that the judgment, which was delivered by Lyndhurst, was superficial, and that "it was due to the character of the judge below, as well as to the importance of the cause, to go into much greater detail, and to reason the case more, and reply to those legal grounds on which Jenner's judgment was grounded". [2] Stephens, op. cit. i 87.

[3] Ibid ii 273; Atlay, op. cit. ii 350. [4] Ibid ii 351.

[5] Stephens, op. cit. ii 246; Selborne, Memorials Personal and Political ii 36. [6] Stephens, op. cit. i 77-79. [7] Ibid i 75. [8] Ibid i 79-80. [9] Ibid i 95-96. [10] 13, 14 Victoria c. 43. [11] Vol. ix 375-376; above 20, 38, 74, 75.

could not spare him, and so he refused it with regret. But in 1852 another Vice-Chancellorship fell vacant which he accepted.

His success as a Vice-Chancellor is shown by the number of able counsel who elected to practise in his court.

Cairns, Rolt, G. M. Giffard, W. M. James, and Amphlett, all in their turns Lords Justices, attached themselves to his dingy little Court in the purlieus of Lincoln's Inn, and no reputation, however high, no personality, however formidable, was able to impose a sophistry upon him or shake him in a conclusion which he had deliberately formed. He was essentially...''a judge for the parties'' who aimed at doing immediate justice rather than at enriching our legal literature. The appeals from his decisions were few in number and seldom successful, and a writer in the ''Solicitors' Journal'' declared that on the judgments of Vice-Chancellor Wood there was undoubtedly placed an amount of reliance unshared by any other living judge.[1]

But his willingness to bear with long and irrelevant arguments,[2] and his habit of never writing his judgments, spun out both the hearing of the case and the length of the judgment.[3] Rolt says that ''judgments in the main undoubtedly right, were often of inordinate length, diffuse, wandering, and in great part unintelligible, many sentences being imperfect, incomplete, or unfinished''.[4] The latter defect was made the subject of so personal and severe a criticism by Lord Campbell that his brethren, with whom Wood was deservedly popular, remonstrated, and extorted from Campbell a sort of apology.[5] And Rolt says that though he was impartial, the warmth of his temperament sometimes led him, as the hearing proceeded, to become a partisan of one of the parties.[6] On the other hand Selborne said that his decisions, though discursive, were almost always sound, and that ''the parties concerned seldom left his court without feeling that everything which they had to say had been properly considered.''[7]

In 1868 he was made a Lord Justice of Appeal. But he only held that office for a few months, for in December of the same year Gladstone made him Lord Chancellor with the title of Lord Hatherley. Roundell Palmer,[8] who had been attorney-general in the last liberal government, would have been the natural successor to that office. But he was opposed to Gladstone's measure for the

---

[1] Atlay, op. cit. ii 358-359.
[2] ''A friend who was walking home with him one day from his court, remarked on the tedious lengthiness of the speech of a junior counsel, and the unnecessary number of cases which he had cited. 'True', the Vice-Chancellor replied, 'it was wearisome, for he assumed that I was ignorant of the ABC of the law; but I recollected how I was once snubbed by Leach when I was a junior, and I resolved to hear him out''', Stephens, op. cit. ii 59
[3] Atlay, op. cit. ii 359.
[4] Rolt, Memoirs 119.
[5] Stephens, op. cit i 87-95.
[6] Memoirs, 118-119, 120.
[7] Stephens, op. cit. ii 282.
[8] Below 97 et seq.

disestablishment and disendowment of the Irish Church, and so refused to take office. As Chancellor, Hatherley presided over the House of Lords with dignity, and efficiently supported the measures of the government. He piloted through the House the Irish Land Act, the Education Act, the Ballot Act, and the University Tests Act, and supported the abolition of purchase in the army by an act of the prerogative. But he failed to carry a bill of his own founded on the report of the Judicature Commission,[1] which was an anticipation of the Judicature Act. It was sketchy in character; it was criticized by Westbury;[2] and, since the judges had not been consulted, they felt an hostility to it which was voiced effectively by Cockburn C. J. in his very able pamphlet on *Our Judicial System*.[3] His speeches on the bill for disestablishing the Irish Church,[4] and in defence of the appointment of Sir Robert Collier to the post of paid member of the Judicial Committee of the Privy Council,[5] are examples of the efficient way in which he defended government measures.

All through his life he had been troubled by bad eyesight. It was for this reason that he resigned in 1872. His sight was to some extent restored by a successful operation for cataract; and he continued to hear cases in the House of Lords, and to support government measures, notably Selborne's Judicature Act. In 1878 he lost his wife—a very heavy blow, for no more devoted couple ever lived.[6] He died July 10, 1881. He was, said Selborne,[7]

A resolute and courageous man; strong in his convictions, and never flinching from them; quick of apprehension, and clear in judgment. But he was also patient and candid, gentle and courteous. . . . He had no egotism, or vanity, or arrogance.

Westbury said of him that "he was a mere bundle of virtues without a redeeming vice".[8] As a Chancellor he is not, as Atlay has said,[9] amongst the great figures. He shone more as a Vice-Chancellor than as a Lord Chancellor, for "he was neither a great master of equity like Cottenham or Cranworth, nor possessed of the deep and subtle intellect of a Cairns or a Selborne".[10] The following are a few specimens of his more notable decisions:

Two of his decisions, one as a Lord Chancellor and the other as Vice-Chancellor, are important in that department of Private International Law which is concerned with the validity of foreign

---

[1] Hansard (3rd Ser.) cc 170-176.   [2] Ibid 176-181.
[3] Atlay, op. cit. ii 415.   [4] See Stephens, op. cit. ii 183-211 for his speech.
[5] For his speech, see, ibid. ii 222-234.
[6] A selection of the sonnets which he was accustomed to write to her on her birthdays and on the anniversaries of their wedding day is printed by Stephens, op. cit. ii 285-305.   [7] Ibid. ii 281.
[8] Atlay, op. cit. ii 367.   [9] Ibid.   [10] Ibid.

judgments. The case of *Castrique v. Imrie*[1] is a leading case upon the effect of a foreign judgment *in rem*, and the case of *Simpson v. Fogo*[2] upon the effect to be given to a foreign judgment *in personam*. In the latter case he held that a judgment which violated the principles of Private International Law is invalid.[3] As Lord Chancellor he took part in *McCormick v. Grogan*,[4] which is a leading case on the subject of secret trusts; and in the case of *Moss v. Cooper*[5] his view as to the conditions in which the communication of such a trust is binding on a legatee, though rejected by the Court of Appeal in 1937,[6] is both more logical and more consistent with principle.[7] In his judgment in *Sackville-West v. Holmesdale*,[8] in which he gave a dissentient judgment, there is a good discussion of the circumstances in which the courts will construe an executory trust in accordance, not with the literal words used by the parties, but with their intention. In *Reese River Mining Co. v. Smith*[9] he discussed the rights of a person induced to become a shareholder by fraudulent statements in a prospectus. In the case of *Knox v. Gye*[10] he adhered to his own decision, and, in a dissenting judgment, held that the Statute of Limitations could not be applied by analogy to a claim by the representatives of a deceased partner against a surviving partner. In the case of *Shaw v. Foster*[11] he discussed the conditions of the application of the equitable principle that the vendor of an estate is, after the date of making a contract a trustee for the purchaser. In one of the many important ecclesiastical cases which arose out of the doctrines and practices of the advanced high church party, he laid down a principle making for that comprehensiveness which has always characterized the Church of England that, "if the Minister be allowed to introduce at his own will variations in the rites and ceremonies that seem to him to interpret the doctrines of the sermon in a particular direction, the service ceases to be what it was meant to be, a common ground upon which all Church people may meet though they differ about some doctrines. But the Church of England has wisely left a certain latitude of opinion in matters of policy, and has not insisted on a rigorous uniformity of thought which might reduce the communion to a narrow compass."[12]

[1] (1870) L.R. 4 H.L. 414.
[2] (1860) 1 J. and H. 18, (1863) 1 H. and M. 195.   [3] Ibid at p. 247.
[4] (1869) L.R. 2 H.L. 82.   [5] (1861) 1 J. and H. 352 at p. 367.
[6] *Re Keen* [1937] 1 Ch. 236.   [7] Holdsworth, Essays in Law and History 199.
[8] (1870) L.R. 4 H.L. 543.   [9] (1869) L.R. 4 H.L. 64.
[10] (1872) L.R. 5 H.L. 656.   [11] (1872) 5 H.L. 321.
[12] *Sheppard v. Bennett* (1872) 9 Moo. P.C.N.S. at pp. 193-194; with this statement Selborne agreed, Memorials Personal and Political i 340.

As Vice-Chancellor, he decided a number of well known and important cases, of which the following are illustrations: the case of *Churton v. Douglas* [1] in which the term "goodwill" was defined, and rules were laid down as to the rights and duties of the vendor and purchaser of goodwill; the case of *Allhusen v. Whittell* [2] which deals with the manner in which executors in administering an estate, must adjust accounts as between tenant for life and remainderman; the case of *Coventry v. Chichester* [3] in which the doctrines of satisfaction and ademption were discussed; and the case of *Thomson v. Shakespeare* [4] in which he discussed the question of the conditions in a bequest which can be held to be charitable. In the case of *Duke of Portland v. Hill* [5] he discussed the question of the ownership of the freehold, and the consequent right to the minerals, in manors where the tenants held by copy of the court roll according to the custom of the manor, but not at the will of the lord; and in the case of *Crossley v. Lightowler* [6] he discussed and decided several important points in the law relating to easements. An important decision in Private International Law is the case of *Boyes v. Bedale*,[7] which decided the question of the status in English law of children legitimated by the subsequent marriage of the father in a country where he had acquired a domicil. Wood's decision that, though born and then legitimated in a country where this form of legitimation was recognized, and though the father was there domiciled at the time of the birth and the legitimation, they were illegitimate, was disapproved in a later case,[8] but it was supported by Jessel M.R.[9] and Leach L.J. On the other hand, his view that if the child was born of a father domiciled in a country where such legitimation was not possible, a change in the father's domicil to a country where it was possible, would not enable him to legitimate his child by a subsequent marriage, has been upheld,[10] and extended to a case of adoption.[11] Lastly, a number of his decisions elucidated the

---

[1] (1859) Johns 174. [2] (1867) 4 Eq. 295.

[3] (1864) 2 H. and M. 149; his decision was affirmed by the Lords Justices (1864) 2 De G.J. and S. 336, dissentient Turner L.J., and reversed by the House of Lords (1867) L.R. 2 H. L. 71.

[4] (1859) Johns 612; see Hanbury, Modern Equity, 8th ed.

[5] (1866) 2 Eq. 765; vol. iii 268.

[6] (1866) 3 Eq. 279, affirmed in part and reversed in part by the Lords Justices (1867) 2 Ch. App. 478.

[7] (1863) 1 H. and M. 798.

[8] *Re Goodman's Trusts* (1861) 17 Ch.D. 266.

[9] (1880) 14 Ch.D. 619; (1881) 17 Ch.D. at pp. 269-290.

[10] *Re Wright's Trusts* (1856) 2 K. and J. 595; *Udny v. Udny* (1869) L.R. 1 Sc. and Div. at pp. 447-484.

[11] *Re Luck's Settlement Trusts* [1940] Ch. 864; see Dicey, Conflict of Laws, 7th ed. 438-441; Hanbury, The Vinerian Chair and Legal Education, 129.

position of foreign sovereigns and their ambassadors or agents who sued or were sued in an English court,[1] some of which arose out of the action of the United States at the close of the civil war.[2]

SELBORNE
(1872-1874, 1880-1885)

The last of the Lord Chancellors of this period—Selborne and Cairns—were two of the greatest equity lawyers of the nineteenth century.

Roundell Palmer, Lord Selborne,[3] was born on November 27, 1812, at Mixbury, Oxfordshire, of which place his father was rector. He was educated at Winchester and Trinity College, Oxford: and at both places his scholastic successes, and his success at Oxford as an orator at the Union, presaged his future fame. In 1835 he became a Fellow of Magdalen College, Oxford. He had been brought up in an ecclesiastical atmosphere; and throughout his life he was a devoted Anglican.[4] He was naturally much interested in the Oxford Movement—though he took no active part in it. But in 1834 the death of his brother in a shipwreck led him to turn his thoughts from the law to the church. His father wisely dissuaded him from taking this step; and he became a student at Lincoln's Inn in 1834. He read in the chambers of Walters, a conveyancer, and of James Booth, an equity drafts-man. Like many others,[5] he felt the change from his literary and classical studies at Oxford to the dull work of copying precedents. In fact he hazarded the conjecture that that contrast helped to explain why Cambridge had turned out more eminent lawyers than Oxford:

---

[1] *Gladstone v. Musurus Bey* (1862) 1 H. and M. 495; *Gladstone v. Ottoman Bank* (1863) ibid 505.

[2] *United States v. Prioleau* (1864) 2 H. and M. 559; *United States v. McRae* (1867) 4 Eq. 327; Hanbury, Current Legal Problems (1955) 1, 11, 19.

[3] Memorials Family and Personal, and Memorials Personal and Political; Atlay, Victorian Chancellors ii 377-432; D.N.B.

[4] "On all that pertains to the history of hymnology he was an acknowledged authority. During his second Chancellorship he found time to contribute to the new edition of the 'Encyclopaedia Britannica' an article on the Hymns of the Latin and Oriental Churches, as well as those of Germany and Great Britain. His addiction to sacred song was the cause of some ribald merriment among his professional brethren", Atlay, op. cit. ii 411.

[5] E.g. Bowen, see Cunningham, Life of Bowen 76-77, cited vol. xii 101 n. 3; and Westbury, Judicial Society Papers ii.

they had come from the austerities of abstract mathematical science, in which the imagination is kept under control and the logical faculty severely tacked to something which was, at all events, human and practical. But an Oxford man seemed to come from humanity in its highest intellectual form to a mundane art so narrow and conventional as to have the austerity without the beauty and dignity of science.[1]

During his first eighteen months at the bar he only earned twenty-six guineas. His first notable success was due to one of his uncles:

His uncle, Mr. Horsley Palmer, was high in influence at the Bank of England, and an intimation in the ear of Messrs. Freshfield, hereditary solicitors of that great corporation, was not long in bearing fruit. Palmer found himself briefed third on the equity side of the Court of Exchequer with instructions to oppose a motion for the appointment of a receiver. When his leaders had urged every point which their ingenuity or experience could suggest, there seemed little left for number three. But Palmer, like Erskine in the memorable Greenwich Hospital case, was not to be daunted. Dropping the argument from the facts disclosed in the affidavits, he pressed upon the Court the established rule in Chancery, not to interfere with the state of possession before the hearing of a cause without some proof of danger to the property. The motion was refused, and Lord Selborne's modesty omits to say how far his speech contributed to the result, but Baron Alderson, to whom Mr. Palmer was a complete stranger, passed a slip of paper down to Mr. James Freshfield warmly commending his young counsel. The latter's fee book for the year registered a hundred and sixty guineas.[2]

For a short period he combined with his growing practice the writing of reviews in learned periodicals, and leaders for *The Times*. But in 1843 the growth of his practice as well as the advice of his friends led him to give up these extraneous activities. In 1845 he was doing so well that he was offered the post of Advocate-General of Bengal—an offer which, on the advice of his father he wisely declined. In 1847 he was returned to the House of Commons for Plymouth as a Peelite. In fact his political opinions were a blend of liberal and conservative. On the one hand he supported the removal of Jewish disabilities, opposed the Ecclesiastical Titles Act, and favoured a large extension of the franchise. On the other hand, he supported the Navigation Acts, and, on all matters relating to the Church of England and the Universities, he was a conservative. He supported Lord Aberdeen's ministry, but he voted for Cobden's vote of censure on the *Arrow Case* in 1857; and that meant the loss of his seat. He did not get back into Parliament till 1861, when, having been made Solicitor-General by the liberal government, a safe seat was found for him at Richmond, Yorkshire.

[1] Memorials, Family and Personal i 200.   [2] Atlay, op. cit. ii 385-386.

That appointment he owed to his growing fame at the bar which had been increasing ever since he had taken silk in 1849. He had an acute and a very subtle mind, a vast knowledge of equitable principles and rules, and a genius for legal strategy which enabled him to adapt his argument to any new turn taken in the hearing of his case. His industry in mastering the facts of his case and his memory were almost superhuman.[1]

Many are the stories of the almost incredible powers of application displayed by Palmer at the Bar, of his swiftness in mastering his briefs, and of the tenacity with which his mind retained their contents. . . . It was stated in print after his elevation to the Woolsack, that he had been accustomed to work night and day for weeks at a stretch, only resting on Sunday, and spending the whole of that day in bed. Lord Selborne repudiated these extravagant stories, but pleaded guilty to having on one exceptional occasion worked from 2 a.m. on Monday to late on Saturday without seeking his couch. His power, indeed, of going without sleep, and yet retaining his mental activity at its highest level, was the wonder and despair of those who knew him. "I have seen him", writes Lord Hobhouse, "all trembling and quivering from over-strain, and yet apparently as quick and alert in mind as ever." [2]

Lord Lindley emphasized his extraordinary industry, his unrivalled knowledge of law, and his consummate skill as an advocate.[3]

As Solicitor-General it fell to him to advise the government upon many points of international law which arose out of the American civil war, such as the *Trent Case* and the *Alabama Case*. In that capacity he and the Attorney-General failed to obtain a verdict for the government in the case of *The Alexandra*—a ship seized by the government under the Foreign Enlistment Act, 1819.[4] Pollock C.B. directed the jury that if the ship was supplied to the confederate government in pursuance of a contract, and not with the intention that it should be fitted out for purposes of aggression, no offence had been committed;[5] and, on the motion for a new trial, the judges being equally divided, this ruling was upheld.[6] In 1863 he became Attorney-General. As Attorney-General he exposed the fraudulent claim of Mrs. Ryves to be the legitimate descendant of the Duke of Cumberland, the brother of

[1] Lord Hobhouse said of Palmer that he excelled "in power of work, in knowledge of his briefs, in ready memory, and vast resources of case law, in subtlety and great skill in addressing himself to unforeseen exigencies. He could perform the most difficult operation of strategy, changing front in face of the enemy", Memorials Personal and Political ii 437.

[2] Atlay, op. cit. ii 392. [3] Memorials Personal and Political ii 439.

[4] *Attorney-General v. Sillem* (1863) 3 F. and F. 646.

[5] Ibid at p. 676; "if", he said, "a man may supply any quantity of munitions of war to a belligerent, why not ships?" ibid.

[6] (1863) 2 H. and C. 431.

George III[1]—a case reminiscent in many ways of the more famous
Tichborne Case. In 1866 the government resigned. While in
opposition he considerably increased his reputation in the House
of Commons.

He played a leading part in transforming the original "ten minutes bill"
of the Derby Cabinet into a sweeping measure of reform, and earned
the compliment of having his name coupled by *The Times* with that of
Mr. Gladstone as one of the twin leaders of the Opposition.[2]

When the conservatives were defeated in 1868 Palmer's
services to his party made his succession to the Chancellorship a
foregone conclusion, and Gladstone offered it to him. But he
could not agree to one of the main planks in Gladstone's programme—the disendowment as well as the disestablishment of
the Irish Church. He therefore refused to take office, and also
refused the Lord Justiceship vacated by Hatherley and a peerage.
During Hatherley's Chancellorship he gave an independent
support to the government. He also gave his support, both in and
out of office, to large proposals for law reform. In 1867 and 1868
he was a member of royal commissions on the neutrality laws and
naturalization; in 1867 he drew up the report of the royal
commission on the marriage laws of the United Kingdom.[3] In
1865 he had carried through the House of Commons the Act for
the rehousing of the Courts;[4] and in 1867 he had proposed the
Judicature Commission upon the report of which the Judicature
Act of 1873 was based.[5] He founded in 1867 an Association for
the Improvement of Legal Education, and tried without success
to found in London a school of law.[6] He supported the Treaty of
Washington, by which the claims of the United States arising out
of the Alabama and other cruisers were submitted to arbitration;
and he acted as counsel for the Government in that arbitration.
In 1872, on Hatherley's resignation, he became Lord Chancellor
with the title of Lord Selborne.

The main achievement of his first Chancellorship was the
passing of the Judicature Act of 1873.[7] Selborne's bill profited
by the experience which he had gained from the discussion of
earlier bills. He took the advice of the judges and the leaders of
the profession; with the result that it was blessed by the lawyers
of all parties. Nevertheless it was essentially Selborne's work. In

---

[1] Memorials Personal and Political i 25-34; Atlay, op. cit. ii 399-431.
[2] Atlay, op. cit. ii 401-402.
[3] Memorials Personal and Political i 44-46.
[4] He was the successful advocate of the Strand site as opposed to a site on the
embankment, Memorials Personal and Political i 23-24.
[5] Ibid 46-47.   [6] Ibid 48-54; vol. xv 245.
[7] Vol. i 638-643; vol. xv 128 *et seq.*

his *Memorials* he understated the part he played, but prophesied truly when he said:

Much as I profited by the experience and wisdom of others, I might, without presumption take to myself some credit for the initiation, advancement, and completion of this work. If I leave any monument behind me which will bear the test of time, it may be this.[1]

We have seen that the Act was modified in one important particular before it came into force. The clauses which deprived the House of Lords of its jurisdiction to hear appeals in English cases were dropped, and in 1876 the Appellate Jurisdiction Act was passed, which retained and strengthened the appellate jurisdiction of the House of Lords.[2] Selborne's labours in preparing the Judicature Bill and seeing it through the House of Lords were increased by the fact that Romilly, the Master of the Rolls, was too ill to do his work, whilst his destined successor, Jessel,[3] because he was in charge of the bill in the House of Commons, could not be spared. Till the bill was passed he did the judicial work of the Master of the Rolls as well as his own.

Selborne ceased to be Chancellor when Gladstone's government fell in 1874. He became Chancellor for a second time when Disraeli's government was defeated in 1880. Just as the great event of his first Chancellorship had been the passing of the Judicature Act, so the great event of his second Chancellorship was the opening of the Law Courts by the Queen on December 4, 1882.

The most impressive part of the day's work had been performed at an earlier hour, when, after breakfasting with the Chancellor in the House of Lords, the judges moved in procession for the last time down Westminster Hall, "taking solemn leave of that ancient home of English justice". The fusion of law and equity, the housing of them both under the same roof, the choice of the Strand for their local habitation were the doing of Lord Selborne more than of any other single man; and the consummation of so many years of toil was fittingly acknowledged by the dignity of an earldom conferred upon him on the morning of that eventful day.[4]

His second Chancellorship was marked by the passing of many important statutes, among which some of the most important are the Settled Land Act, the Conveyancing Act, and the Married Women's Property Act. But Gladstone's tendency to adopt increasingly democratic views made him uneasy—"it may be doubted whether he was ever thoroughly at home in the Cabinet during his second Chancellorship".[5]

---

[1] Memorials, Personal and Political i 300.   [2] Vol. i 643-644.
[3] Below 121 *et seq.*   [4] Atlay, op. cit. ii 427-428.   [5] Atlay, op. cit. ii 425.

His second Chancellorship ended with the fall of the government in 1885. When Gladstone took office in 1886 his fear that the Church of England would be attacked, and the government's policy of Home Rule, led him to refuse office, and to throw in his lot with the new liberal unionist party. He defended the Union on the platform, and the Church of England both on the platform and with his pen.[1] After a short illness he died May 4, 1895.

Of the impression which Selborne as a statesman made upon his fellow statesmen the best description is given by Lord Rosebery:[2]

We have one or two great qualities associated with Lord Selborne which cannot perish with his name or generation. We have the memory of an industry which was in reality sleepless, and of which the traditions surpass, perhaps, all that is known of human industry. We have that disregard for worldly position, of worldly temptation, which led him in 1868 to refuse the great prize of his profession rather than palter with principles which he held higher than any prize or any profession. I think he showed something of that in his appearance. There was something in his austere simplicity of manner which I think must have recalled to every onlooker something of those great lawyers of the Middle Ages who were also great Churchmen, for to me at any rate, Lord Selborne always embodied that great conception and that great combination.

Of his merits as a judge Lord Davey has said:[3]

First, Lord Selborne was distinguished by a rapid and accurate appreciation of the relevant and material facts and a rare power of sifting the wheat from the chaff in the complicated mass of evidence and documents which too often fill the appeal books in the House of Lords and Privy Council. This was no doubt partly due to his training and experience at the Bar. But his power of reproducing these facts and documents in a lucid and intelligible form in his Judgments was a gift of his own. In those days it was more common for both the House of Lords and Privy Council to deliver judgment at the end of the argument than it is now, and I often thought that Lord Selborne's oral judgments so delivered were quite as good as his written judgments. Secondly, I should mention his great industry in the performance of his judicial duties. Judgments when he presided were seldom delayed for at most a few weeks. . . . In connection with this I should mention his great knowledge not only of legal principles, but of . . . previous judicial decisions. In writing his judgments it was his habit to comment on the previous decisions and point out the distinctions between them, and put them into their proper places. The result has been to increase the value to the practitioner of his judgments, which are often a complete commentary on the particular branch of the law, and recognised as the *dernier mot* on the subject. . . . Needless to say that Lord Selborne was the master of his authorities and not their slave. The third judicial quality in Lord Selborne that

---

[1] In 1886 he published *A Defence of the Church of England against Disestablishment*, and in 1888 *Ancient Facts and Fictions concerning Churches and Tithes*.
[2] Memorials, Personal and Political ii 431.
[3] Memorials, Personal and Political ii 442-443.

struck me was his absolute fairness and obedience to law. All English judges are impartial, but not all have the power of divesting themselves of prejudice. Lord Selborne had this power in an eminent degree. . . . I never knew any judge less disposed to strain the law in a hard case than Lord Selborne. . . . Some writers have thought that his subtlety of mind led him sometimes (as also was said of the late Lord Bowen) to give refined reasons for his judgment when it might be rested on plainer or broader grounds. There may be some truth in this criticism, but if it is meant that Lord Selborne was wanting in breadth of legal vision I do not agree. I may point to the judgments he delivered in the constitutional questions which came before the political committee of the Privy Council chiefly from Canada, but also from other parts of the Empire.

Let us look at one or two of the cases in which these qualities were displayed.

Selborne's practice at the bar was principally an equity practice. Therefore it is by his decisions on equity that he made his greatest contribution to the development of the law. But as law officer, as Lord Chancellor, and as a member of the Judicial Committee of the Privy Council he made also considerable contributions to other branches of the law.

In the sphere of *equity* he surveyed and explained important equitable doctrines in the following cases: In the case of *Ewing v. Orr Ewing* [1] he explained why the fact that equity acts *in personam* gives to courts of equity a wider jurisdiction than that possessed by courts of law.[2] In the case of *Speight v. Gaunt* [3] he restated the law as to the circumstances in which a trustee could delegate his powers and duties. His judgment in the case of *Maddison v. Alderson* [4] is the leading authority upon the meaning and scope of the equitable doctrine of part performance. In the case of *Scarf v. Jardine* [5] he explained the principle upon which a retired partner may be held liable for the debts of the firm incurred after his retirement, and the rights of a creditor as against the retired and continuing partners. In the case of *Kendall v. Hamilton* [6] he exposed the fallacy of the view that in equity the liability upon partnership debts was always joint and several, and explained why, in the single case where a partner had died, equity made the liability joint and several. In the case of *Earl of Aylesford v. Morris* [7] he surveyed the equitable doctrines relating to "catching bargains" with expectant heirs and

---

[1] (1883) 9 App. Cas. 34.
[2] "In the exercise of this personal jurisdiction they have always been accustomed to compel the performance of contracts and trusts as to subjects which were not either locally or nationally domiciled within their jurisdiction. They have done so as to land, in Scotland, in Ireland, in the Colonies, in foreign countries", ibid at p. 40.
[3] (1883) 9 App. Cas. 1.   [4] (1883) 8 App. Cas. 467.
[5] (1882) 7 App. Cas. 345.   [6] (1879) 4 App. Cas. 504.
[7] (1873) L.R. 8 Ch. 484.

reversioners, and considered the effect upon them of the repeal of the usury laws and the Act of 1868[1] as to the sale of reversions. In the case of *Ayerst v. Jenkins* [2] he summed up the law as to the circumstances in which equity would give relief against covenants or settlements of property made upon an illegal consideration.

In the law of *real property* his judgment in the case of *Dalton v. Angus* [3] surveys the law as to the easement of support, its capacity to be acquired by prescription, and the application to it of the Prescription Act. The case of *Lyell v. Kennedy*[4] contains an elaborate survey of the law about the non-application of the Real Property Limitation Act of 1833 [5] to persons who are in a fiduciary relation to the true owner. Several of his judgments contain valuable surveys of common law doctrines. Instances are the case of *Debenham v. Mellon* [6] which deals with the husband's liability for his wife's post-nuptial debts; the case of *Foakes v. Beer,*[7] which finally settled an important point in the law as to consideration; the case of *Drummond v. Van Ingen,*[8] which stated the law as to the conditions as to quality which the law implies on a sale of goods; and the case of *Bank of England v. Vagliano,*[9] in which he considered the application of the doctrine of equitable estoppel to the conduct of the parties to forged bills made payable to a fictitious person.

In the sphere of *colonial constitutional law* he laid down, in *R. v. Burah,*[10] the important principle that a subordinate legislative body, when acting within the limits of its authority, "is not in any sense an agent or delegate of the Imperial Parliament, but has, and was intended to have, plenary powers of legislation, as large, and of the same nature, as those of Parliament itself". In the sphere of *ecclesiastical law* he examined, in the case of *Mackonochie v. Lord Penzance,*[11] the limits of the jurisdiction of the ecclesiastical courts with respect to suits against clergy for unlawful practices in the performance of divine service.

[1] 31, 32 Victoria c. 4.
[2] (1873) 16 Eq. 275.
[3] (1881) 6 A.C. 740.
[4] (1889) 14 App. Cas. 437.
[5] 3, 4 William IV c. 27.
[6] (1880) 6 App. Cas. 24.
[7] (1884) 9 App. Cas. 605; vol. viii 40.
[8] (1887) 12 App. Cas. 284.
[9] [1891] A.C. 107.
[10] (1878) 3 App. Cas. at p. 904.
[11] (1881) 6 App. Cas. 424.

CAIRNS
(1868, 1874-1880)

Hugh McCalmont Cairns, Lord Cairns,[1] was born at Belfast on December 27, 1819. He was something of an infant prodigy, for it is said that he gave a lecture on chemistry at the age of eight, and contributed articles to the *Church Missionary Gleaner* before he was eleven. But his career, unlike that of most infant prodigies, fulfilled the promise of his youth. He was educated at the Belfast Academy and Trinity College, Dublin. His tutor, George Wheeler, who had already had distinguished lawyers amongst his pupils,[2] persuaded his father to allow his son to go to the bar. He became a a student at Lincoln's Inn in 1841, and learned pleading from Chitty, and equity from Malins, who persuaded him not to return to Ireland, but to practise at the English bar. In 1844 he was called to the bar by the Middle Temple, whither he had migrated from Lincoln's Inn. His abilities soon procured him a growing practice. At a very early stage in his career Bethell, after meeting him in consultation, prophesied that he would rise to the top of his profession. He took silk in 1856, and soon became one of the three leaders of the Chancery bar. Of his position at the Chancery bar, and of his merits as an advocate, Bryce has said:[3]

At the Chancery bar he was one of a trio who had not been surpassed, if ever equalled, during the nineteenth century . . . The other two were Mr., afterwards Lord Justice, Rolt,[4] and Mr. Roundell Palmer, afterwards Lord Chancellor Selborne.[5] All were admirable lawyers, but, of the three, Rolt excelled in his spirited presentation of a case and in the lively vigour of his arguments. Palmer was conspicuous for exhaustless ingenuity, and for a subtlety which sometimes led him away into reasonings too fine for the court to follow. Cairns was broad, massive, convincing, with a robust urgency of logic which seemed to grasp and fix you, so that while he spoke you could fancy no conclusion possible save that toward which he moved. His habit was to seize upon what he deemed the central and vital point of the case, throwing the whole force of his argument upon that one point, and holding the judge's mind fast to it.

In 1852 he had been elected member for Belfast in the conservative interest; and in a few years he had won a position in the House of Commons as distinguished as that which he had won in

---

[1] Atlay, Victorian Chancellors, ii 292-333; Brief Memoirs of the first Earl Cairns, which deals mainly with his religious and kindred activities; Bryce, Studies in Contemporary Biography, 184-195; D.N.B.—a sketch by Lord Sumner.
[2] Willes, Fitzgibbon, Palles, and Law, Atlay, op. cit. ii 293 n. 2.
[3] Studies in Contemporary Biography 191-192.
[4] Below 134.   [5] Above 97.

the courts. It is not surprising therefore that he was made Solicitor-General in 1858. From that time onwards he was one of the leaders of the Conservative party. His speech in 1858 in defence of Lord Ellenborough's censure of Lord Canning's Oude proclamation was said by Lord Granville to have been one of the best speeches ever made in the House of Commons;[1] and Disraeli said of his speech on the government's Reform Bill of 1859 [2] that it "charmed everyone by its lucidity and controlled everyone by its logic".[3] It should be noted that he approved Mackintosh's arguments for a diversity of franchise, and insisted on the desirability of keeping a balance between the voting power of different classes in the community.[4]

The government fell in that year. During the ensuing seven years of opposition Cairns increased his reputation both at the bar and in the House of Commons.

His chief practice at the bar was in the court of Chancery and before the House of Lords. He appeared also in ecclesiastical cases before the Privy Council. In the case of *The Alexandra* [5] he defeated the government in the courts, and got damages for the detention of the ship;[6] and in Parliament he criticized very effectively the policy pursued by the government in relation to *The Alabama* and other ships supplied to the Confederate States.[7] One of his best speeches before a jury was made in defence of the sanity of Windham, the result of which was that Windham was able "to continue his career of reckless profligacies".[8] The case illustrated the need for some such law as the Romans had for dealing with prodigals; and, though no such law was passed, it helped Westbury to pass his Act to amend the law as to the procedure under commissions of lunacy.[9] In the House of Commons,

He was not only among the highest authorities in the House on purely legal questions, but his general knowledge of public affairs was wide and exact, and his speeches breathe the genius of one whose natural bent was for statesmanship quite as much as for law. Whether discussing the clauses of a Bankruptcy or a Land Registration Bill, whether criticizing the details of a commercial treaty, or denouncing some palpable sham in the shape of a Parliamentary Reform Bill, he seemed equally at home and equally secure in his hold on an assembly which is morbidly quick

---

[1] Atlay, op. cit. ii 297. [2] Hansard (3rd Ser.) cliii 599-623.
[3] Monypenny and Buckle, Life of Disraeli i 1606.
[4] Hansard, cliii 610-611, 613.
[5] *Attorney-General v. Sillem* (1863) 3 F. and F. 646; above 99.
[6] Costs and damages were compromised at £3,700, Wheeler, Foreign Enlistment Act, 1870, 57.
[7] Hansard (3rd Ser.) clxx 718, clxxiii 987.
[8] Atlay, op. cit. ii 301-302. [9] 25, 26 Victoria c. 86; above 85.

to resent the readiness of the professional advocate. As became the Member for an Orange stronghold, and himself a Protestant of the Protestants, Cairns was a most vigilant and effective champion of the Irish Establishment.[1]

In 1865 the Conservatives regained office, and Cairns became Attorney-General. But he had never been a strong man, and so, when a few months later a Lord Justiceship fell vacant, he took it—much to the dismay of Disraeli.[2] He was made a peer, and in the House of Lords he distinguished himself as a defender of the government. Though he disliked Disraeli's Reform Bill, he defended it, and introduced a clause, designed to protect minorities, by which electors in three membered constituencies only had two votes.[3] When Derby resigned and Disraeli became Prime Minister in 1868, his first act was to give the Great Seal to Cairns —much to Chelmsford's chagrin.[4] He was as successful as a Cabinet Minister as he had been as Member of Parliament and as a law officer;[5] and his efforts contributed largely to the defeat in the House of Lords of the Irish Church Suspensory Bill. But he only held office for a few months, since the government fell in the following December.

Cairns did not succeed as a speaker in the House of Lords so well as he had succeeded in the House of Commons.[6] But his speeches in defence of the Irish Church were very effective; and it was his efforts as leader of the opposition which secured a favourable compromise, and averted a conflict between the Lords and Commons.[7] On other matters, too, he was an effective critic of the government. He was particularly bitter over the Geneva Arbitration, denouncing it lock, stock, and barrel—the treaty, the negotiations, the award.[8]

In 1874 Cairns again became Chancellor. He had co-operated with Selborne to pass the Judicature Act;[9] and the final settlement of the jurisdiction of the House of Lords by the Appellate Jurisdiction Act, 1876, was his work.[10] We shall see that he had

---

[1] Atlay, Victorian Chancellors, ii 303.
[2] He said, "with him I was not afraid to encounter Gladstone and Roundell Palmer", Monypenny and Buckle, Life of Disraeli ii 214.
[3] Hansard (3rd Ser.) clxxxix 310-323.   [4] Above 66, 67.
[5] Disraeli said on one occasion "Cairns is a great success at the Council Board" and on another occasion that he was a "tower of strength" to him, Monypenny and Buckle, op. cit. ii 414, 1056.
[6] Bryce, op. cit. 189, says that the reason was that "the heart of the House of Commons warmed his somewhat chilly temperament and roused him to a more energetic and ardent style of speaking than was needed in the Upper Chamber, where he and his friends . . . had things all their own way".
[7] Disraeli said of this compromise that it saved the honour of the Lords and satisfied moderate men, but that the "decided spirits" on either side would not like it.
[8] Atlay, op. cit. ii 314.   [9] Above 100, 101.   [10] Above 100, 101.

prepared the way for the important reforms in the land laws which were effected by his successor.[1] In 1878 he was raised to the dignity of an earldom—a promotion fairly earned by his services to the government. For instance, "his speech in defence of the summons of the Indian troops to Malta was a masterpiece, and carried conviction to many waverers outside the walls of the chamber in which it was delivered".[2]

He ceased to hold office in 1880. In opposition he was again a most effective critic of the government's Irish policy; and his attack upon the treaty made with the Boers after the battle of Majuba Hill was one of his most eloquent pieces of oratory. The last speech which he made in the House of Lords was in March 1885, when he opposed successfully a motion to open on Sundays the Natural History Museum at South Kensington. Later in the month he caught a chill. His chest and lungs, which had always been weak, were attacked, and he died on April 7.

Throughout his life Cairns had been an enthusiastic supporter of the Evangelical and Protestant side of the Church of England. Every day he set apart the early morning hours for his private devotions, and nothing would induce him to work on Sunday. He taught in Sunday school even after he was Chancellor. He gave largely to such bodies as the Bible Society, the Church Missionary Society, the Young Men's Christian Association, and Dr. Barnardo's Homes, and he was always ready to advocate these and similar causes. He is even said to have declared that "to hear Moody and Sankey was the richest feast he could enjoy". The strictness of his religious beliefs, and his cold ungenial manner, did not make for popularity. He had very few intimate friends amongst his fellow statesmen and judges; and it was this incapacity to mix with his colleagues in Parliament and the courts which prevented him from becoming the leader of the opposition after Beaconsfield's death. He naturally inclined to look with favour upon those who shared his religious beliefs; and it was said that the knowledge of this fact induced barristers who wanted County Court judgeships to attend prayer meetings at his home with regularity.[3] But Coleridge testified to his honesty and care in his appointments to the bench; and said that though he had a reputation for want of geniality and a sense of humour, he "had always found him most cheerful and amusing", and possessed of a keen sense of humour.[4]

---

[1] Below 101.   [2] Atlay, op. cit. ii 327; Hansard ccxl 211-216.

[3] For a good story which illustrates this failing, see Atlay, op. cit. ii 323-324; but, as Atlay says, most of his appointments to the High Court bench were very good; they included Bowen, Lindley and Fry.

[4] Hansard (3rd Ser.) ccxcvi 1438-1439; cf. Atlay, op. cit ii 333.

His defects of manner were more than compensated for by his powers of oratory and debate, and by his outstanding achievements as a lawyer and a statesman. Atlay tells us of the impression which his oratory made upon him in 1882:[1]

The occasion was the annual dinner of the Canning and Chatham Clubs . . . and for nearly an hour Lord Cairns held us . . . spell-bound. Unhappily the custom of the country excluded reporters, and to my shame be it said, I cannot, at this distance of time, recall a single one of the stately and incisive phrases which fell from the lips of the man whom Lord Beaconsfield delighted to honour. But I can well remember that the first impression, among the younger of us at any rate, was that of surprise. We could hardly believe that this glowing, virile orator, with the grand presence and the lofty ideals of public duty, who roused our post-prandial enthusiasm to frenzy with his flood of arguments and sarcasm, could be the cold, austere, and cautious lawyer whom fondness for Moody and Sankey's hymns had been the fount of so much indifferent humour.

Speaking, after his death, of his achievements as a lawyer and a statesman, Lord Salisbury said, "he had an eminence not very often granted to a single man—he was equally great as a lawyer, as a statesman, and as a legislator".[2]

We are concerned with him as a legislator and a judge, and under these two heads I shall consider his contribution to the development of the law.

There is only one Act actually associated with his name—the Act of 1858 [3] which allowed the court of Chancery to give damages in addition to or in substitution for specific performance or an injunction. But he had a share in passing the Judicature Act;[4] he settled the question of the jurisdiction of the House of Lords and reformed its constitution as the final court of appeal by the Appellate Jurisdiction Act, 1876;[5] he supported the Public Worship Regulation Act, 1874;[6] and he passed the Vendor and Purchaser Act, 1874,[7] and the Real Property Limitation Act, 1874.[8] The Conveyancing Acts, 1881 and 1882, the Settled Land Act, 1882, and the Married Women's Property Act, 1882, were passed in the Chancellorship of his successor;[9] but "they were prepared by his directions and under his instructions",[10] and he assisted their progress through the House of Lords. He tried in 1875 to simplify title by a Land Transfer Act which introduced a system of registration of title;[11] but his Act which, like Westbury's, was optional and not compulsory, was, like Westbury's Act,[12] a

---

[1] The Victorian Chancellors, ii 329-330.   [2] Hansard (3rd Ser.) ccxcvi 1436.
[3] 21, 22 Victoria c. 27.   [4] Above 100, 101, 107.   [5] Above 101, 107.
[6] 37, 38 Victoria c. 85; vol. i 613-614.   [7] 37, 38 Victoria c. 78.
[8] 37, 38 Victoria c. 57.   [9] Above 101.   [10] Atlay, op. cit. ii 320.
[11] 38, 39 Victoria c. 87.   [12] Above 85.

failure. The reasons for their failures have been summarized as follows:

Three things were needed for real success. First, there must be a perfect survey of the whole country; secondly, every estate must be vested in some person with the powers of an absolute owner, reducing all derivative interests, as in the case of stock, to equitable rights; and lastly, the State must compensate owners for the consequences of official errors. The survey did not exist; opinion was not . . . fully ripe for the needful changes; and it casts no discredit on the efforts of Lord Cairns and those who worked in the same direction that complete success was not achieved.[1]

It is upon his qualities and work as a judge that he made his greatest contribution to the development of the law. Bryce said that his command of principles and his capacity to state them luminously and apply them to the facts of a case, made him the greatest of the judges of the Victorian era.[2] Benjamin said that he was the greatest lawyer before whom he had argued.[3] G. W. Hemming, who had also practised before him, emphasized "his largeness of view which brought the world of law into touch with the world of business", and the convincing power of his judgments which made them command universal assent.[4] Like Westbury he decided cases by the application of broad and simple principles.[5] But Cairns's character, and more accurate knowledge of the law, secured for his statements of principle a respect which Westbury's statements often failed to secure, and so they obtained a far more universal consent, and effected a permanent settlement of the law. Then, too, Cairns's behaviour on the bench was perfect. G. W. Hemming says:[6]

A judge's function is to hear and decide, and, from the point of view of the Bar at any rate, a judge who knows how to hear is quite as highly prized as one whose strength consists exclusively in his capacity to decide. Lord Cairns was equally great in both. To hear well means for a judge to get the greatest amount of aid which can be got from the arguments of counsel, and at the same time to check effectually the waste of time upon ingenious sophistry. Few judges ever combined these ends more satisfactorily than Lord Cairns. No one ever complained of him that he was too reticent or too outspoken. If he never kept Counsel in the dark as to what was passing in his mind . . . or silenced them with contradictions [7] . . . he knew well how to curtail an argument in which a

---

[1] L.Q.R. i 367.   [2] Studies in Contemporary Biography 184.
[3] Atlay, op. cit. ii 316.   [4] L.Q.R. i 365.
[5] Above 87.   [6] L.Q.R. i 366.
[7] "Lord Blackburn . . . had acquired in the Queen's Bench a somewhat unpleasing notoriety for his habit of extinguishing argument by deftly delivered posers. His initial effort in this direction was checked, when an answer could be given, by an icy voice from the Woolsack, 'I think the House is desirous of hearing the arguments of counsel, and not of putting questions to him'", Atlay, op. cit. ii 316-317.

fallacy was veiled in periphrastic amplitude of language. Without a trace of assertion he would cut short the flow of sophistry with a grave question whether the argument did not come to this or that, and then would follow a terribly accurate paraphrase so unmistakeably clear as to close once for all any further contention on the point. And yet with all this power of criticism and irony he was patient beyond most; a virtue not to be lightly esteemed in any, and, unlike other virtues, most difficult of all to minds as strong and clear as his.

The following are a few of the many cases in which Cairns helped to make our modern law.

It is generally agreed that his greatest contribution to legal development was in the sphere of *company law*. The following cases are a few illustrations of the many fundamental doctrines which originate in his decisions: in the case of the *Ashbury Carriage Co. v. Riche* [1] he defined the functions and effect of the memorandum of association of a limited company, and distinguished the function and effect of a company's articles of association. In the case of *Gardner v. London, Chatham and Dover Railway* [2] he settled the rights of the holders of debentures over the undertaking of a railway—they were a security, he said, upon a "fruit-bearing tree", and this "living and going concern" created by the Legislature could not "under a contract pledging it as security, be destroyed, broken up or annihilated". In the case of *Erlanger v. New Sombrero Phosphate Co.*[3] he defined the position and duties of the promoters of a company. In the case of *Peek v. Gurney* [4] he defined the class of persons who could sue the company for false statements contained in its prospectus. In the case of *Princess of Reuss v. Bos* [5] he emphasized the conclusiveness of a company's certificate of incorporation, and commented upon the absence of any power to take proceedings to forfeit a company's charter if it has been guilty of illegal acts.

Several of his decisions in the sphere of *contract and tort* are leading cases. Illustrations are *Ward v. Hobbs*,[6] in which the circumstances in which an action for deceit will lie are discussed; *Cundy v. Lindsay* [7] in which the effect upon a contract of a mistake induced by fraud, as compared with a contract induced by fraud, is discussed; *Lamare v. Dixon*,[8] which dealt *inter alia* with misrepresentation as a defence to an action for specific performance; *Rylands v. Fletcher*,[9] in which he distinguished the

---

[1] (1875) L.R. 7 H. L. 653 at pp. 667-668.
[2] (1867) L.R. 2 Ch. 201 at p. 217.   [3] (1878) 3 App. Cas. 1218 at p. 1236.
[4] (1873) L.R. 6 H. L. 377 at pp. 411-412.
[5] (1871) L.R. 5 H. L. 176 at pp. 199-202; cf. vol. ix 66.
[6] (1878) 4 App. Cas. 13 at pp. 19-24.   [7] (1878) 3 App. Cas. 459 at pp. 463-466.
[8] (1873) L.R. 6 H. L. 414 at p. 428.
[9] (1868) L.R. 3 H. L. 330 at pp. 338-340; vol. viii 471-472.

liabilities arising from the natural user of land from those arising from its non-natural user, and expressly approved Blackburn J.'s statement of law; *Metropolitan Railway Co. v. Jackson,*[1] in which he defined the functions of judge and jury in an action for negligence. One of the very few cases in which his opinion was not accepted by the House of Lords was the case of *Hammersmith Railway Co. v. Brand,*[2] which dealt with the liability of railway companies to pay compensation for damage caused by vibration, without any negligence on their part. In the sphere of *mercantile law* he took part in the decision of the case of *Goodwin v. Robarts.*[3] The actual question at issue in that case he thought could be decided by the application of the doctrine of estoppel; but he approved the principles that the quality of negotiability could be annexed to instruments by the custom of the merchants.

In the sphere of *property law* his judgment in the case of *Lyon v. Fishmongers' Co.*[4] contains a valuable survey of the rights of the owners of land abutting upon a navigable river. In the sphere of *equity* his judgment in the case of *Brown v. Gellatly*[5] settled the rights of tenants for life and remaindermen to the income of residuary personalty directed by a testator to be converted, where conversion was postponed under a power in the will; the case of *Carver v. Cartwright*[6] affirmed the power of executors to sell and give a good title to property vested in them by law or by the will of the deceased; and in the case of *Doherty v. Allman,*[7] the question when the court ought to grant an injunction, when damages are a sufficient remedy, and the treatment by equity of ameliorating waste, were considered. In the sphere of *public law* his judgment in the case of *United States v. Wagner*[8] settled the law as to the right of a foreign state to sue in an English court, and the conditions under which that right is recognized.

---

[1] (1877) 3 App. Cas. 193 at pp. 197-198.   [2] (1868) L.R. 4 H.L. 171.
[3] (1876) 1 App. Cas. 476 at pp. 489-490.
[4] (1876) 1 App. Cas. 662 at pp. 670-677.   [5] (1867) L.R. 2 Ch. 751.
[6] (1875) 7 H. L. 731.   [7] (1877) 3 App. Cas. 709 at pp. 716-723.
[8] (1867) L.R. 2 Ch. 582 at pp. 593-595.

MASTERS OF THE ROLLS

LANGDALE
(1836-1851)

The three Masters of the Rolls during this period were Henry Bickersteth, Lord Langdale; John Romilly, Lord Romilly; and Sir George Jessel.

Bickersteth [1] was born on June 18, 1783, at Kirkby Lonsdale. He was the son of a medical practitioner, and was originally destined for that profession. He studied medicine at London and Edinburgh, and then went to Caius College, Cambridge to complete his medical education. At the end of his first term he broke down, and to provide him with a rest and change of scene, he was recommended for, and accepted the post of, medical attendant to the Earl of Oxford, who in 1803 was setting out on a European tour. He returned in 1804, and, having brought the Earl safely through a serious illness, the foundation of a life-long friendship was laid, which in 1835 was cemented by his marriage with the Earls' daughter. But when Bickersteth went back to Cambridge he gave up medicine, and took to the study of mathematics. [2] He was so successful that in 1808 he graduated as senior Wrangler and Smith's prizeman. He was elected to a Fellowship at Caius, [3] and became a student at the Inner Temple in the same year. At the Temple he read with Bell, who became one of the leading practitioners of the court of Chancery.

While on his travels abroad he had been introduced to the brother of Sir Francis Burdett; and it was through him that he was introduced to Sir Francis and Bentham. He became a friend and adviser of Burdett, and a disciple of Bentham. [4] In 1818 he suggested that Bentham should draw up a plan of Parliamentary reform which Burdett should introduce to the notice of Parliament and the nation, [5] and he supported Burdett against Romilly in the

---

[1] T. Duffus Hardy, Memoirs of Lord Langdale; Foss, Lives of the Judges ix 136-146; D.N.B.; Quart. Rev. xci 461-503—a carping and not very fair review of Hardy's book.

[2] He considered the project of going into the army, but was dissuaded.

[3] At a later period he came to the conclusion that the Master and Fellows had distributed to the Fellows the Perse trust funds on a wrong principle, and returned to the college the amount which he had wrongly received and interest—a sum of £773 15/-; in 1837, with the consent of the parties, the question of the construction of the Perse trust came before him as Master of the Rolls, *Attorney-General v. Caius College* (1837) 2 Keen 150; in all the circumstances he held that the Master and Fellows were not liable to refund their overpayments, ibid at pp. 667-668.

[4] He helped Bentham with his "Equity Despatch Court Bill", and Bentham in 1830 referred to him as "a cordial friend to law reform to its utmost extent", Works, xi 21, 39.   [5] Bentham, Works x 492-493.

Westminster election of that year. Though his progress at the bar was at first slow, he gradually acquired a good practice, and in 1824 he gave valuable evidence before the Chancery commission in which *inter alia* he stressed the defects in the procedure used by the court to compel the defendant's appearance, the length of time during which suits lasted, and the unnecessary length of pleadings.[1] Copley consulted him as to his bill for the reform of the court, and, in 1827, when Copley became Chancellor, he gave him a silk gown. In 1831 Bickersteth declined the offer of the chief judgeship of the new court of bankruptcy; and in 1834 he refused the office of Baron of the Exchequer since he did not feel competent to perform the common law duties attached to it. He was no admirer of Brougham, with whom he had had a brush in the Privy Council in 1834 when, as counsel for Cambridge University, he was opposing the grant of a charter to London University;[2] and it was largely because he felt that he could not get on with him that he refused the office of Solicitor-General later in 1834.[3]

When Melbourne took office in 1835 he applied to Bickersteth for his views as to the measures which ought to be taken to reform the court of Chancery. Bickersteth wrote a valuable memorandum in which he advocated an increase in the judicial strength of the court, both original and appellate, and a division of the duties of the Lord Chancellor.[4] In 1836, when it became necessary to appoint a new Chancellor, some favoured Bickersteth.[5] But Pepys was appointed; Bickersteth, much to Campbell's disappointment, succeeded Pepys as Master of the Rolls;[6] and, in spite of his reluctance, was raised to the peerage with the title of Lord Langdale. In the House of Lords he abstained from taking an active part in political conflicts, and devoted his energies to the promotion of reforms in the law.[7] He took some

---

[1] Vol. ix 351-352, 374, 402.

[2] "The most striking incident occurred in an answer of Bickersteth's to one of the Chancellor's interruptions. He said, talking of degrees, 'Pray, Mr. Bickersteth, what is to prevent the London University granting degrees *now*?' To which he replied, 'the universal scorn and contempt of mankind'. Brougham said no more; the effect was really fine", Greville, Memoirs iii 84.

[3] Ibid iii 145 n; in 1845 Greville said that Langdale would not sit in the Judicial Committee of the Privy Council with Brougham, because Brougham would take precedence of him, ibid v 271.

[4] Memoirs of Lord Langdale i 421-443.

[5] Greville, Memoirs iii 335 n; above 28.

[6] Campbell, Chancellors viii 110, 147.

[7] Campbell says that he was of no use to the government in the House of Lords, Chancellors viii 480; but it would seem that he had stipulated, when he was made a peer, that he was not to be regarded as a political supporter of the government, Foss, Judges ix 142.

share in the preparation of the Wills Act, and saw it through the
House of Lords.[1] Though he criticized Cottenham's bill for the
reform of the court of Chancery, he supported other Acts with the
same object,[2] as well as an Act which regulated attorneys and
solicitors,[3] and the Act which reformed the law as to imprisonment
for debt.[4] Foss, from personal experience, testifies to the pains
which he took in the preparation and progress of all schemes of
legal reform.[5] In 1847 he presided over a commission to enquire
into schemes for the registration of title and reforms in the law
of conveying land.[6] He waged war against the pernicious system
by which the suitor at every stage in an action was charged with
fees for the benefit of the officials of the court;[7] for though in
many cases the officials had come to be paid by a fixed salary, the
fees were still charged.[8] It was largely due to his efforts that the
Act of 1838 for establishing a Public Record Office was passed,
and that the initial steps were taken to preserve and catalogue
the records, and make them available to students.[9] Foss, who
dedicated to him his Lives of the Judges, said that he had
"subjected the chaotic mass [of the public records] to an arrangement, which even now, in its unfinished state, affords facilities
to the statesman, the historian, and the biographer, which they
never before enjoyed".[10] He also did good work as a Trustee of the
British Museum, and as the head of a commission to enquire
into its organization.[11]

In 1850 the Chancellorship was offered to him. But he refused
it because he was still of the opinion that no one man could
adequately perform its duties; and he was conscious that he had
not the strength to perform them.[12] In fact the month that he
held the Great Seal as first commissioner, after Cottenham's
resignation and till Truro was made Chancellor, caused a break-
down in his health. He partially recovered, but he was no longer
able to fulfil the duties of his office, and resigned on March 28,
1851. He died three weeks later on April 18.

As a counsel he reasoned closely and vigorously. He was
always the master of every detail of his case, and he was quick to
detect the weak points in his opponent's case.[13] As a judge he was
equally industrious in mastering the facts of his cases, and could

---

[1] 7 William IV and 1 Victoria c. 26; Hardy, Memoirs of Lord Langdale ii 215.
[2] E.g. 5, 6 Victoria c. 103, vol. i 444; 5 Victoria c. 5, vol. i 443.
[3] 6, 7 Victoria c. 73; vol. xv 224.   [4] 1, 2 Victoria c. 110; above 31.
[5] Judges ix 143.   [6] Memoirs of Lord Langdale ii 222-223.
[7] Ibid ii 224.   [8] Vol. i 444; above 37.
[9] Memoirs of Lord Langdale ii 111-193; vol. ii 601-602.
[10] Judges iii n. 1.   [11] Memoirs of Lord Langdale ii 195 et seq.
[12] Ibid ii 243-245; 249-250, 257-258.   [13] Memoirs of Lord Langdale i 473.

state them shortly and clearly. His manner, Selborne says, was dignified—"perhaps a little too much so". But in Selborne's opinion he did not on the bench quite maintain the reputation which he had gained at the bar, and was somewhat overshadowed by the leading counsel in his court [1]—Pemberton Leigh and later Turner.[2]

Nevertheless some of his decisions have settled important points of equitable doctrine. The two most important of his decisions are *Tullett v. Armstrong* [3] in which many points as to the incidents of the separate estate of married women and of the restraint upon anticipation were settled, and *Tulk v. Moxhay*,[4] in which, as we have seen, his statement of the law as to covenants running in equity with the land was affirmed by Cottenham.[5] Other notable decisions are *Croft v. Day*,[6] which raised the question of the fraudulent use of a trade name; *Duke of Brunswick v. King of Hanover* [7] in which the liability of a foreign sovereign, who was also a British subject, to be sued in the English courts was discussed; and *Colyear v. Mulgrave*[8] which raised the question of the distinction between a mere contract between two persons for the benefit of a third, and a contract between two persons which creates a trust for a third person. The most famous of his decisions in his own day was given by him, not as Master of the Rolls upon a point of equity, but in the Privy Council upon a question of ecclesiastical law. This was his decision in the case of *Gorham v. Bishop of Exeter*,[9] in which he reversed the decision of the court of the Arches and held that Gorham's views as to baptism and regeneration were not contrary to the doctrines of the Church of England, so that the bishop was wrong in refusing to institute him to a living. Langdale laid down the important principle that in these cases the Privy Council had

no jurisdiction or authority to settle matters of faith, or to determine what ought to be in any particular the doctrine of the Church of England. Its duty extends only to the consideration of that which is by law established to be the doctrine of the Church of England, upon the true and legal construction of her articles and formularies; and we consider that it is not the duty of any court to be minute and rigid in cases of this sort. We agree with Sir William Scott . . . "that if any Article is really a

---

[1] Memoirs, Family and Personal i 372.
[2] Below 133; Rolt says, Memoirs 91, that when his judgments did not consist in saying ditto to Pemberton Leigh, they consisted of a luminous statement of the facts "with the addition that, upon the whole of the case, he thought the plaintiff or defendant (as the case might be) was entitled".
[3] (1838) 1 Beav. 1.   [4] (1848) 11 Beav. 571.
[5] Above 34; (1848) 2 Ph. 774.   [6] (1843) 7 Beav. 84.
[7] (1844) 6 Beav. 1.   [8] (1836) 2 Keen 81.
[9] (1850) Moore, Special Report.

subject of dubious interpretation, it would be highly improper that this Court should fix on one meaning, and prosecute all those who hold a contrary opinion regarding its interpretation".[1]

This principle was approved, and effect was given to it, by Lord Westbury in the later case arising out of the publication of *Essays and Reviews*.[2]

ROMILLY
(1851-1873)

Langdale's successor was John Romilly, Lord Romilly.[3] He was the second son of Sir Samuel Romilly, and was born on January 10, 1802. He was called to the bar by Gray's Inn in 1827, and took silk in 1843. He was made Solicitor-General in 1848, and Attorney-General in 1850. While Attorney-General he procured the appointment of the commission for the reform of the court of Chancery, which suggested the valuable and extensive reforms effected in 1852.[4] In 1851 he succeeded Langdale as Master of the Rolls, and was raised to the peerage in 1865. He held his office of Master of the Rolls till ill-health compelled him to resign in 1873. He died on December 23, 1874. From 1847 till 1852 he represented Devonport in the House of Commons. He was the last Master of the Rolls to sit in Parliament, since the Master of the Rolls, in common with other judges, was incapacitated from sitting in the House of Commons by the Judicature Act.[5]

Romilly was an industrious and conscientious judge, and decided an immense number of cases during his long tenure of office. Some of these lay down important principles of equity. Two of them lay down important principles as to charitable trusts. In the case of *Philpott v. St. George's Hospital* [6] he defined the limits of the power of the court to order a *cy-près* application of funds left on trust for a charity;[7] and in the case of *Attorney-General v. Dean and Canons of Windsor* [8] he considered the question of the circumstances in which trustees, who have been

---

[1] (1850) Moore, Special Report, 472; the defendant tried in vain to stop the execution of the judgment by means of a writ of prohibition, see *Gorham v. Bishop of Exeter* (1850) 15 Q.B. 52, 10 C.B. 102, 5 Exch. 630.
[2] *Williams v. Bishop of Salisbury* (1863) 2 Moo. P.C.N.S. at p. 424.
[3] Foss, Judges ix 253-255; D.N.B.—biography by Lord Sumner.
[4] Vol. i 444-445; vol. ix 375-376.
[5] 36, 37 Victoria c. 66 § 9.
[6] (1859) 27 Beav. 107.
[7] At p. 112.
[8] (1858) 24 Beav. 679.

directed to make certain payments, are entitled to take beneficially the surplus of the fund. In the case of *Newsome v. Flowers* [1] he laid down the important principle that trustees cannot, as against a *cestui que trust,* set up a *jus tertii*; and in the case of *Thrupp v. Collett* [2] he applied the rule that a trust to effect an illegal purpose is void. He gave two important decisions on the law of mortgage. In the case of *Perry Herrick v. Attwood* [3] he defined the conditions in which the conduct of a first mortgagee, though holding the legal estate, will postpone him to later equitable incumbrancers; and in the case of *Rolt v. Hopkinson* [4] he laid down the principle, which was affirmed by the House of Lords, [5] that a further advance made by a first mortgagee, with notice of an intermediate advance, cannot be tacked to the original sum lent. His decision in the case of *Money v. Jorden* [6] on the question of misrepresentation caused a difference of opinion amongst the Lords Justices [7], and did not commend itself to the House of Lords [8]—though Lord St. Leonards dissented from the majority of the House. On the other hand two of his decisions on the effect of mistake in equity [9] and one of his decisions as to the limits within which the rule in *Penn v. Lord Baltimore* [10] is applicable, [11] have been approved. These cases show that Romilly's contribution to the development of equity was not inconsiderable. On the other hand, as Lord Sumner has said, [12] his decisions were often reversed on appeal, because "he was prone to decide cases without sufficiently considering the principles they involved and the precedents by which they were governed".

But though Romilly cannot be considered to be a great lawyer, there is no doubt that he performed a very great service to historical learning of all kinds by the way in which he carried on Langdale's work at the Record Office. He rendered the records accessible to students; and his initiation of the policy of printing calendars of state papers, and of issuing, in the Rolls Series, well edited editions of chronicles and other documents which were under his care. [13] He stimulated historical research, by making important parts of the contents of the Record Office available to the world.

[1] (1861) 30 Beav. 461.
[2] (1858) 26 Beav. 125.
[3] (1857) 25 Beav. 205.
[4] (1858) 25 Beav. 461.
[5] (1861) 9 H.L.C. 514.
[6] (1852) 15 Beav. 372.
[7] (1852) 2 De G.M. and G. 318.
[8] (1854) 5 H.L.C. 185.
[9] *Webster v. Cecil* (1861) 30 Beav. 62; *Garrard v. Frankel* (1862) ibid 445.
[10] (1750) 1 Ves. Sen. 444; vol. xii 264, 265.
[11] *Norris v. Chambres* (1861) 29 Beav. 246.
[12] D.N.B.
[13] Foss, Judges ix 254; vol. ii 601 n. 9.

JESSEL

(1873-1883)

Romilly's successor, Sir George Jessel, was the greatest of the Masters of the Rolls since Sir William Grant.

Jessel [1] was born on February 13, 1824. He was the son of a Jewish merchant and was himself a Jew. He was educated at University College, London, where he took honours in mathematics and branches of natural science. He became a Fellow of University College in 1846, and in later life, as a member of the Senate and Vice-Chancellor of the University of London, he took an active part in its government. He was called to the bar by Lincoln's Inn in 1847, and soon got a large and increasing practice at the bar. Westbury refused to give him silk in 1861, but he was induced [2] by Roundell Palmer to give it to him in 1865. He became a member of Parliament in the liberal interest in 1868, where, in 1869, he attracted Gladstone's notice by his speeches on the bankruptcy bill of that year. But, "though lucid and powerful in his treatment of legal topics, he was never popular with the House of Commons, for he presented his views in a hard, dry, dogmatic form, with no graces of style or delivery".[3] He was made Solicitor-General in 1871. In that capacity he piloted the Judicature Act of 1873 through the House of Commons. In the same year he succeeded Lord Romilly as Master of the Rolls. He continued to hold that office till his death on March 21, 1883.

Jessel was something of a jurist. He had studied Roman law, and foreign codes founded upon it. He used that knowledge in his speech on the bankruptcy bill, delivered on April 5, 1869.[4] He pointed out that Roman law was the basis of the bankruptcy legislation of the civilized world, but that English lawyers had used Roman principles in a very unintelligent way—using it "as the Turks used the remains of the splendid temples of antiquity".[5] In particular our law differed from Roman law and the law of all other nations in Europe in exempting the bankrupt's after-acquired property when he had paid 10/- in the £; [6] and in making large and irrational differences, which worked much injustice, in the distribution of an insolvent's estate according as he died the day after, or the day before, adjudication.[7] But his place in English legal history rests upon his profound knowledge of

---

[1] D.N.B.; Bryce, Studies in Contemporary Biography, 170-183.
[2] Above 87; Selborne, Memorials Personal and Political ii 93.
[3] Bryce, op. cit. 173.   [4] Hansard (3rd Ser.) cxcv 142-154.
[5] At p. 143.   [6] At p. 146.   [7] At pp. 150-152.

equity, and his capacity not only to explain its principles and
rules with clarity, but also in many cases to rationalize them, by
refusing to allow merely technical objections and decisions which
stood in his way to stop him from laying down what he considered
to be the right and sensible rule. As I said in my first volume,[1] he
was a profound equity lawyer with the mind of an acute juryman,
who, by reason of that unique combination of qualities, was able
to apply to the rules of equity the touchstone of common sense.

Jessel's genius for law, his knowledge of affairs, his extraordinary quickness of apprehension, and his retentive memory
made him one of the most powerful advocates at the equity bar.
Though his manners, and conduct to other counsel, made him
unpopular at the bar,[2] he was always willing to help a young
student. Witt tells us [3] that when he was a pupil, and he and his
fellow pupils were unable to solve a problem, they adopted the
following plan:

We went off to lunch in the room at Lincoln's Inn below the hall, and
sat down opposite George Jessel, who was then doing a fine business at
the Junior Bar. We at once began to talk about the point which had
baffled us. Jessel instantly pricked up his ears, and in less than five
minutes we had the problem solved, with full information as to all the
cases and references to the reports in which they were to be found.

Birrell [4] has said that, when on the bench, his "civility to a
barrister was always in inverse ration to the barrister's practice",
and that "his friendly zeal in helping young and nervous practitioners over the stiles of legal difficulties was only equalled by the
fiery enthusiasm with which he thrust back the Attorney and
Solicitor-General and people of that sort".

His method of hearing cases was unique, and possible only to
a judge with his profound knowledge of law and his peculiar
combination of intellectual gifts. It is thus described by Bryce:[5]

When the leading counsel for the plaintiff was opening his case, Jessel
listened quietly for the first few minutes only, and then began to address
questions to the counsel, at first so as to guide his remarks in a particular
direction, then so as to stop his course altogether and turn his speech
into a series of answers to the Judge's interrogations. When, by a short
dialogue of this kind, Jessel had possessed himself of the vital facts, he
would turn to the leading counsel for the defendant and ask him whether
he admitted such and such facts alleged by the plaintiff to be true. If
these facts were admitted, the Judge proceeded to indicate the view he
was disposed to take of the law applicable to the facts, and by a few
more questions to counsel on the one side or the other, as the case might

---

[1] Vol. i 350.   [2] Bryce, op. cit. 181.
[3] J. G. Witt, Life in the Law 31.   [4] Obiter Dicta (2nd Ser.) 126-127.
[5] Studies in Contemporary Biography 173-176.

be, elicited their respective legal grounds of contention. If the facts were not admitted, it of course became necessary to call the witnesses or read the affidavits, processes which the rigorous impatience of the Judge considerably shortened. . . . But more generally his searching questions and the sort of pressure he applied so cut down the issues of fact that there was little or nothing left in controversy regarding which it was necesssary to examine the evidence in detail, since the counsel felt that there was no use in putting before him a contention which they could not sustain under the fire of his criticism. Thus Jessel proceeded to deliver his opinion and dispose of the case. . . . Thus business was despatched before him with unexampled speed, and it became a maxim among barristers that, however low down in the cause list your case might stand, it was never safe to be away from the court, so rapidly were cases "crumpled up" or "broken down" under the blows of this vigorous intellect. It was more surprising that the suitors, as well as the Bar and the public generally, acquiesced, after the first few months, in this way of doing business. Nothing breeds more discontent than haste and heedlessness in a judge. But Jessel's speed was not haste. He did as much justice in a day as others could do in a week; and those few who, dissatisfied with these rapid methods, tried to reverse his decisions before the Court of Appeal, were very seldom successful.

The style of his judgments was as unique as his manner of hearing his cases. He never wrote them. They were given almost always immediately after the close of the argument,[1] however complicated the facts or however obscure the law; for, at the close of the argument, Jessel had always made up his mind both as to facts and the law—he said once "I may be wrong, but I never have any doubts".[2] A good instance of his power of rapid and correct decision in the most complicated case is his judgment in the case of *Commissioners of Sewers v. Glasse*.[3] The hearing lasted twenty-three days, and one hundred and fifty witnesses were examined. Jessel gave judgment immediately after the case was finished, and there was no appeal from his decision. The style of these judgments is conversational—the learned conversation of a man who, because he is the master of his subject, is able to make his meaning perfectly clear, sometimes with the help of a homely illustration, and to explain not only the rule which he is applying but its *rationale*. And in the course of this conversation he explains not only the rule and its *rationale*, but also the authorities on which it is based—applying, distinguishing, and, if necessary, disapproving the earlier cases on the subject. He could be very critical of cases or the reasoning in cases of which he disapproved; and that criticism was expressed caustically, and

[1] Bryce, op. cit. 180, says that he only reserved judgment on two occasions at the request of his colleagues in the Court of Appeal.   [2] Ibid 181.

[3] (1874) 19 Eq. 134; there was an appeal from his decision at an earlier stage of the case overruling a demurrer to the bill, and his decision was affirmed (1872) L.R. 7 Ch. 456.

occasionally with considerable humour. One instance of the caustic way in which he dealt with decisions of which he did not approve is to be found in the case of *Johnson v. Crook*,[1] where he said of a dictum of Lord Chelmsford, "I am no Oedipus and I do not understand the passage. It cannot be right as it stands";[2] and of a dictum of Lord Selborne in which he stated the effect of a dictum of Lord Thurlow, "There is a very good answer to that— he did not say so".[3] Another instance is to be found in *In re International Pulp Co.*[4] when he said:

It is very dangerous for a judge who does not agree with particular decisions to deal in distinctions from those decisions. Now I will not attempt to distinguish this case from the cases before the Court of Appeal which have been cited, but I will say this, that I do not consider them absolutely binding upon me in the present instance; and for this reason, that I do not know the principle on which the Court of Appeal founded their decisions, I cannot tell whether I ought to follow them or not. If those decisions do lay down any principle I am bound by it, but I have not the remotest notion what that principle is.

An instance of his humorous handling of a rule of law is to be found in his judgment in the case of *Couldery v. Bartrum*[5] in which he described the shifts which the doctrine of consideration had rendered necessary before the common law could recognize the validity of a composition with creditors.[6] He said:[7]

According to English common law a creditor might accept anything in satisfaction of his debt except a less sum of money. He might take a horse, a canary, or a tomtit if he chose, and that was accord and satisfaction; but, by a most extraordinary peculiarity of the English common law, he could not take 19/6 in the pound; that was *nudum pactum*. . . . But, that being so, there came a class of arrangements between creditors and debtors, by which a debtor who was unable to pay in full offered a composition of something less in the pound. Well, it was felt to be a very absurd thing that the creditors could not bind themselves to take less than the amount of their debts. . . . Therefore it was necessary to bind the creditors; and as every debtor had not a stock of canary birds or tomtits, or rubbish of that kind, to add to his dividend, it was felt desirable to bind the creditors in a sensible way by saying that, if they all agreed, there should be a consideration imported from the agreement constituting an addition to the dividend, so as to make the agreement no longer *nudum pactum*, but an agreement made for valuable consideration.

The only serious criticism passed upon his judgments was that he took "a somewhat hard and dry view of a legal principle, over-looking its more delicate shades"; and that in interpreting

---

[1] (1879) 12 Ch.D. 639.   [2] At p. 651.   [3] At pp. 652-653.
[4] (1877) 6 Ch.D. at p. 559.   [5] (1881) 19 Ch.D. 394.
[6] Vol. viii 85.   [7] (1881) 19 Ch.D. at pp. 399-400.

statutes and documents he stuck too closely to the letter, over-looking their spirit. In these respects, some thought he was inferior to Cairns, whose outlook was more broad and philo-sophical.[1]

Such a man necessarily made a large contribution to the development of equitable doctrine. He decided a large number of leading cases,[2] and in them he did a great work, not only in explaining and settling and developing equitable principles, but also, as I have said, in rationalizing equitable doctrines. The following cases are a very few out of the many illustrations which could be given of his achievement in all these directions:

Cases in which Jessel settled important *principles of equity* are *Re Hallett's Estate*,[3] in which he settled the main principles of the doctrine of following trust property; *Richards v. Delbridge*,[4] in which he enforced the rule that validity cannot be given to an imperfect gift by construing it as a declaration of trust; *Pooley v. Driver*,[5] in which he analysed the considerations which must be taken into account to determine whether an agreement to share profits will or will not create a partnership; *Re Johnson*,[6] in which he explained the position of an executor, and the creditors of an executor, when the executor has carried on his testator's trade in pursuance of a power given him by the will. Many of his decisions elucidate important principles in the law of *real property*. Instances are *Honywood v. Honywood*,[7] in which the rights of the tenant for life and the remainderman in respect of timber are considered; *Cooper v. Macdonald*, in which the rights of a married woman restrained from anticipation over her equitable estate tail are explained; *Re D'Angibau*,[8] in which he considered various kinds of powers of appointment, and held that an infant could exercise a power in gross; *Abbiss v. Burney*,[9] in which he held that the rule against perpetuities applied to equitable contingent remainders; *London and South Western Railway v. Gomm*,[10] in which he held that a covenant which gives an interest in land falls within the rule against perpetuities, and explained the juridical character of negative covenants which run with the land in equity. In the law of *contract* he considered, in *Printing Co. v. Sampson*,[11] the doctrine of public policy, and in *Wallis v. Smith* [12] the question

---

[1] Bryce, op. cit. 180.
[2] A summary of Jessel's decisions with notes thereon was published by A. P. Peter in 1883.
[3] (1879) 13 Ch.D. 196.
[4] (1874) 18 Eq. 11.
[5] (1876) 5 Ch.D. 458.
[6] (1880) 15 Ch.D. 548.
[7] (1874) 17 Eq. 306.
[8] (1880) 15 Ch.D. 228.
[9] (1881) 17 Ch.D. 211.
[10] (1882) 20 Ch.D. 562.
[11] (1875) 19 Eq. 462.
[12] (1882) 21 Ch.D. 243.

whether a stipulation for the payment of a fixed sum for breach of a contract was a penalty or liquidated damages. In two cases on the effect of the *Judicature Act*—*Walsh v. Lonsdale* [1] and *Smith v. Chadwick* [2]—his views were in the first case expressed too widely, and in the second case have not been followed. [3]

---

[1] (1882) 21 Ch.D. 9.   [2] (1882) 20 Ch.D. 27.
[3] L.Q.R. li 145-146; Hanbury, Modern Equity, 8th ed.

LORDS JUSTICES IN CHANCERY

SOME LORDS JUSTICES IN CHANCERY

The Court of Appeal in Chancery, set up in 1851,[1] had a short history, but most of the Lords Justices who sat in it were very eminent lawyers, and some of them made a considerable contribution to the development of the principles of equity. The full list will be found at the foot of the page.[2] Of the three of them who became Chancellors—Cranworth, Cairns, and Hatherley—I have already given an account.[3] Of the others the three most notable were Knight-Bruce, Mellish, and James. Of these I shall speak in the first place, and then give a shorter account of the others.

KNIGHT-BRUCE

Of all the Lords Justices Knight-Bruce[4] (1791-1866), who was one of the two first appointed under the Act of 1851, had the most striking personality and the keenest sense of humour, to which full effect was given by his literary gifts and his talent for epigram. At the outset of his career he was articled to a solicitor, but he turned over to the bar, was called by Lincoln's Inn in 1817, and took silk in 1829. He became Vice-Chancellor and Chief Judge in Bankruptcy in 1841. He was Treasurer of Lincoln's Inn in 1843, and in that capacity laid the foundation stone of the new hall and library. He was made a Lord Justice in 1851. He held that office till failing sight compelled him to resign on November 7, 1866. He died a fortnight later.

Knight-Bruce had great industry, great learning, a wonderful memory, a power of quickly mastering facts, and therefore a capacity for getting through business quickly and well. In 1850,

---

[1] 14, 15 Victoria c. 83.
[2] Knight-Bruce (1851-66)   Page Wood (Lord Hatherley) (1868-69)
Cranworth (1851-52)   Selwyn (1868-69)
Turner (1853-67)   Giffard (1869-71)
Cairns (1867-68)   Mellish (1870-76)
Rolt (1867-68)   James (1870-81).
[3] See also Atlay, Victorian Chancellors.
[4] Foss, Judges ix 152-154; D.N.B.; his original name was Knight. He assumed the name of Bruce—his mother's maiden name.

shortly before the beginning of the long vacation, the other two Vice-Chancellors were taken ill. He did the work of all three with such skill and accuracy "that a public expression of respect and admiration was elicited from the whole bar, in an address from the Attorney-General".[1] He had never got on with Cottenham since the days when they were rival leaders in Shadwell's court; and since Knight-Bruce was always willing to relax procedural rules to secure substantial justice, whilst Cottenham was a great stickler for the observance of technical forms, it is not surprising that the feud continued.[2]

It showed itself in indecorous ways, and was a commonplace of professional gossip. Under the easy sway of Lyndhurst Knight-Bruce had indulged freely in those "short cuts", with the view of effectuating the administration of justice, which were so abhorrent to the soul of the Chancellor. On one occasion, when an amendment had been granted at the hearing of a cause, Lord Cottenham, on the appeal, asked for precedents, and when none were forthcoming, be blazed out on the "relaxation of the practice of the Court upon which he had frequently of late taken occasion to express his opinion." [3]

We have seen that he had had a quarrel with Bethell;[4] and the feud continued when Bethell became Lord Chancellor—Westbury always disliked sitting with Knight-Bruce in the court of Appeal in Chancery.[5] But Knight-Bruce's ideas as to the manner of treating the technicalities of procedure commended themselves to the Legislature; and it was not likely that Bethell's capacity for cruel phrases and biting epigrams would assort well with Knight-Bruce's more genial talent both for epigrams and humorous and caustic statement. There is no doubt that Knight-Bruce was a most learned and capable judge, and that his epigrams and his humorous and caustic statements give him a unique place amongst the Chancery lawyers of his time. Here are two instances of his gift for epigram: "Some breaches of good manners are breaches of law also." "The decree in this case is a matter of course unless the court and the laws of this country are to be reconstructed with a view to this particular case." [6] A famous instance of his gift of caustic and humorous

---

[1] Foss, Judges ix 153; Rolt, Memoirs, 115-116, says, "his orders all stood the test of the sifting such orders get in the Registrar's Office, in the course of being drawn up, and of subsequent lapse of time. As far as I know no error was ever discovered in them."

[2] "The seeds of mutual dislike between him and Lord Cottenham were sown when that great lawyer, plain and dull of speech had to endure what he regarded as daily affronts from his eloquent competitor. They bore fruit when the one sat as Judge of Appeal over the other", Selborne, Memorials, Family and Personal i 375.

[3] Atlay, Victorian Chancellors i 412-413.

[4] Above 73, 74   [5] Atlay, op. cit. ii 261.

[6] Cited by Veeder, A Century of Judicature, Essays, A.A.L.H. i 801.

statement is the opening paragraph of his judgment in the case of *Burgess v. Burgess* [1]—a case which established the right of a manufacturer to use (without fraud) his own name, although a rival manufacturer had the same name. It runs as follows:

All the Queen's subjects have a right, if they will, to manufacture and sell pickles and sauces, and not the less that their fathers have done so before them. All the Queen's subjects have a right to sell their articles in their own names, and not the less so that they bear the same name as their fathers; nor is there anything else that this defendant has done.

Another less known illustration is his description, in *Small v. Currie* [2] of the steps taken in the middle of the nineteenth century to preserve the Parliamentary interest of the member for the borough of Petersfield. These are the opening sentences of his judgment:

A small country town in Hampshire, which, at least since the Reform Act, has returned but one representative to the House of Commons, happened to possess also but one bank, a bank unluckily conducted upon opposition principles, that is to say, upon principles unfavourable to what in the language of those who deal in Members of Parliament, is called, I believe, the old influence. And this bank was supposed, whether regularly or irregularly, whether by means as to which

Più è il tacer che 'l ragionare, onesto

or otherwise to disturb and endanger that influence so much that the gentleman by whom the influence was at or soon after the time of passing the Act impersonated, and an active and intelligent London solicitor . . . appears to have thought that an additional bank, a bank having more correct views of the public interest, might be beneficially set up in the borough. . . . The plan was resolved on, but as neither of the gentlemen could or would be the resident manager, and it seemed necessary to have a sound man in that capacity, they looked about and found a young farmer of the place whose opinions upon the theory and practice of government were suitable, and to his great pleasure, as well as surprise, no doubt, turned him into a banker and their partner; a choice additionally recommended by the fact that his wife was the niece and adopted daughter of an elder agriculturist well to pass in the world who, being also a right-minded politician, might fill the character of surety for the other rustic.

Knight-Bruce and Selborne had always been friends, and, on his death Selborne testified to his "splendid powers and generous character". [3]

[1] (1853) 3 De G.M. and G. at pp. 903-904; another good example is to be found in his judgment in the case of *Thomas v. Roberts* (1850) 3 De G. and Sm. 758, 772 recounting the doings of a man who had deserted his wife and retired to an "Agape mone" which Knight-Bruce described as a kind of "spiritual boarding house—though to what kind of religion, if any, the inmates belong, does not appear".
[2] (1854) 5 De G.M. and G. at pp. 149-150.
[3] Memorials, Personal and Political i 42.

MELLISH

Mellish (1814-77) [1] was a great commercial lawyer. His opinions, says Bryce, [2] were considered "to be equal in weight to a judgment of the Court of Exchequer Chamber"; and his arguments on points of law were remarkable for their lucidity and their logic. Bryce tells us that he heard him argue the case of *The Alexandra*, and that his argument outshone even Cairns's—"one felt as if the voice of pure reason were speaking through his lips". [3] Rolt welcomed his appointment as Lord Justice because it seemed to him the appointment of a common lawyer to the Court of Appeal in Chancery was a step towards the fusion of law and equity. [4] On the bench he did not quite live up to his reputation at the bar. [5] That was probably due to the fact that he had little knowledge of equity and equity procedure. There were more difficulties in setting common lawyers to decide equity cases and *vice versa* than whole-hearted advocates of the fusion of law and equity imagined. For all that his judgments are lucid and learned, and show a power to state principles clearly and tersely. [6] His colleague James L. J. said that his only defect as a judge was that "he was too anxious to convince counsel that they were wrong, when he thought their contention unsound, seeming to forget that counsel are paid not to be convinced". [7]

JAMES

James (1807-81) was created a Vice-Chancellor in 1869 and Lord Justice in 1870. Bramwell said of him that,

he possessed every quality and accomplishment that a judge needed. He had a great intellect, at once keen and profound. He was a consummate lawyer, thoroughly imbued with legal principles. He was a man of vast experience, not merely in the law, but in those things which make a man what is commonly called a man of the world, fitted to deal with the affairs of the world. [8]

[1] D.N.B.   [2] Studies in Contemporary Biography 177.
[3] Ibid 177-178.   [4] Memoirs 180, 186.   [5] Bryce, op. cit. 178.
[6] An illustration is his dictum in *Farhall v. Farhall* (1871) L.R. 7 Ch. at p. 128 that "no contract can be made with an executor which will not charge him personally".   [7] Bryce, op. cit. 178 n.
[8] *The Times*, June 15, 1881, cited Veeder, A Century of Judicature, Essays, A.A.L.H. i 802.

Lord Sumner praises his power "of terse and clear enunciation of principles".[1] And there is a passage in his judgment in the case of *Salvin v. North Brancepeth Coal Co.*[2] which shows that he had considerable gifts. He was stating the rule that substantial present damage must be proved before an action could be brought for nuisance, and in the course of his statement he said:

It would have been wrong, as it seems to me, for this Court in the reign of Henry VI to have interfered with the further use of sea coal in London, because it had been ascertained to their satisfaction, that by the reign of Queen Victoria both white and red roses would have ceased to bloom in the Temple Gardens. If some picturesque haven opens its arms to invite the commerce of the world, it is not for this Court to forbid the embrace, although the fruit of it should be the sights, and sounds, and smells of a common seaport and ship building town, which would drive the Dryads and their masters from their ancient solitudes.

TURNER

Turner (1798-1867) [3] did good work on the commission whose work was the foundation of the Chancery Procedure Act of 1852. He and Knight-Bruce made a very satisfactory court of appeal— his steadiness and gravity contrasting well with Knight-Bruce's vivacity and dry humour.[4] One of his best known expositions of the law is his clear statement in the case of *Milroy v. Lord* [5] of the conditions of the validity of a voluntary settlement. He was jealous in preserving his court's jurisdiction. Following Eldon,[6] he denied the rule, which had once prevailed,[7] that the assumption by courts of law of a jurisdiction once exercised by the court of Chancery could narrow the sphere of equity.[8] On the contrary, where necessary he helped to expand the jurisdiction of the court to meet new needs.

[1] D.N.B.
[2] (1874) L.R. 9 Ch. at pp. 709-710; see Holdsworth, Essays in Law and History 229.   [3] D.N.B.
[4] Selborne, Memorials, Personal and Political i 44, said that "he was a first rate judge; patient, painstaking, and accurate".
[5] (1862) 4 De G.F. and J. at pp. 274-275.
[6] Vol. xii 596-597.   [7] Ibid 595 and n. 3.
[8] "It is new to me that the creation of jurisdiction in courts of law can oust the jurisdiction of this court in matters originally within its cognisance", *Jenner v. Morris* (1861) 3 De G.F. and J. at p. 56.

ROLT

Rolt (1804-71),[1] like many other successful lawyers, was a self-made man. As he says in his memoirs, he was educated at a "common commercial school" till he was fourteen and then was "placed behind the counter of a shop in Oxford Street", and left to shift for himself.[2] He educated himself, and managed to save enough money to get called to the bar in 1837. He soon acquired a practice, took silk in 1846, and entered Parliament in the conservative interest in 1857. In 1862 he got Parliament to pass what was known as Rolt's Act,[3] which was a step towards the fusion of the jurisdiction of the courts of law and equity. In 1866 he was made Attorney-General. He helped Disraeli to carry his Reform Act of 1867, but otherwise he made no great figure in Parliament. He was made a Lord Justice in July 1867. But his private practice and his duties as Attorney-General had overtaxed his strength.[4] An attack of paralysis compelled him to resign in February 1868. He died in June 1871. Rolt was a skilful advocate and a good equity lawyer. But his knowledge of other branches of law does not seem to have been great. An opinion he gave as Attorney-General as to what constitutes an unlawful assembly states the law very inaccurately.[5] But his memoirs, which have been recently published, are very valuable to legal historians because they throw light on the legal life of his day, and give valuable sketches of some of his contemporaries which we get nowhere else. Instances are his accounts of two eminent Chancery reporters, Jacob [6] and James Russell.

SELWYN

Rolt was succeeded by Selwyn (1813-1869) who was the son of the reporter.[7] He was a distinguished Chancery practitioner, and represented the University of Cambridge in the House of Commons.[8] He was a sound, but not a very distinguished judge.

---

[1] Memoirs of Sir John Rolt, published by the Inner Temple; D.N.B.
[2] Memoirs 124.
[3] 25, 26 Victoria c. 42; Memoirs 181-186; vol. xv 124.
[4] Memoirs 173.
[5] Ibid 159; he notes at p. 163 that Thring had questioned the correctness of his statement of the law.   [6] Vol. xiii 440.
[7] Vol. xiii 437.   [8] D.N.B.

His most eminent pupil, Lord Lindley, has preserved one of his sayings to the effect that it was the duty of a trustee to commit "judicious" breaches of trust.[1]

GIFFARD

Giffard (1813-70) [2] had a leading equity practice in Page Wood's court. He succeeded Page Wood as Vice-Chancellor in 1868, and later in the same year he succeeded him as Lord Justice. James L. J. said of him that his intellect was acute, his judgment sound, and his knowledge of legal principles was unsurpassed.[3]

[1] *Perrins v. Bellamy* [1899] 1 Ch. at p. 798.
[2] D.N.B.   [3] *The Times*, July 16, 1870.

IX
THE CIVILIANS

THE CIVILIANS

I pass now to those parts of the law which fell within the sphere of the civilians' practice, but which, before the end of this period, had come to form part of the practice of the common law and equity bars.

In a preceding volume I have described the professional organization of the civilians.[1] We have seen that statutes of 1857 [2] and 1859 [3] merged the advocates and proctors who practised in the ecclesiastical courts and the court of Admiralty with the barristers, attorneys and solicitors who practised in the courts of common law and equity.[4] It is true that for some time longer a King's Advocate and a King's Proctor continued to be appointed. But we have seen that the post of King's Advocate was not filled after 1872,[5] and that the post of King's Proctor is combined with the post of Treasury Solicitor.[6] Nevertheless just as the differences between law and equity necessitated a *de facto* separation between the common law and equity bars, which have survived the Judicature Acts,[7] so the differences between those bodies of law which formerly fell within the sphere of the civilians' practice and both common law and equity, necessitated a *de facto* separation between the common law and equity practitioners and those who practised in the probate, divorce, and admiralty courts.

I shall given an account, first, of the judges of the court of Admiralty; secondly, of the judges of the ecclesiastical courts; thirdly, of the judges of the probate and divorce courts; and fourthly of some of the members of the Judicial Committee of the Privy Council to which, as we have seen,[8] appeals lay from the court of Admiralty and the ecclesiastical courts.

---

[1] Vol. xii 6-8, 46-51.
[2] 20, 21 Victoria c. 77 §§ 40-45.   [3] 22, 23 Victoria c. 6.
[4] Vol. xii 6, ibid at p. 77 mention should have been made of the amalgamation of the proctors with the attorneys and solicitors by the Act of 1857, 20, 21 Victoria c. 77 §§ 43-45.   [5] Vol. xii 6 n. 5.
[6] Ibid 13.   [7] Ibid 604-605.   [8] Vol. i 518.

JUDGES OF THE COURT OF ADMIRALTY

The judges of the court of Admiralty during this period were Nicholl (1833-38), Lushington (1838-67), and R. J. Phillimore (1867-83). All of them were also at different periods of their careers judges of some of the ecclesiastical courts.

With Nicholl, whose judicial career began in the period 1792-1832, I have already dealt.[1]

LUSHINGTON

His successor, Stephen Lushington (1782-1873),[2] was a more brilliant lawyer than Nicholl; Westbury, when asked who was the best judge he had ever known, put Lyndhurst first and Lushington second.[3] He had better opportunities than his predecessor of leaving his mark upon the branches of law which fell within the jurisdiction of the court of Admiralty. His tenure of the office of judge was much longer; during that tenure the jurisdiction of the court was enlarged by the Legislature;[4] and the outbreak of the Crimean War gave him an opportunity of exercising the prize jurisdiction of his court. In the sphere of that part of ecclesiastical law which is concerned with the doctrines of the Church of England, the differences of opinion which arose out of the impact of new scientific discoveries and of new criticism of the Bible, and out of the divergencies of opinion between low, broad, and high churchmen, gave rise to more cases upon questions of doctrine than had come before the courts during the preceding century.

Lushington was educated at Eton and Christ Church, Oxford, and gained a Fellowship at All Souls' College, Oxford, in 1802. He was called to the bar by the Inner Temple in 1806, and in 1808 became a member of Doctors' Commons. He was a member of the House of Commons from 1806 to 1808, and from 1820 to 1841. He was a consistent Whig, and, in his later days, he developed some radical tendencies. He was a consistent opponent of the slave trade, and a supporter of Roman Catholic emancipation and Parliamentary reform; and in 1833 he supported motions for the

---

[1] Vol. xiii 691-696. [2] D.N.B.
[3] Atlay, Victorian Chancellors i 85 n. 3.
[4] Vol. i 558-559; vol. xv 127.

ballot and triennial Parliaments. In 1840 he supported a motion
for the abolition of capital punishment, and in 1841 a bill for the
abolition of church rates. It was in the years between 1808 and
1820 that he was building up his reputation as a lawyer. In 1820
he was retained as one of the counsel for Queen Caroline, and
made an eloquent speech in her defence. She appointed him one
of her executors, and he attended her funeral at Brunswick. He
was also counsel for Mrs. Serres, who pretended to be the daughter
of the Duke of Cumberland, when she claimed a legacy under the
will of George III.[1] He was appointed judge of the consistory
court of the Bishop of London in 1828, and judge of the court of
Admiralty in 1838. In 1858, on the resignation of Dodson, he
became Dean of the Arches and Master of the Faculties. He
resigned his offices as judge of the court of Admiralty and Dean
of the Arches in 1867; but he retained the office of Master of the
Faculties till his death in 1873.

Lushington's contributions to the development of the law are
in the sphere of maritime law, prize law, and ecclesiastical law.

Maritime law

We have seen that an Act of 1840 had given the court of
Admiralty jurisdiction over claims of the mortgagees of a ship,
over the title to ships, and over all questions of salvage services
whether or not they were rendered on the high seas;[2] that an Act
of 1850 had given it an extended jurisdiction in cases of piracy;[3]
and that in 1861 its jurisdiction had been still further extended
to certain claims for building or equipping ships, for damage to
cargo, for damage caused by a ship, and for wages and disburse-
ments by the master of a ship.[4] In addition, some of the clauses
of the Merchant Shipping Act, 1854 [5] had added to its jurisdiction.
These statutes put the jurisdiction of the court on its modern
basis; and it was Lushington's decisions upon the cases which
arose under these Acts which laid the foundation of many of the
modern principles of maritime law. He so interpreted these
statutes that he brought the new law to which these new pieces
of jurisdiction gave rise into harmony with the old law of his
court. It was a task which required a thorough knowledge of the
old principles, a capacity to adapt them to new uses, and a power
to give a clear and reasonable interpretation of the wide and
often vague provisions of those statutes. These powers were
shown by Lushington in very many cases, and entitled him to be

[1] *In the goods of George III* (1822) 1 Add. Eccl. 255.
[2] 3, 4 Victoria c. 65; vol. i 558-559.   [3] 13, 14 Victoria c. 26.
[4] 24, 25 Victoria c. 10.   [5] 17, 18 Victoria c. 104; vol. xiv 93.

regarded as one of the ablest of the Admiralty judges of this period.
It is true that a few of his decisions have not been approved. For
instance, his view that the Act of 1840 gave a lien on the ship for
the supply of necessaries has been disapproved by the House of
Lords;[1] and his view that a sale of a British ship by the master,
which was valid by the law of the place where the ship was sold,
did not pass the property in the ship, was disapproved by the court
of Exchequer Chamber.[2] But for the most part his decisions have
been accepted as sound law. The following are a very few out of
their very large number.

Two decisions define the rights of salvors and the circumstances in which a salvage reward was due.[3] In the case of *The
Araminta*[4] he held, following the case of *Stilk v. Myrick*,[5] that a
promise to give the wages of seamen who had deserted to those
who had not, if they worked the ship home, was void for want of
consideration, and that therefore, if these wages had been paid
over, the amount paid could be deducted from the wages payable
at the end of the voyage. In the case of *The William F. Safford*[6]
he considered the rule as to the priority of various claims against
a ship—wages, holders of a bottomry bond, and those who have
supplied necessaries. In the case of *The Victor*[7] he laid down the
rule that the cargo laden on a ship which had damaged another
by a collision is not liable for the damages:

Damage is said to be done by the ship, but this is a mere form of expression; the truth being that it is done by the master or crew employed by
the owner of a ship, who is therefore responsible for their conduct. But
the master and crew are not the agents nor the servants of the owner of
the cargo; upon what principle, then, are the owners of the cargo
responsible?[8]

The same principle was applied in the case of *The Milan*.[9] In that
case Lushington rightly refused to follow the case of *Thorogood
v. Bryan*;[10] but he refused to allow the owner of the cargo to
recover the whole damages from one of the two delinquent ships.[11]
In the case of *The Magellan Pirates*[12] there is an interesting
discussion of the crime of piracy at common law.

[1] *The Flecha* (1854) Sp. Ecc. and Ad. at p. 441; *The Henrich Bjorn* (1886) 11
App. Cas. at p. 279.
    [2] *The Segredo, otherwise Eliza Cornish* (1853) 1 Sp. Ecc. and Ad. 36; *Cammel v.
Sewell* (1860) 5 H. and N. at pp. 745-746.
    [3] *The E.U.* (1853) 1 Sp. Ecc. and Ad. 63; *The Silver Bullion* (1854) 2 Sp. Ecc.
and Ad. 70.   [4] (1854) 1 Sp. Ecc. and Ad. 224.
    [5] (1809) 2 Camp. 317.   [6] (1860) Lush. 69.   [7] (1860) Lush. 72.
    [8] Ibid at p. 76.   [9] Ibid at p. 388.
    [10] (1849) 8 C.B. 115, overruled in *The Bernina* (1888) 13 App. Cas. 1.
    [11] See *The Devonshire* [1912] A.C. at pp. 646-647 for some criticism of this ruling.
    [12] (1853) 1 Sp. Ecc. and Ad. 81.

Prize law

We have seen that in the case of *The Franciska* Lushington recognized the great authority of both Lord Stowell and Sir William Grant [1] upon questions of prize law; and in the case of *The Leucade* [2] he said "my first guide will be the principles adopted by Lord Stowell". In very few cases did he question the authority of Stowell's rulings. In one case he dissented from his ruling as to the evidence upon which the court could sit;[3] and in another case he pointed out that he had given a judgment in ignorance of the existence of a statute of 1812 which exempted owners from liability for the default of licensed pilots.[4] It should be noted that he agreed with Stowell in his view,[5] which was overruled by *The Zamora*,[6] that the Crown by its prerogative could alter the rules of prize law.[7]

Many of the principles of prize law are examined and explained in Lushington's judgments. The case of *The Franciska* [8] is a mine of information on the subject of blockade. Several of his decisions deal with the question of the validity of the sale or disposal of enemy ships to neutrals.[9] The court, he said, must not "sin against a great principle of prize law by prohibiting to neutrals a transference of property perfectly lawful in time of peace"; but it was entitled to make certain, especially if one of the parties was an enemy, that the transfer was made in good faith.[10] And, since a prize court always looks at the real intentions of the parties and the substance of the transaction, it will hold that if a transfer of a British ship to an enemy is merely fictitious and made to avoid seizure, and the ship is afterwards captured, it must be restored to the owners.[11] But since all trading with the enemy is illegal, the sale of a ship by an enemy to a British subject is illegal and void.[12] In the case of *The Ida* [13] he held that in the prize court the test is who is the legal owner of the cargo, and that the rights of lienors or pledgees must be disregarded. In the case of *The Aina* [14] he

---

[1] (1854) 2 Sp. Ecc. and Ad. at pp. 114-115.
[2] (1855) 2 Sp. Ecc. and Ad. at p. 230.
[3] *The Aline and Fanny* (1856) Sp. P.C. at pp. 332-333.
[4] *The Wild Ranger* (1862) Lush. at p. 561.
[5] *The Fox* (1811) Edw. at pp. 312-314.   [6] [1916] 2 A.C. at pp. 95-96.
[7] *The Neptune* (1855) Sp. P.C. at p. 286; see vol. i 566-568.
[8] (1854) 2 Sp. Ecc. and Ad. 113.
[9] E.g. *The Rapid* (1854) Sp. P.C. 80; *The Baltica* (1855) ibid 264—reversed by the Privy Council (1857) 11 Moo. P.C. 141.
[10] *The Benedict* (1855) Sp. P.C. 314.
[11] *The Ocean Bride* (1854) 2 Sp. Ecc. and Ad. 8 at pp. 20-23.
[12] *The Neptune* (1855) Sp. P.C. 281.
[13] (1854) 1 Sp. Ecc. and Ad. 331; followed in *The Odessa* [1916] 1 A.C. 145.
[14] (1854) 1 Sp. Ecc. and Ad. 313; for commercial domicil, see vol. ix 99-102.

emphasized the fact that it was the commercial domicil of the claimant which was the important question, so that a neutral trading in an enemy's country must be regarded as an enemy; and in *The Primus* [1] and *The Industrie* [2] he held that a neutral's share in a ship sailing under the enemy's flag was forfeited.[3] In the case of *The Ionian Ships*,[4] he defined, for the first time, the legal position of the inhabitants of a protected state. Lastly, in the case of *The Banda and Kirwee Booty* [5] he performed very skilfully the difficult task of determining the principles upon which booty captured on land by the army was to be distributed. This jurisdiction had been given to the court of Admiralty by the Act of 1840 which directed that the court shall proceed "as in cases of prize of war". Lushington in his very elaborate judgment adapted the prize law on the subject of joint capture to this new field.

Ecclesiastical law

Lushington's decisions cover the whole field of ecclesiastical law. In the sphere of *divorce* his views as to acts which constitute legal cruelty have been followed;[6] and in the case of *Davidson v. Davidson* [7] he laid down the principle that proof of attachment, criminal intention, and opportunity creates a presumption that adultery has been committed. In the sphere of *probate* one of the most important of his decisions in the Privy Council was in the case of *Cutto v. Gilbert*,[8] which dealt with some of the rules and presumptions as to the revocation of a will. It was a case in which the testator made a will in 1825, and another in 1852 which was not forthcoming at his death. The contents of the latter will were not known, except that it was described as a "last will". It was held that the burden of proving that the later will revoked the earlier was on those who propounded the later will, that the execution of a later will, although it was called a "last will", was not sufficient to prove revocation of the earlier will, and that a later will, the contents of which are not known, cannot revoke an earlier will. In the sphere of that part of *ecclesiastical law* which relates to the Church of England and its discipline and doctrine, the cases of *Long v. Bishop of Cape Town* [9] and *In re Lord Bishop of Natal*,[10] in which he took part, are important both in ecclesiastical

---

[1] (1854) 1 Sp. Ecc. and Ad. 353.   [2] (1854) Ibid 444.
[3] These decisions were followed in *The Marie Glaeser* [1914] P. 218.
[4] (1855) 2 Sp. Ecc. and Ad. 212.   [5] (1866) L.R. 1 Ad. and Ecc. 109.
[6] *Ciocci v. Ciocci* (1853) 1 Sp. Ecc. and Ad. 121; *Chesnutt v. Chesnutt* (1854) ibid 196; *Browning v. Browning* [1911] P. 161.
[7] (1856) Deane 132.   [8] (1854) 1 Sp. Ecc. and Ad. 417.
[9] (1863) 1 Moo. P.C.N.S. 411 at pp. 461-462.
[10] (1864) 3 Moo. P.C.N.S. 115 at pp. 152-154; see vol. xi 242 and n. 2.

and in constitutional law, for they define the position of the Church of England and its members in colonies where there is no church established by law, and laid down the rule that the ecclesiastical law of England and the ecclesiastical courts were not imported into these colonies. But in this sphere it was the cases dealing with the question of church rates, and cases dealing with the doctrines of the Church of England which excited the greatest interest then, and are of permanent importance as statements of the law upon the matters with which they deal.

The hostility of the radical party to the established church, and the jealousy of their allies, the Protestant dissenters, of its privileges, was the cause of the growing feeling against compulsory church rates. That feeling resulted in much litigation in which the legality of a rate or liability to pay it was disputed. The most famous of these cases was the *Braintree Case* [1] in which Lushington, as Chancellor of the diocese of London, held that where a rate had been rejected by a majority of the parishioners, and then, the majority having left, the minority carried the rate, the rate so carried was not legally imposed. His decision was reversed by Jenner-Fust, the Dean of the Arches, [2] and that reversal was held to be good law by the courts of Queen's Bench [3] and Exchequer Chamber. [4] But the House of Lords, in accordance with the opinion of a bare majority of the judges, [5] reversed these decisions, and, in effect upheld Lushington's opinion. [6]

The cases dealing with the doctrines of the Church of England were, as we have seen, caused by the differences of opinion between different parties in the Church. The three most important of these cases in which Lushington took part were *Gorham v. Bishop of Exeter*, [7] *Heath v. Burder*, [8] and *Bishop of Salisbury v. Williams*. [9] In the first of these cases he held in a very learned judgment that Gorham's views upon infant baptism were contrary to the doctrines of the Church of England. This decision was reversed by the Privy Council, Knight-Bruce L.J. dissenting; [10] and it was this reversal which decided Manning that he could no longer remain a member of the Church of England. In the second of these cases he held that sermons preached by Heath were

---

[1] *Velez v. Gosling* (1843) 3 Curt. 253.   [2] Ibid at pp. 304 *et seq.*
[3] *Gosling v. Veley* (1847) 7 Q.B. 406.   [4] (1850) 12 Q.B. 328.
[5] Four judges thought that the rate was valid, five judges thought that it was invalid, and one expressed no opinion as to its validity but agreed with the majority on a technical point of procedure.
[6] (1853) 4 H.L.C. 679.   [7] (1849-50) Moore, Special Report.
[8] (1860-62) 15 Moo. P.C. 1.   [9] (1862-63) 2 Moo. P.C.N.S. 390.
[10] This is one of the three cases in which any mention is made of a dissenting opinion in the Privy Council, see vol. i 519.

contrary to the Thirty-nine Articles; and this decision was upheld by the Privy Council. In the third of these cases which, as we have seen,[1] arose out of the publication entitled *Essays and Reviews*, his decision against the appellant Williams for propounding heretical doctrine as to the inspiration of the Bible and eternal punishment was reversed. Lushington's judgments in these cases prove his competence as an ecclesiastical lawyer; and it should be noted that in the last mentioned case the Archbishops of Canterbury and York did not concur in the reversal of his decision as to certain of the articles charged against the appellant.

PHILLIMORE

Lushington's successor as judge of the court of Admiralty and Dean of the Arches, Sir Robert Phillimore (1810-85),[2] was a distinguished representative of a famous legal family. He was the son of Joseph Phillimore, an able civilian advocate of the Admiralty, and Regius Professor of Civil Law at Oxford, who, as we have seen,[3] edited two series of reports. He was educated at Westminster and Christ Church, Oxford: in 1839 he became an advocate at Doctors' Commons; and in 1841 he was called to the bar by the Middle Temple. He soon got a good practice in the ecclesiastical courts. In 1855 he succeeded his father as advocate of the Admiralty, in 1858 he took silk, and in 1862 became Queen's Advocate. In that capacity his knowledge of international law, which was displayed in his book on that subject,[4] stood him in good stead, for many delicate problems were set to him and to the law officers by the events of the American Civil War. From 1852-57 he was a member of the House of Commons. He supported Aberdeen's ministry, proposed bills to amend the law as to simony and next presentations, and carried Acts to amend the procedure of the ecclesiastical courts,[5] and to abolish their jurisdiction over defamation.[6] On his own subjects—ecclesiastical and international law—he was an effective speaker. In 1867 he succeeded Lushington as judge of the court of Admiralty and Dean of the Arches,[7] In 1871 and 1872 he also held the office of Judge Advocate-

[1] Above 78.   [2] D.N.B.   [3] Vol. xiii 441.   [4] Vol. xv 330, 331.
[5] 17, 18 Victoria c. 47.   [6] 18, 19 Victoria c. 41; vol. i 620.
[7] Lushington retained the office of Master of the Faculties till his death. Since the main emolument of the Dean of the Arches was derived from the Mastership of the Faculties, he served as Dean practically without pay till Lushington's death in 1873.

General. Section eight of the Judicature Act, 1875,[1] which provided that if the judge of the court of Admiralty resigned his ecclesiastical offices he should have the same rank, salary and pension as the other judges, made it advisable for him to resign his position of Dean of the Arches, but he continued to sit as a judge in the Probate, Divorce and Admiralty Division of the High Court until he resigned that office in 1883. He died in 1885.

Lord Sumner has said of him [2] that "he belonged to a class of lawyers that has now passed away. He was a scholar both in classical and in modern languages, and a jurist of wide reading. As an advocate he displayed great industry and tact, and he had a polished address and a considerable gift of eloquence. . . . On the bench he was dignified, painstaking, and courteous; and he delivered a series of important judgments full of historical and legal knowledge, and luminously expressed." But more of his judgments in important cases were reversed than Lushington's, so that, though they have many merits, it cannot be said that he was as sound a lawyer as his predecessor. Nevertheless they make an important contribution to the development of the law; and, as we have seen,[3] he made another important contribution by his writings on many various topics.

His main contributions to the law as a judge are in maritime law, divorce and probate law, and ecclesiastical law.

Maritime law

Several of the more important cases decided by Phillimore on this topic were connected with or raised questions relating to international law, public and private. In the case of *The Teutonia* [4] he held that if the performance of the contract of carriage was made illegal by the outbreak of war, the contract was at an end; and that if the goods were delivered at another port and there accepted, a *pro rata* freight must be paid. The two cases of *The Charkieh* [5] and *The Parlement Belge* [6] raised the question of the immunity of foreign sovereigns and their property from the process of an English court. In the first of these cases the court held that historical and other evidence showed that the Khedive of Egypt, the owner of *The Charkieh*, was not a sovereign; and that, if he was a sovereign, his immunity extended only to property "connected with the *jus coronae* of the sovereign", so that it would extend to a public ship but not to a merchant ship; and that if, as in this case, the sovereign's ship was engaged in trade, such

---

[1] 38, 39 Victoria c. 77.   [2] D.N.B.   [3] Vol. xv 330, 331.
[4] (1871) L.R. 3 Ad. and Ecc. 395.   [5] (1873) L.R. 4 Ad. and Acc. 59.
[6] (1879) 4 P.D. 129.

engagement in trade amounted to an implied waiver of the sovereign's immunity. In the second of these cases he held that a ship carrying mails and merchandise and belonging to the King of the Belgians, although given by treaty the privileges of a public ship, was not entitled to have privileges and was therefore amenable to the process of the court. Following the first of these cases, he held that such a ship had not by the rules of international law the immunity of a public ship; and that a treaty which gave it that immunity was inoperative, because it was a treaty which, without the consent of Parliament, altered the rights of British subjects and so changed the law. This decision was reversed by the Court of Appeal [1] on the ground that the property of a foreign sovereign was immune from legal process, and that, in the case of a ship, this immunity was not lost by the fact that the ship was engaged in trade. The court therefore disapproved some of Phillimore's reasoning in the case of *The Charkieh*.[2] Moreover, it was said in the case of *Mighell v. Sultan of Johore* [3] that he ought not in that case, to have looked at any other evidence as to the existence of the status of sovereignty than the statement of the Secretary of State. Nevertheless his judgments in both these cases show a profound knowledge of the rules of English law, of foreign law, and of international law, and in these and other cases a power of criticizing rules of English law by the light of this knowledge;[4] and his view that a treaty which varies the rights of British subjects, and so in effect changes English law, cannot be enforced by English courts, has been approved by the Privy Council in the case of *Walker v. Baird*.[5]

His decision in the case of *The Halley* [6] upon an important and a new point in private international law, though learned and well reasoned, was reversed by the Privy Council,[7] which laid it down that an act which is wrongful by the law of the place where it is done is not actionable in England unless it is also actionable by English law; and, conversely, his decision in the case of *The Mary Moxham* [8] that a person liable by English, but not liable by the law of the place where the wrongful act was committed, could be made liable in an English court, was also reversed.[9] As we shall now see, some of his most important decisions in divorce cases were also decisions upon this branch of the law.

---

[1] (1880) 5 P.D. 197. [2] Ibid at pp. 215-217, 219-220. [3] [1894] 1 Q.B. at p. 158.
[4] Thus in *The Teutonia* (1871) L.R. 3 Ad. and Ecc. at p. 44, he said of the rule in *Paradine v. Jane* (1648) Aleyn 26, vol. viii 64, 353, n.l. that it was "not in harmony with the jurisprudence of any other European state".
[5] [1892] A.C. 491.   [6] (1867) L.R. 2 Ad. and Ecc. 3.
[7] (1868) L.R. 2 P.C. 193; Cheshire, Private International Law, 3rd ed., 373-375.
[8] (1875) 1 P.D. 43.   [9] (1876) 1 P.D. 107.

Divorce and probate law

His decision in the case of *Sottomayor v. de Barros*,[1] that the *lex loci contractus* governs the validity of a marriage, so that incapacities existing by the law of the domicil of the parties must be disregarded, was reversed by the Court of Appeal.[2] In the case of *Le Sueur v. Le Sueur*,[3] he held that a deserted wife could not sue her husband in England if he was neither resident not domiciled in England. His decision in the case of *Niboyet v. Niboyet*[4] that an English court had no jurisdiction to dissolve the marriage of persons not domiciled in England, though reversed by the Court of Appeal,[5] was in effect approved by the Privy Council,[6] and is now regarded as settled law.[7] Most of the probate cases came before the President of the Probate, Divorce and Admiralty Division and not before Phillimore. One of his decisions—*In the goods of Tharp*[8]—which was upheld in a learned judgment by Jessel M.R., decided that since the Judicature Act the Probate Division has jurisdiction to decide whether a married woman has separate estate, and, if she had, to grant probate of her will limited to that separate estate.

Ecclesiastical law

The same causes which had brought cases upon doctrinal questions before the ecclesiastical courts before Phillimore's predecessor[9] continued to operate during the tenure of his office as Dean of the Arches. In his very long and elaborate judgment in the first case of *Martin v. Mackonochie*[10] he considered the question of the legality of certain ceremonial practices used by the defendant in the communion service; and in the second case between the same parties he considered the legality of other practices.[11] In the case of *Elphinstone v. Purchas*[12] he considered the interpretation of the ornaments rubric of the Book of Common Prayer, and the legality of various rites and ceremonies used by the defendant; and in the case of *Sheppard v. Bennett*[13] he considered the question of the limits within which a clergyman is allowed to affirm the doctrine of a real presence in the consecrated elements in the communion service. In the case of *Boyd v. Phillpott*,[14] he

[1] (1877) 2 P.D. 81. [2] (1877) 3 P.D. 1. [3] (1876) 1 P.D. 139.
[4] (1878) 3 P.D. 52. [5] (1878) 4 P.D. 1.
[6] *Le Mesurier v. Le Mesurier* [1895] A.C. 519.
[7] Cheshire, Private International Law, 5th ed. 366, 368.
[8] (1878) 3 P.D. 76. [9] Above 144 *et seq.*
[10] (1868) L.R. 2 Ad. and Ecc. 116, at pp. 121-247.
[11] (1874) L.R. 4 Ad. and Ecc. 279.
[12] (1870) 3 Ad. and Ecc. 66. [13] (1870) 3 Ad. and Ecc. 167.
[14] (1874) 4 Ad. and Ecc. 297; L.R. 6 P.C. 435.

considered the question of the legality of a reredos erected in Exeter cathedral, and the jurisdiction of the Bishop to order its removal.

JUDGES OF THE ECCLESIASTICAL COURTS

The most notable judges of the ecclesiastical courts were the Deans of the Arches and judges of the Prerogative Court.[1] The three men who held this office before 1857, when their probate and divorce jurisdiction was turned over to the state, were Nicholl (1809-34), Jenner-Fust (1834-52) and Dodson (1852-57).

JENNER-FUST

Of Nicholl's career, I have already spoken. His successor, Sir Herbert Jenner-Fust (1778-1852),[2] was a member of Trinity Hall, Cambridge. He was called to the bar by Gray's Inn in 1800, and admitted as an advocate at Doctors' Commons in 1803. From 1828 to 1834 he was King's Advocate, and in the latter year he was appointed the judge of the Prerogative and Arches courts. In 1843 he became, like Hervey [3] in the sixteenth and Marriott [4] in the eighteenth centuries, Master of Trinity Hall—thus preserving the old connection between Trinity Hall and Doctors' Commons.[5] He was regarded as an authority on international law, and his decisions show that he was a very sound ecclesiastical lawyer. He died on February 20, 1852.[6]

Some of his decisions on *doctrinal questions*, which aroused considerable interest at the time when they were given, are notable contributions to this branch of the law. As we have seen, the progress of science and the reactions of that progress upon

---

[1] For these courts, see vol. i 601, 602.
[2] D.N.B.; he added Fust to his name in 1842 on succeeding to the estate of his cousin, Sir John Fust.
[3] Vol. iv 235.　　　　[4] Vol. xii 674.　　　　[5] Vol. iv 235-236; vol. xii 47.
[6] 2 Rob. Ecc. 422 n; during his illness his successor Dodson acted for him in the court of the Arches, and Lushington acted for him in the Prerogative court; Lushington cleared off the arrears, and, after Dodson's appointment, decided those cases in which Dodson had been retained as counsel, ibid 419 n.

theology, as well as the controversies excited by the Oxford Movement, had brought doctrinal questions to the front. Two of the most famous of these cases were concerned with the doctrine of baptism. In the case of *Mastin v. Escott*[1] he held that an infant not baptized by a clergyman of the Church of England but by a Wesleyan minister, was not an unbaptized person, and that a clergyman could not refuse to perform the burial service over such a person on the ground that he was unbaptized. This decision was upheld by the Privy Council.[2] But in the second and more famous of these cases—*Gorham v. Bishop of Exeter*[3]—which turned on the doctrine of baptismal regeneration, his very learned judgment was, as we have seen, reversed by the Privy Council.[4] In the case of *Breeks v. Woolfrey*[5] he held that prayers for the dead are not prohibited by the Church of England.

As judge of the Prerogative Court the Wills Act of 1837 set him a number of new problems in the law as to *probate*. In the case of *The Countess Ferraris v. Marquis of Hertford*[6] he held *inter alia* that a testator cannot, by a direction in his will, give validity to future testamentary papers not executed in accordance with the Wills Act. This strict interpretation of the provision of the Wills Act that the testator's signature must be at "the foot or end" of the will,[7] the reason for which he explained in the case of *Smee v. Bryer*,[8] was so inconvenient that the Legislature was obliged to intervene.[9] On the question whether the will has been duly executed, e.g. whether the testator signed before the witnesses, he held that the court can draw its own conclusions from all the circumstances, and need not regard the statements of the witnesses as conclusive if they do not appear to recollect the facts accurately.[10] In the case of *Ilott v. Genge*[11] he made it clear that the witnesses must attest the signature of the testator, so that they must either see him sign, or, if he has already signed, he must acknowledge his signature to them. In the case of *Hobbs v. Knight*[12] he held that a testator who had cut out his signature had revoked his will, for "it is difficult to comprehend when that which is essential to the existence of a thing is destroyed, how the thing itself can exist";[13] and in the case of *Townley v. Watson*[14] he

[1] (1840) 2 Curt. 692.   [2] (1842) 4 Moo. P.C. 104.
[3] (1849) 2 Rob. Ecc. 1.   [4] Moo. Special Report; above 145.
[5] (1838) 1 Curt. 880.
[6] (1843) 3 Curt. 468; the defendant was the original of Thackeray's Marquis of Steyne and Disraeli's Duke of Monmouth.
[7] 7 William IV and 1 Victoria c. 26 § 9.
[8] (1848) 1 Rob. Ecc. at pp. 623-624.   [9] 15, 16 Victoria c. 24.
[10] *Cooper v. Bockett* (1843) 3 Curt. 648; (1846) 4 Moo. P.C. 419; see also *Blake v. Knight* (1843) 3 Curt. 547.   [11] (1842) 3 Curt. 160; 4 Moo. P.C. 265.
[12] (1838) 1 Curt. 768.   [13] At p. 777.   [14] (1844) 3 Curt. 761.

held that if passages in a will are obliterated by a testator *animo revocandi*, so that they are not legible without extrinsic aid, they are revoked. In the case of *Barry v. Butlin* [1] he explained the law as to the presumptions made by the law, and the manner in which they must be rebutted, when a legatee propounds a will which he has drawn. His judgment in the case of *Drummond v. Parish* [2] is the leading case on the subject of soldiers' wills. As a judge of the Arches Court he gave a few decisions on points of *divorce law*, e.g. in the case of *Dysart v. Dysart* he considered the legal definition of cruelty. But the majority of these cases came before Lushington as the judge of the Consistory Court of London, since this was the court in which most of the important divorce cases were tried. [3]

DODSON

Jenner-Fust's successor was Sir John Dodson (1780-1858). [4] Dodson was educated at Merchant Taylors' School and Oriel College, Oxford. He was admitted as an advocate at Doctors' Commons in 1808. He was a Tory member of Parliament, 1819-23, and became advocate to the Admiralty in 1829 and King's Advocate in 1834. In 1841 he became Master of the Faculties, and in 1849 Vicar-General. In 1852 he became judge of the Prerogative and Arches Courts, and held those offices till the jurisdiction over probate and divorce was taken from the Prerogative and Arches Courts in 1857. [5] He died in 1858. We have seen that he was the editor of a series of Admiralty reports. [6] His decisions were sometimes reversed, [7] but on the whole they show that he was a learned and sound ecclesiastical lawyer.

One remarkable case which came before him concerned the will of Napoleon Bonaparte. The Secretary of State applied for the delivery up of the will that it might be sent to the French

---

[1] (1837) 1 Curt. 614.   [2] (1843) 3 Curt. 522.

[3] " Suitors in heavy and important cases preferred to have their cases tried in the Consistory Court of London, not only for the advantage of having it heard before an experienced judge and in a Court remarkable for the rapidity of its proceedings, but also to enable them to have it conducted by the London proctors and members of Doctors' Commons Bar, instead of its being tried in the county diocesan courts where they have had no such advantages ", Halsbury, Laws of England (2nd ed.), xi 600 n.(b).

[4] D.N.B.   [5] Above 150; below 153.   [6] Vol. xiii, 432, 441, 679.

[7] E.g. *Cutto v. Gilbert* (1853) 1 Sp. Ecc. and Ad. 276, 417; *Bremer v. Freeman* (1856) Dean. 192, 10 Moo. P.C. 306.

government—an application which was acceded to.[1] In the case of *Clarke v. Scripps* [2] he considered the effect of the mutilation of a will, which as he said depended upon whether an intention to revoke could be inferred from the nature of the mutilation or proved by extrinsic evidence. In the case of *Ekins v. Brown* [3] he explained the law as to paraphernalia; and in the case of *In the goods of Cockayne* [4] he applied the principle of dependent relative revocation. In the sphere of *ecclesiastical law* his most learned judgment was given in the case of *Westerton v. Liddell*,[5] in which he considered the question of the legality of certain ornaments and observances used at the church of St. Paul's, Knightsbridge, and St. Barnabas', Pimlico. His judgment was varied by the Privy Council, but on many points it was affirmed, and it is a mine of historical and legal learning as to the law of these matters.

The Act of 1840 which extended the jurisdiction of the Court of Admiralty had provided that the Dean of the Arches should be able to sit as assistant to the judge of the Admiralty, and amalgamated the bars of the Admiralty and Arches Court.[6] A link was thus created between the two courts, and we have seen that, from 1857 when the probate and divorce business was taken from the ecclesiastical courts and entrusted to a new probate and a new divorce court, the judge of the Court of Admiralty was the Dean of the Arches, till the two offices were separated as the result of the Judicature Act, 1875.[7] That is the reason why in the first series of the Law Reports, 1865-75, the reports of admiralty and ecclesiastical cases are grouped together. A further measure of amalgamation was contemplated by the Acts which established the new probate and divorce courts. The former Act, after providing for the appointment of a judge of the new courts and giving him the status of a puisne judge of a common law court,[8] gave the Crown power to appoint this judge on the next vacancy, to be judge of the Court of Admiralty, or, if he died or resigned first, to appoint the judge of the Court of Admiralty to be judge of the Court of Probate; and it provided that after the union of the two offices they should thenceforth be held by the same person.[9] The latter Act provided that the Lord Chancellor, the chiefs and the senior puisne judges of the three common law courts, and the

---

[1] *In the matter of the will and codicil of the late Emperor Napoleon Bonaparte* (1853) 2 Rob. Ecc. 606.   [2] (1852) 2 Rob. Ecc. 563.
[3] (1854) 1 Sp. Ecc. and Ad. 400; vol. iii 523, 527, 544.
[4] (1856) Deane 177.
[5] Moore, Special Report; he affirmed the very learned judgment of Lushington before whom, as judge of the Consistory Court of London, the case originally came.
[6] 3, 4 Victoria c. 65 §§ 1 and 2.   [7] Above 147.
[8] 20, 21 Victoria c. 77 §§ 5-8; vol. i 630.   [9] § 10.

judge of the Court of Probate should be judges of the Divorce Court,[1] and that the judge of the Court of Probate should be the judge ordinary of the Court with power to exercise alone the jurisdiction given to the Court except in certain defined cases.[2] The result was that jurisdiction in probate and divorce cases came to be exercised by a single judge, and, since the addition of the Admiralty business would have been too much for a single judge, the power to make the judge of the Court of Probate the judge of the Court of Admiralty was not exercised. It is for that reason that in the Law Reports the probate and divorce cases are grouped together in a series separate from the admiralty and ecclesiastical cases.

Having said something of the judges who presided during this period in the admiralty and ecclesiastical courts, I must now say something of the judges who presided over the Probate and Divorce courts in the period between 1857 and 1875.

JUDGES OF THE PROBATE AND DIVORCE COURTS

The judges of the Probate and Divorce Courts during this period were Cresswell (1858-63), Wilde, Lord Penzance (1863-72), and Hannen (1872-91).

CRESSWELL

Of the first judge in ordinary of the Divorce Court and judge of the Probate Court Sir Cresswell Cresswell (1794-1863) I have already said something. We have seen that he was called to the bar by the Inner Temple in 1819, became leader of the Northern Circuit, and took silk in 1834; that he was member for Liverpool in the Conservative interest, 1837-42, and that in the latter year he was made a judge of the Court of Common Pleas, and discharged

---

[1] 20, 21 Victoria c. 85 § 8; vol. i 624; the other judges of the common law courts were added in 1859, 22, 23 Victoria c. 61 § 1.

[2] § 9; the excepted topics were petitions for the dissolution of marriage, applications for new trials, bills of exception, and special cases; these exceptions were got rid of by 21, 22 Victoria c. 108 § 18 and 23, 24 Victoria c. 144 § 1, though he could direct matters to be heard by the full court, ibid § 2.

his duties in that capacity to the satisfaction of all.[1] In 1858 he became the first judge of the Probate and Divorce Court. That position was not an easy one to fill. The difficult task of adapting the ecclesiastical rules of procedure and the ecclesiastical law to the new situation fell upon him; and his success in making this adaptation caused a far larger flow of business to his court than had been anticipated. But he disposed of the business rapidly, and his decisions were so sound that he was only once reversed. Sir Robert Phillimore, then Queen's Advocate, addressing the court after his death, spoke of his "conscientious care and unceasing assiduity" which "so moulded, formed and shaped the practice" of his court that it was able "to discharge the functions for which it had been created". He referred to his tenacious memory, to his power of accurate and logical thought and luminous statement, to his knowledge of the common law, to his swift mastery of the ecclesiastical law and procedure, and to his performance of the difficult task of adapting that law and procedure to a trial by a jury. On July 17, 1863, he was knocked off his horse on Constitution Hill, and died of heart failure twelve days later.

PENZANCE

His successor, James Wilde, Lord Penzance (1816-1899) [2] was the nephew of Lord Truro.[3] He was educated at Winchester and Trinity College, Cambridge, and was called to the bar by the Inner Temple in 1839. He devilled for his uncle, was made counsel to the Commissioners of Customs in 1840, and soon got a good practice on circuit and at Westminster. He took silk in 1835, and in 1860 was made a Baron of the Exchequer. In 1863 he succeeded Cresswell as judge of the Probate and Divorce Court; and it was in those courts that his best work as a judge was done. In 1869 he was raised to the peerage with the title of Lord Penzance. As a peer he supported the disestablishment of the Irish Church, an Act to allow the parties in actions for breach of promise of marriage and divorce proceedings to give evidence,[4] and Acts to abolish imprisonment for debt and to reform the law as to absconding debtors,[5] married women's property,[6] and naturalization.[7] He also supported a bill to legalize marriage with a deceased wife's

---

[1] Vol. xiii 436, 437; Foss, Judges ix 184-187; D.N.B.
[2] D.N.B.   [3] Above 37-39.   [4] 32, 33 Victoria c. 68.
[5] 32, 33 Victoria c. 62.   [6] 33, 34 Victoria c. 93.   [7] 33, 34 Victoria c. 14.

sister. He retired in 1872; but in 1874 he consented to serve as judge under the Public Worship Regulation Act.[1] It was not a comfortable position. His status, and the status of his court, were not defined, and it was not till 1881 that the House of Lords, reversing the Queen's Bench Division, held that he could commit for contempt.[2] The orders of his court were disregarded because the Erastian character of the Act caused the bishops to dislike the court created by it, and many laymen disapproved the policy of prosecuting the ritualists. Moreover, the Act and the court created by it was unnecessary, because the powers conferred on the Court of the Arches by the Church Discipline Act, 1840, were sufficient.[3] It is not surprising therefore that the court came "to be all but deserted". Penzance retired in March, 1899, and died in the following December.

HANNEN

His successor, Sir James Hannen (1821-94),[4] was educated at St. Paul's School and Heidelberg University. He was called to the bar by the Middle Temple in 1848. He succeeded so well at the common law bar that in 1863 he was appointed attorney-general's devil. In 1868 he was appointed a judge of the Court of Queen's Bench, and in 1872 judge of the Probate and Divorce Court. In 1876 he became the President of the Probate, Divorce, and Admiralty Division of the High Court. In 1888 he presided over the Parnell Commission which was composed of himself and Day and A. L. Smith JJ. In 1891 he was appointed a Lord of Appeal in Ordinary, and in 1892 he acted as arbitrator in the Behring Sea fishery dispute between Great Britain and the United States. He died in 1894. Sir Herbert Stephen said of him [5] that his,

personal appearance and manner accorded in the most striking manner with the popular conception of a judge, as a grave, tranquil, impartial, and venerable officer. He had a peculiar gift for making his meaning perfectly clear in the fewest words, and could indicate rebuke by a word or an intonation. He was consequently master of his own court, and of everyone who appeared before him, to an unusual degree, and the business before him was conducted with the happiest combination of deliberation and despatch.

[1] 37, 38 Victoria c. 85, vol. i 613-614.
[2] *Mackonochie v. Lord Penzance* (1881) 6 App. Cas. 424; *Green v. Lord Penzance* (1881) ibid 657; *Enraght v. Lord Penzance* (1882) 7 App. Cas. 240.
[3] Vol. i 613-614; 3, 4 Victoria c. 86.   [4] D.N.B.   [5] Ibid.

These three judges laid the foundations and settled many of the principles and rules of the modern law as to probate and divorce. Let us look at one or two illustrations of their achievements in these two spheres.

Probate. Both Penzance and Hannen held that where a testator has left two or more duly executed testamentary papers the later will not revoke the earlier unless the testator so intended. His intention must be ascertained by looking at the documents to see what his intentions were, and all the papers which carry them out must be admitted to probate.[1] Cresswell held that a joint will, if unrevoked, must be admitted to probate as the last will of the deceased.[2] But one of Penzance's decisions [3] as to the evidence admissible to establish the existence and contents of a lost will was overruled by the decision of Hannen and the Court of Appeal in the case of *Sugden v. Lord St. Leonards*.[4] Penzance's decision in the case of *Parfitt v. Lawless* [5] is the leading case on the difference between the application of the law as to undue influence to legacies and its application to gifts *inter vivos*; and in the case of *Wingrove v. Wingrove* [6] Hannen gave a lucid explanation of the kind of influence which is undue in the eyes of the law. In the case of *Dancer v. Crabb* [7] Hannen gave the best and most concise account of the doctrine of dependent relative revocation that has ever been given;[8] and the explanations which he gave to juries in the cases of *Boughton v. Knight* [9] and *Smee v. Smee*,[10] of the conditions which must be satisfied before a person can be said to be not of sufficiently sound mind, memory and understanding to make a will, are models of lucid exposition and unequalled as clear statements of the law. Penzance's decision in *Charter v. Charter* [11] is a leading case on the question of the extrinsic evidence admissible to interpret the words used by a testator in his will— though his view that the case was a case of equivocation, so that evidence of the testator's intention was admissible, was not acceded to by the House of Lords.[12]

[1] *Lemage v. Goodban* (1865) L.R.1 P. and D. 57; *In the goods of De la Saussaye* (1873) L.R. 3 P. and D. 42.
[2] *In the goods of Letitia Lovegrove* (1862) 2 Sw. and Tr. 453, following *Hobson v. Blackburn* (1822) 1 Add. 274.   [3] *Quick v. Quick* (1864) 3 Sw. and Tr. 442.
[4] (1876) 1 P. and D. 154.   [5] (1872) L.R. 2 P. and D. 462.
[6] (1885) 11 P.D. 81.   [7] (1873) L.R. 3 P. and D. 98.
[8] "If the testator's act can be interpreted thus: 'Whatever else I may do, I intend to cancel this as my will from this time forth,' the will is revoked; but if his meaning is, 'As I have made a fresh will my old one may now be destroyed', the old will is not revoked if the new one be not in fact made", ibid at pp. 104-105.
[9] (1873) L.R. 3 P. and D. 64.   [10] (1879) 5 P.D. 84.
[11] (1871) L.R. 3 P. and D. 315; in the House of Lords the House was equally divided so that his decision stood, L.R. 7 H.L. 364.
[12] Ibid; see Stephen, Digest of the Law of Evidence, Note xxxiii.

Divorce. Penzance's decision in the case of *Hyde v. Hyde* [1] established the principle that English law will only recognize as marriage a monogamous union, so that the machinery of the divorce court cannot be used to enforce or dissolve the rights and duties arising out of a polygamous marriage, although it was valid by the law of the place where it was contracted. In the case of *Wing v. Taylor* [2] Cresswell and the full court interpreted the law as to what marriages were void because they came within the prohibited degrees of relationship. In the case of *Keats v. Keats* [3] Cresswell gave the accepted definition of the term "condonation", and distinguished it from the term "forgiveness". In the case of *Hope v. Hope* [4] he held that where both husband and wife were guilty of adultery, so that neither could get a divorce, the wife could not get restitution of conjugal rights; and his decision has been approved by the Court of Appeal.[5] Cases in this court raised many important questions in Private International Law. The following are a few illustrations: In the case of *Mette v. Mette* [6] Cresswell held that the marriage of a domiciled English man to his deceased wife's sister, who was a German woman in Germany, was invalid, although the marriage was valid by German law; and in *Simonin v. Mallac* [7] he held that the law of the place where a marriage is celebrated governs the formal validity of the marriage, so that a marriage in England between two domiciled French subjects, who had come to England to evade a formality required by French law, was valid. In the case of *Shaw v. Attorney-General* [8] Hannen laid down the accepted principle that English courts will not recognize the validity of a foreign divorce, unless the parties were domiciled in the jurisdiction of the foreign court; and in the case of *Manning v. Manning* [9] that temporary residence within the jurisdiction will not give an English court jurisdiction to grant a divorce or a separation.

[1] (1866) L.R. 1 P. and D. 130. See Cheshire, Private International Law, 5th ed. 293.

[2] (1861) 2 Sw. and Tr. 278.   [3] (1859) 1 Sw. and Tr. 334 at pp. 345-348.

[4] (1858) 1 Sw. and Tr. 94; his decision was in accordance with the weight of opinion in the English ecclesiastical courts, but the opposite opinion had been reached by the Consistory Court in Dublin in the case of *Seaver v. Seaver* (1846) 2 Sw. and Tr. 665.

[5] *Brooking Phillips v. Brooking Phillips* [1913] P. 80, in which *Seaver v. Seaver* was overruled.   [6] (1859) 1 Sw. and Tr. 416.

[7] (1860) 2 Sw. and Tr. 67; see Cheshire, Private International Law, 3rd ed., 287, 420, 448.

[8] (1870) L.R. 2 P. and D. 156.   [9] (1871) L.R. 2 P. and D. 223.

SOME MEMBERS OF THE JUDICIAL COMMITTEE OF THE PRIVY COUNCIL

Some members of the Judicial Committee of the Privy Council.

Though the Acts which created the probate and divorce courts provided that appeals from them should go to the House of Lords,[1] appeals from the ecclesiastical and prize courts go,[2] and, till 1875, appeals from the court of Admiralty went,[3] to the Judicial Committee of the Privy Council. The Act of 1833 which created that Committee provided that the Crown could appoint two other persons besides those named in the Act to be members, and an Act of 1871 provided that the Crown could appoint four paid members,[4] Some of the lawyers appointed under those Acts have helped forward the development of those branches of law which fell within the sphere of the civilians' practice as well as helping forward the development of Indian and Colonial law. Therefore, at this point, I must say something of some of those members of the Judicial Committee of whom I have not already given some account as Chancellors, Lords of Appeal, Lords Justices, Vice-Chancellors, or Judges.

KINGSDOWN

The most eminent of these members was Pemberton Leigh, Lord Kingsdown (1793-1867).[5] He was the son of a successful Chancery barrister who was a descendant of Sir Francis Pemberton, a Chief Justice successively of the King's Bench and Common Pleas in Charles II's reign.[6] But his father died young and left his family poorly off. At the age of sixteen he went for a year to a solicitor's office, at the end of which time he went into the chambers of his uncle, Edward Cooke, who had a good practice at the Chancery bar. In his chambers, by means of his own reading, and with his uncle's help he got his education in the theory and practice of equity, and, before his call, he earned a little money as an equity draftsman. He was called to the bar by Lincoln's Inn in 1816, and his connections and abilities enabled him to earn the unprecedented sum of £600 in the first year after his call. He

---

[1] Vol. i 624, 630.   [2] Ibid 518, 524.   [3] Ibid 565, 643.   [4] Ibid 518.
[5] Lord Kingsdown's Recollections; Ed. Rev. cxxix 40-68; D.N.B.—article by Lord Sumner.   [6] Vol. vi 503.

never looked back, and, before he was thirty he was earning £3000 a year. From the first his main practice had been in the Court of Chancery; and, though he joined the Northern Circuit, he only attended once at Lancaster where there was a Chancery court, in which court he "earned but was not paid the sum of half a guinea".[1] He was so prosperous that he was able to refuse briefs in bankruptcy and lunacy cases and to give up the drafting of pleadings, and his practice in the court of Exchequer. In 1829 he took silk, and settled down in the court of the Master of the Rolls. In 1831 he entered Parliament for Rye in the conservative interest after a contest which, as was to be expected in the height of the Reform Bill agitation, was extremely riotous.[2] He lost his seat in 1832, but in 1835 he became member for Ripon, which seat he retained till he retired from Parliament in 1843. He made no great mark in the House of Commons. His most successful speech was made in opposition to the exaggerated claims of privilege made by the House of Commons in the case of *Stockdale v. Hansard*.[3]

Pemberton's forensic talents had made him the leader of the Chancery bar. Of those talents it has been said:[4]

His was not the suaviloquence of Follett or the grandiloquence of Wetherall, but a lucid simplicity and subdued strength, which seemed, without an effort, to assume the most appropriate forms of argument and language. Usually more succinct than the advocates of his own day, and infinitely less prolix than the advocates of our time, Pemberton marshalled the facts of his case, with an unerring perspicuity and then led the mind of the judge, by a natural train of thought, to the legal principles which ought to govern his decision. A crowd of ingenious and apposite illustrations served to strengthen his own position or to rebut the arguments of his opponent. The bearing of the whole case was by this process distilled into an essence, and a subject, originally complex, reduced at last to one or two questions so simple that the determination of them appeared easy and irresistible. To the ordinary purpose of English eloquence . . . oratory of his exquisite refinement would have been inapplicable. But in a court of equity or at the bar of a court of appeal . . . the merit of Mr. Pemberton's style of argument has never been surpassed.

In 1825 he was offered and refused both the Solicitor-Generalship —a refusal which he said was due to "moral cowardice",[5] and a puisne judgeship—thinking, very erroneously, that he was not qualified for the judicial office.[6] In 1843 he retired both from the bar and from Parliament. This step was due to what was the most extraordinary episode in his career.

---

[1] Lord Kingsdown's Recollections 24.   [2] Ibid 81-92.
[3] (1839) 9 A. and E. 1.   [4] Ed. Rev. cxxix, 55.
[5] Lord Kingsdown's Recollections 103.   [6] Ibid 102.

A distant relative, Sir Robert Leigh, was a wealthy landowner with an income of some £14,000 a year. In 1831 Pemberton was briefed in a case, set down for hearing in the Rolls Court, concerning a tithe modus, in which Leigh was the defendant. He was briefed because Bickersteth had been retained on the other side. He won the case in spite of a flaw in it which his opponent did not detect; and Leigh was so pleased that he left him a life interest in his estates. As Pemberton says,[1]

It has always seemed to me that my introduction to Sir R. Leigh is one of the most remarkable examples which I have ever seen of the important effects produced by circumstances apparently trivial, and which we are accustomed to call fortuitous. If the cause had come on for hearing some months earlier, or been set down in another court, I should probably have had nothing to do with it. If Bickersteth had not been already retained for the plaintiff, no doubt I should have been his counsel, and should have been obliged, probably, to make the observations which gave so much offence to Sir Robert. . . . At all events, I must have contended against his interest, and probably might have defeated him by observing the blot to which I have alluded, and which he would naturally have considered as a mere trick. In any event, the chance is that I should have lost or have failed to gain some £12,000 or £14,000 a year.

Sir Robert Leigh died in 1842, and it was this accession of wealth which was the cause of Pemberton's retirement. He added the name of Leigh to his own, settled down to the life of a large landowner, and, he says,[2]

I provided myself with microscopes, telescopes, painting implements, a chest of turners' tools, and I know not how many other resources against ennui, none of which I ever used; and after the lapse of seventeen years I can safely say that I have never had one hour hang heavy on me, nor felt anything but regret at being called upon to attend the sittings of the Judicial Committee or the Duchy Councils.

On his retirement Peel made him Chancellor of the Duchy of Cornwall and a Privy Councillor in order that he might attend the sittings of the Judicial Committee. In the former office he did good work, in conjunction with Prince Albert,[3] in making reforms in the finances of the Duchy, which resulted in the accumulation of a considerable fund during the minority of the Prince of Wales. But it is his work in the latter capacity which gives him his place in legal history. It was work for which he was unpaid; and

[1] Lord Kingsdown's Recollections 80-81.   [2] Ibid 128-129.
[3] Of the Prince he says, "his aptitude for business was wonderful; the dullest and most intricate matters did not escape or weary his attention; his judgment was very good; his readiness to listen to my suggestions, though against his own opinion, was constant; and though I saw his temper very often tried, yet in the course of twenty years I never once saw it disturbed, nor witnessed any signs of impatience", ibid 129-130; he added, ibid 131, that he was the best shot he ever saw.

it was only after he had four times refused a peerage and once the office of Lord Chancellor that he was at last, in 1858, induced to take a peerage, and became Lord Kingsdown. In 1857 Greville had very justly said of him that,[1]

it is a very singular thing that in such times as these, and when there is such a dearth of able men and so great a demand for them, he should voluntarily condemn himself to a state of comparative obscurity, and refuse to take the station in public life which it would be difficult to find any other man so well qualified to fill.

His achievement as a member of the Judicial Committee was twofold. In the first place, he took the chief part in the reform of its practice, the reduction of the costs of an appeal, and the elimination of delays in the hearing of cases. In the second place, he took a leading part in the framing of many of its most important decisions. It is this work which, in Lord Sumner's opinion,[2] puts him "in the front rank of English judges". As a judge he showed in an even higher degree the same qualities as he had shown as an advocate, with the result that his judgments were, as Lord Sumner says, "at once standard decisions and models of judicial expression".

Many of them he wrote and rewrote several times over. His legal knowledge was extraordinarily varied, and he was especially versed in the minutiae of Indian land tenures. His grasp of principles was great, and led him to place little dependence on reported decisions.[3]

After he became a peer he gave valuable help in the hearing of cases in the House of Lords. He died in 1867.

A few out of the very many of the important decisions in which he took the leading part will illustrate the versatility and breadth of his legal knowledge.

Kingsdown's learning in the ecclesiastical law of the Church of England is illustrated by his judgments in such cases as *Westerton v. Liddell*,[4] *Liddell v. Beal*[5] which raised questions similar to those raised in *Westerton v. Liddell*, and *Heath v. Burder*[6] which was a case of a clergyman who preached false doctrine. Of his judgment in the first of these cases Greville said:[7]

It was a very able judgment and prepared with great care and research, and so moderately and fairly framed that it was accepted unanimously by the Committee, and even by the Bishops of Canterbury and London, both Low Churchmen. It was drawn up by Pemberton Leigh himself, and its publication will give the world in general some idea of his great ability, with the extent of which few are acquainted.

[1] Memoirs viii 101.   [2] D.N.B.   [3] Ibid.
[4] Moore, Special Report; above 153.   [5] (1860) 14 Moo. P.C. 1.
[6] 15 Moo. P.C. 1; above 145.   [7] Memoirs viii 101.

In the case of *Long v. Bishop of Capetown* [1] his decision as to the authority of a colonial bishop over his clergy, and the jurisdiction of so-called ecclesiastical courts in a self-governing or settled colony, is recognized as one of the leading cases on this subject.

Many of Kingsdown's decisions are concerned with the other branches of the law which fell within the sphere of the civilians' practice. In the sphere of the *probate* jurisdiction the case of *Dyke v. Walford* [2] is a leading case on the history of the testamentary jurisdiction of the ecclesiastical courts, on the right of the Crown to *bona vacantia*, and on the *jura regalia* of the Duchy of Lancaster. In the case of *Austen v. Graham* [3] he delivered the judgment which reversed the decision of the Prerogative Court on the question of the sanity of a testator who had turned Mahomedan, and left a will which was not irrational for a Mahomedan to make. The case of *Allen v. Maddock* [4] is the leading authority on the law as to the condition in which unattested papers may be incorporated into a later duly attested will. In the spheres of *prize and admiralty law* the case of *The Ostsee* [5] is an authority for the rules as to the payment of the costs and expenses of capture by captor or claimant when restitution of a ship is decreed. In the case of *The Franciska* [6] many of the rules as to blockade were reviewed, and in the case of *The Panaghia Rhomba* [7] the rule as to the liability of the cargo upon a ship captured for breach of blockade was considered. In the case of the *The Gerasimo* [8] the law as to commercial domicil,[9] as to the distinction between "hostile occupation and possession clothed with a legal right by cession or conquest",[10] and as to the duty of the captor to bring the ship in for adjudication by a Prize Court and the consequences for the breach of this duty, were considered. In the case of *The Minnehaha* [11] the law as to salvage, and the circumstances in which a contract to tow may be superseded and a claim to salvage services may be made, was considered; and in the case of *Cleary v. M'Andrew* [12] the law as to the liens of the master of a ship for freight and general average, and the lien of the holder of a respondentia bond were considered.

Several of Kingsdown's decisions lay down important principles of *colonial and Indian constitutional law*. The case of *The*

---

[1] (1863) 1 Moo P.C.N.S. 411.
[2] (1846) 5 Moo. P.C. 434.
[3] (1854) 8 Moo. P.C. 493.
[4] (1858) 11 Moo. P.C. 427.
[5] (1855) 9 Moo. P.C. 150.
[6] (1855) 10 Moo. P.C. 37.
[7] (1858) 12 Moo. P.C. 168.
[8] (1857) 11 Moo. P.C. 88.
[9] Vol. ix 99-102.
[10] 11 Moo. P.C. at p. 100.
[11] (1861) 15 Moo. P.C. 133.
[12] (1863) 2 Moo. P.C.N.S. 216; vol. viii 261-263.

Falkland Islands Co. v. The Queen [1] lays down the principle that the Crown can review the decisions of all colonial courts in both civil and criminal cases, but that it is only in very special circumstances that it will do so in criminal cases. In the case of the *Secretary of State v. Sahaba* [2] it was held that the transactions of independent foreign states *inter se* are acts of state with which a municipal court cannot interfere, so that the dealings of the Government of India with an Indian prince could not be made the subject of enquiry in a municipal court. In the case of *The Advocate-General of Bengal v. Ranee Surnomoye Dossee* [3] it was held that the rules of the English criminal law, though applicable to Englishmen in India, do not apply to Hindus, so that the property of a Hindu who had committed suicide was not forfeited to the Crown.

Problems of *Private International Law* frequently came before the Privy Council. Kingsdown took no part in the decision of the case of *Bremer v. Freeman;* [4] but it was that decision which caused him to propose and carry the Act as to the forms of wills of personalty made by British subjects abroad which is generally known by his name. [5] Other rules of English law are illustrated by the cases of *Barnhart v. Greenshields,* [6] which lays it down that vague rumours or statements by strangers will not affect the purchaser of property with notice, but that "a notice in order to be binding must proceed from some person interested in the property"; [7] and of *Miner v. Gilmour* [8] which discussed the rights of riparian owners to water flowing past their land.

We have seen that under the Judicial Committee Act of 1871 [9] the Crown was empowered to appoint four paid members of the Judicial Committee from among the judges of the superior courts or the chief justices of the High Courts in Bengal, Madras, or Bombay. The result of this Act was to strengthen the Judicial Committee by the addition of four able lawyers. Two were appointed from retired Indian Chief Justices, and two were English lawyers.

---

[1] (1863) 1 Moo. P.C.N.S. 299; following *R. v. Joykissen Mookerjee* (1862) ibid 272; vol. i 523. [2] (1859) 13 Moo. P.C. 22.
[3] (1863) 2 Moo. P.C.N.S. 22. [4] (1857) 10 Moo. P.C. 306; above 21, 152.
[5] 24, 25 Victoria c. 114; Cheshire, Private International Law, 5th ed. 533 *et seq.*
[6] (1853) 9 Moo. P.C. 18. [7] At p. 36.
[8] (1858) 12 Moo. P.C. 131. [9] 34, 35 Victoria c. 91; vol. i 518.

COLVILLE

The two retired Indian Chief Justices were Sir James Colville and Sir Barnes Peacock. Colville (1810-80) [1] was educated at Eton and Trinity College, Cambridge. He was called to the bar by the Inner Temple in 1835, and in 1845 went to India as Advocate-General of the East India Company. In 1845 he was made a puisne judge, and in 1855 Chief Justice of the High Court of Bengal. After his retirement in 1859 he was for some years Indian assessor to the Judicial Committee. In 1865 he was made one of its members, and in 1871 a paid member. He was a very learned Indian lawyer and also a sound English lawyer. One of the notable decisions in which he gave the judgment of the Committee was the case of *Doyle v. Falconer*,[2] which laid down the rule that a colonial assembly has not got the powers possessed by the House of Commons of punishing for contempt, even though the contempt had been committed in its presence.[3]

PEACOCK

Sir Barnes Peacock (1810-90) [4] was called to the bar by the Inner Temple in 1836. He made his name by pointing out the technical objection to the decisions in O'Connell's case [5] which induced the House of Lords to reverse them. He took silk in 1850, and became legal member of the Viceroy's Council in India, in which capacity he was responsible for several codifying Acts. On the termination of this appointment he succeeded Colville as Chief Justice of the High Court of Bengal. He resigned in 1870, and in 1872 he was appointed a paid member of the Judicial Committee under the Act of 1871. Lord Sumner says of him [6] that "his great knowledge of Indian customs, his persevering industry, and his painstaking accuracy made him a specially useful member of the court". One of his decisions—the case of *Lindsay Petroleum Co. v. Hurd*[7]—contains one of the best expositions of the equitable doctrine of lâches; and another—the

---

[1] D.N.B.   [2] (1866) 4 Moo. P.C.N.S. 203.
[3] Earlier cases, *Kielley v. Carson* (1842) 4 Moo. P.C. 63 and *Fenton v. Hampton* (1858) 11 Moo. P.C. 347, had decided that a colonial assembly had no power to punish for contempts committed outside the assembly.
[4] D.N.B.   [5] Above 10.   [6] D.N.B.   [7] (1874) L.R. 5 P.C. 221.

case of *Godfrey v. Poole* [1]—is an authority upon the interpretation of the statutes, 13 Elizabeth I c. 5 and 27 Elizabeth I c. 4,[2] the first of which avoids conveyances made with intent to delay or defeat creditors, and the second, conveyances made with intent to defraud purchasers.

The two English lawyers were Sir Montagu Smith and Sir Robert Collier.

SMITH

Sir Montagu Smith (1809-91) [3] was called to the bar by Gray's Inn in 1835, took silk in 1853, and entered Parliament as member for Truro in 1859. He sponsored the Act of 1862 for the limitation of crown suits,[4] and motions made by him in 1863 and 1864 kept before Parliament the question of the housing of the courts which had long been a very pressing question.[5] A commission appointed in 1858 had reported in favour of the concentration of the courts in one place, and recommended as that place their present site; and in 1865 Smith was appointed one of the commissioners of Works and Buildings who, by an Act passed in that year, were entrusted with the acquisition of the land needed for this purpose.[6] In 1865 he was appointed a judge of the Court of Common Pleas, and in 1871 he became a paid member of the Judicial Committee, which post he held till his resignation in 1881. His work there shows that he was a sound lawyer. He gave the judgment of the Committee in the case of *Mollwo, March & Co. v. The Court of Wards* [7] which is an important case on the criteria which determine whether or not profit sharing connotes a partnership, on the definition of partnership, and on the doctrine of holding out; and in the case of *Yeap Cheah Neo v. Ong Cheng Neo*,[8] in which the question what rules of English law were, and what were not applicable to the Straits Settlements, was discussed.

---

[1] (1888) 13 App. Cas. 497.
[2] Vol. iv 480-482. [They were replaced by sections 172 and 173 of the Law of Property Act, 1925. Eds.]
[3] D.N.B.   [4] 24, 25 Victoria c. 62.
[5] Hansard (3rd Ser.) clxxii 605-607; ibid clxxvi 363-366; vol. i 648; Holdsworth, Charles Dickens as a Legal Historian, 12-36.
[6] 28, 29 Victoria c. 49.   [7] (1872) L.R. 4 P.C. 419.
[8] (1875) L.R. 6 P.C. 381.

COLLIER

Sir Robert Collier (1817-86) [1] was called to the bar by the Inner Temple in 1843. He made his name by his defence of the Brazilian pirates in 1845. Platt B. had refused to reserve a point for the consideration of the Court for Crown Cases Reserved. Collier induced the Home Secretary and Peel to put pressure on the judge to reserve the point, with the result that his clients were acquitted. He was elected member for Plymouth in 1852, and took silk in 1854. He was appointed counsel to the Admiralty in 1859, Solicitor-General in 1863, and Attorney-General in 1868. In 1885 he was made a peer with the title of Lord Monkswell. His appointment as a paid member of the Judicial Committee in 1871 raised a storm in Parliament, because the Government had made him a judge of the Court of Common Pleas for a few days merely to give him the qualification required by the Act. This attempt to treat the statutory qualification of judicial rank in the same way as the common law qualification of admission to the order of the coif was generally condemned, [2] and the Government narrowly escaped censure in both Houses of Parliament. [3] There was no question of the competency of Collier who, besides being a good lawyer and a legal author, [4] was a classical scholar who had written a translation of Demosthenes *de corona*, and an artist. One of his decisions is concerned with the evidence admissible against a prisoner. [5] Another settles the question of the persons entitled to take action in a suit in the ecclesiastical courts—in a criminal suit any one can take action: in a civil suit only a person who has an interest in it. [6]

BERNARD

Another member of the Judicial Committee was Montague Bernard (1820-82), [7] the first Professor of International Law and Diplomacy at Oxford, and Fellow of All Souls' College. He served on the commission which suggested the changes in the law as to

---

[1] D.N.B.   [2] Above 94.

[3] Their majority in the House of Lords was only two, and in the House of Commons twenty-seven.

[4] In 1845 he published a small book on the Railway Clauses Act, and in 1849 a small book on Mines.   [5] *R. v. Coote* (1873) L.R. 4 P.C. 599.

[6] *Lee v. Fagg* (1874) L.R. 6 P.C. 38.   [7] D.N.B.

naturalization and allegiance which were made in 1870;[1] he helped to negotiate the Treaty of Washington in 1871; and he helped in the arbitration in the Alabama case provided for by that treaty. He took a leading part in the Oxford University commission of 1877. His reputation as an international lawyer at home and abroad was deservedly high. His successor T. E. Holland has said of him that "he inclined rather to the historical than to the systematic exposition of his subject, dwelling by preference upon the analysis of treaties, the character of politicians, and the by-play of diplomacy".[2] He left no systematic treatise on his subject, but some of his lectures and essays upon aspects of it are valuable.[3]

We have seen that under a power conferred by the Act which established the Court of Probate Doctors' Commons was dissolved.[4] That was the end of the civilians as a separate branch of the legal profession. Henceforward the branches of English law which they had developed were administered not by advocates and proctors, but by barristers, attorneys and solicitors,[5] and not by judges who had been educated as civilians, but by judges who had been educated as English lawyers. Gibbon's picturesque description of the English civilians and canonists,[6] though not wholly true when it was written,[7] had become true—"the double jurisprudence of Rome", had at length been entirely "overwhelmed by the enormous profession of the common lawyers". It was a development which was inevitable. The fact that the tripartite division of the English legal system into common law, equity and the civilians' sphere of practice was illogical and inconvenient, was coming to be generally recognized. The Act of 1857 which put an end to Doctors' Commons and the separate existence of the civilian branch of the legal profession, and the legislation as to the procedure of the ecclesiastical courts and the Court of Admiralty which preceded and followed it[8] had begun the work of effecting some amalgamation of the sphere of law and equity;[9] and this movement towards uniformity was completed by the Judicature Act of 1875.[10] But though uniformity in the jurisdiction of the courts and in procedure and pleading was to a large extent attained,[11] historical causes prevented the complete amalgamation of the substantive law which the old separate courts had developed.[12] For that reason

---

[1] 33, 34 Victoria c. 14.   [2] D.N.B.   [3] Vol. xv 333.
[4] Vol. xii 49; 20, 21 Victoria c. 77 § 117.   [5] Vol. xii 684; above 139.
[6] Autobiographies of Gibbon, Memoir F, 69, cited vol. xii 605.
[7] Vol. xii 701.   [8] Vol. xii 683-684; above 146.
[9] Vol. i 636-638; above 45, 60, 134.   [10] Vol. i 638-643.
[11] Vol. i 638-643; vol. xii 683-684.   [12] Vol. xii 602-604.

their memory is, as I have said, perpetuated in the different Divisions of the High Court, which are therefore an ever present reminder of the diversity of the origins of different parts of the English legal system.[1]

There is no doubt that the considerable measure of uniformity thus attained has been beneficial to the litigant and the law. But one of the results of the disappearance of the civilians as a separate branch of the legal profession has not been so beneficial. We have seen that the advocates were required to take a degree in Roman law;[2] and though the arrangements for its teaching in the universities were as defective as the arrangements for teaching English law in the Inns of Court,[3] the fact that the procedure of the ecclesiastical courts and the Court of Admiralty was based on the civil and canon law,[4] and that some of the law there administered was influenced by these two bodies of law,[5] made it necessary for the civilians to study Roman law. But with their disappearance this practical incentive to the study of Roman law has disappeared. This was unfortunate, since this study is necessary to a scientific knowledge of the law and legal theory, and to an understanding both of international law and of foreign systems of law. As both Maine and Girard have pointed out [6] Roman law is the "*lingua franca* of universal jurisprudence"; [7] an unrivalled instrument of legal education performing in that sphere the same function as the classical languages perform in a literary education;[8] and a necessary adjunct to the study of legal history by enabling comparisons to be made which illumine the sociological problems underlying legal developments, and guard against two opposite fallacies—the idea that the laws of one particular place or period are ultimate facts which are universally true, and the idea that they are merely accidents dependent upon the arbitrary will of the legislator.[9] Moreover since at different periods our own legal history has been directly influenced by Roman law, it is impossible, as this History has shown, to understand its development without a knowledge of the technical language and doctrines of that law. It is true that a superficial knowledge of Roman law is required by English universities for a degree in law, and a still more superficial knowledge is required by the Council of Legal Education for a call to the bar. But it is also true that the number of students who make a serious study

---

[1] Vol. xii 604, 702. [2] Vol. iv 236; vol. xii 47. [3] Vol. xii 78-85.
[4] Ibid 678-680. [5] Vol. xii 685; vol. viii 245 *et seq.*
[6] Maine, Village Communities, Essay on Roman Law and Legal Education, 330-383; Girard, L'Enseignement du Droit Romain en 1912, Nouvelle Revue Historique de Droit Français et Étranger, xxxvi 557-572.
[7] Maine, op. cit. 361; Girard, op. cit. 562. [8] Ibid. [9] Ibid 562-563.

of it is so small that we can repeat and apply literally to our time, the words which in the sixteenth century the Protector Somerset wrote to Ridley—"We are sure you are not ignorant how necessary a study that study of civil law is to all treaties with foreign princes and strangers, and how few there be at present to do the King's Majesty service therein."[1]

It is true that Roman law has not the same practical use today that it had in the eighteenth and early nineteenth centuries. The codes, beginning with the Code Napoleon in 1804, in which the European nations have embodied their law, have deprived Roman law of its position as the positive law of very many countries in Europe,[2] with the result that "the tradition of treating Justinian's law books chiefly and primarily as a Code to be interpreted and adapted to practical use belongs to the past".[3] Nowadays interest is centred in recovering from the text of Justinian's *Corpus Juris* "dogmatic differences between every age and every jurist, in underlining those discrepancies of thought, expression, and decision which, so long as the *Corpus Juris* was considered as a Code, it was our object to suppress and explain away".[4] This change in the mode of studying Roman law, which is due to the emergence of national codes of law, no doubt accounts for the large decrease in the number of persons who now devote their lives to its serious study; for though it does not invalidate the reasons why some study and knowledge of Roman law is necessary to a liberal education in, and knowledge of, law, it does mean that the practical importance of its intensive study is diminished. The number of persons willing to acquire knowledge for its own sake is always limited. But it is the same reason—the emergence of national codes of law—which accounts for the growing importance of a study which is taking the place once occupied by the intensive study of Roman law on the old lines— the study of comparative law. It is a study which is as necessary to the modern lawyer who wishes to make intelligent reforms in his own legal system, or to assimilate the rules of those parts of it which have an international character to the rules of other systems of law, as it is to the historian of any system of law, for, as Maitland says, "history involves comparison".[5]

---

[1] Cited vol. iv 233.   [2] Girard, op. cit. 559-560.
[3] de Zulueta, The Study of Roman Law Today (Mangurd Lecture, 1920) 6-7.
[4] Ibid 7.   [5] Collected Papers i 488.

INDEX OF NAMES

*An appendix to this index is included on page 175, containing names of persons
dealt with in detail in the text*

APPENDIX TO NAME INDEX

SUBJECT INDEX